W9-CTA-696

LAKE, RIVER AND SEA-RUN FISHES OF CANADA

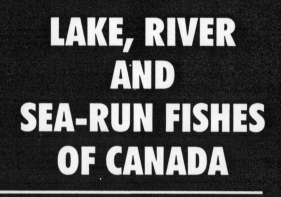

LAKE, RIVER
AND
SEA-RUN FISHES
OF CANADA

Frederick H. Wooding

Foreword by Professor Joseph S. Nelson,
Department of Zoology, University of Alberta

Special chapter *Canada's Aquatic Heritage* by
Dr. Robert R. Campbell,
Chairman, Committee on the Status of Endangered Wildlife in
Canada (COSEWIC), Fish and Marine Mammals
Subcommittee, Canadian Wildlife Service, Environment Canada

HARBOUR PUBLISHING

HARBOUR PUBLISHING
P.O. Box 219
Madeira Park, BC Canada V0N 2H0

Copyright © 1994 by Frederick H. Wooding

All rights reserved. No part of this book may be reproduced in any form by any means without the written permission of the publisher, except by a reviewer, who may quote brief passages in a review.

Published with the assistance of the Canada Council and the Government of British Columbia, Cultural Services Branch
Cover design by Roger Handling
Line illustrations by Gordon Fairbairn
Colour plates courtesy John Camp, Communications Directorate, Department of Fisheries and Oceans, Ottawa

Canadian Cataloguing in Publication Data

Wooding, Frederick H.
  Lake, river and sea-run fishes of Canada

  First ed. (1959) has title: The angler's book of Canadian fishes; 1973 printing has title: The book of Canadian fishes.
  Includes index.
  ISBN 1-55017-113-5

  1. Freshwater fishes—Canada. 2. Fishing—Canada. I. Title.
  II. Title: Angler's book of Canadian fishes. III. Title: Book of Canadian fishes.
QL626.W6 1994   597.092'0971   C94-910752-2

Printed in Canada

*This book
was written for
and is lovingly dedicated to
my grandson
Christopher Paul Michael Wooding*

BY THE SAME AUTHOR

Canada's Atlantic Salmon
> Department of Fisheries, Ottawa, 1954
> Second Edition, 1956

The Angler's Book of Canadian Fishes
> Collins, Toronto, 1959
> Braille Edition, 1960

The Book of Canadian Fishes
> Revised Editions of *The Angler's Book of Canadian Fishes*
> McGraw Hill-Ryerson,
> Toronto, 1973. Reprinted 1974

Wild Mammals of Canada
> McGraw Hill-Ryerson, Toronto, 1982

Les Mammifers Sauvages du Canada
> Marcel Broquet, LaPrairie, Quebec, 1983

Fishing, if I a fisher may protest,
Of pleasure is the sweet'st of sports the best,
Of exercises the most excellent
Of recreation the most innocent.
But now the sport is mard, and wotte ye why?
Fishes decrease, and fishers multiply.

Thomas Bastard: Book VI, Epigrams 14: *De Piscatione.*
From Chresteleros, *Seven Bookes of Epigrames* (1598)

Contents

Sunfish, Bass, Perch & Drum

Catfish, Bullhead, Stonecat & Madtom

Author's Note

I n his preface to the first edition of *The Angler's Book of Canadian Fishes*, Dr. J.R. Dymond, then Professor Emeritus of Zoology at the University of Toronto, made this observation: "Fishes have the right to share the earth with us; they are not here on sufferance." A simple statement but a profound one, nonetheless.

The dangers facing our fish today are cause for alarm. In 1994, Canadian authorities were forced to place an indefinite ban on their once great Atlantic cod fishery. No one knew how long it would take the stocks to replenish themselves. Freshwater fish are also in peril. One has but to examine the list of rare, endangered and extinct species published by the Committee on the Status of Endangered Wildlife in Canada (COSEWIC) (page 281) to understand how serious the problem has become.

For example, some runs of east coast Atlantic salmon and west coast steelhead trout, two of the world's most admired game and food fish, are only trickles of what they once were. And now there is talk of their extinction. Extinction, as Prof. Dymond observed, is forever.

Scientists estimate that fifty to one hundred species of vertebrates and invertebrates are vanishing every day, and they predict that by the year 2050 about half the world's existing species will have been extirpated.

Lake, River and Sea-Run Fishes of Canada, it is hoped, will do more than help readers increase their knowledge of these remarkable and often beautiful creatures. It is hoped that it will play its part in encouraging anglers, commercial fishers, governments and industry to work to minimize the perils facing these fragile resources.

An acknowledgement I made in the first edition of *The Book of Canadian Fishes* applies as well to *Lake, River and Sea-Run Fishes of Canada*—to claim sole authorship of this book would be wrong, for to a large extent it is based on the lifetime studies of some of Canada's most distinguished fisheries scientists. My particular job has been to cull from scientific literature the data that would be of the most interest to anglers and others who are interested in fishes—in itself, I must confess, a very formidable undertaking. This I did with great care and with a sincere determination to interpret the scientists' findings with the highest possible degree of accuracy.

This book could not have been written without the encouragement and support of a number of Canada's most outstanding fisheries scientists. I am especially grateful to Prof. Joseph S. Nelson, professor of zoology, University of Alberta, who advised me wisely and with much patience; he was a source of inspiration throughout. Thanks also go to Dr. Robert R. Campbell, who contributed the special treatise, *Canada's Aquatic Heritage.*

Yorke Edwards, for many years director of the Royal British Columbia Museum, and Dr. Alex Peden, the museum's present curator of fishes, also gave much valuable advice. I am especially indebted to Dr. Peden, who generously made a number of important documents available to me; without them, and without his ongoing counsel, this book could not have been brought to completion.

I acknowledge as well the help of Dr. Cornelis Groot, one of the world's leading authorities on Pacific salmon, and of Dr. Lionel Johnson, an internationally recognized authority on Arctic charr.

Thanks also go to Bob Dunfield of Fisheries and Oceans in Halifax, author of the important study, *The Atlantic Salmon in the History of North America*, for his help in dealing with that species, and to Prof. Richard C. Hoffmann of York University for his advice on the chapter dealing with pike (*Esox lucius*). Ron Ptolemy, senior fisheries biologist of the Recreational Fisheries Branch of BC's Ministry of Environment and Parks, gave careful assessments of all the sections dealing with the trout species in that province and John Bruner, M.Sc., of the Department of Biological Sciences, University of Alberta, checked the entire manuscript for scientific accuracy.

Although great care has been taken to assure the correctness of the statements made in this book, the author assumes full responsibility for any errors or omissions that may have occurred.

FREDERICK H. WOODING
Saanichton, BC

Foreword

Prof. Joseph S. Nelson

Department of Zoology, University of Alberta

This is a book for anglers, naturalists and people in general who want to learn more about fishes in Canada. A good angler is a naturalist, of course, but not all naturalists are anglers. One might think that a book on fishes designed primarily for anglers would include only salmon, trout, bass and a few other species. Hardly so. Almost any fish can be the subject of an angling experience. A good angler, as well as the concerned lay person, takes an active interest in all fishes—both in their biology and in their welfare—not just those that are old-time favourites or in a certain body of water.

Furthermore, we can angle or otherwise enjoy a fish in the field without eating it. It is curious that some people perceive two kinds of fishes, however: those that are edible and those that are inedible. Their worth seems to be judged accordingly by people who use the contemptible adjectives "trash," "rough" or "coarse" for some of our fishes. I recall an experience I once had when collecting fishes in a stream near Burns Lake, British Columbia. I had just seined some northern squawfish and was putting them into a bucket to save for a museum. A local resident expressed dismay that I might be going to eat them and issued a dire warning that these trash fish were poisonous! Some fish are indeed more of a challenge than others to prepare for a tasty meal, but I know of no fish in Canada that is inedible. Furthermore, northern squawfish may give the fish watcher as much pleasure as a peregrine falcon gives the bird watcher.

Fishes show enormous diversity in body form, body function and life history. Their origin extends back at least five hundred million years and they comprise over one-half of the species of animals with backbones known as vertebrates. People have had a long association with fishes. Today they provide us with food, income, enjoyment (from sport to home aquariums) and sometimes misfortune such as the rare shark attack or poisoning.

Fishes, from the time of their origin, have been caught and eaten by other species. From the beginning of human existence, we surely have included fish in our diet as well. It seems most curious that in addition to catching fishes for food and other uses, we make a significant effort to catch them for sheer enjoyment (not necessarily to kill or put in some collection). I am not sure any other group of animals is sought after in this way to such an extent.

The Canadian fish fauna, while seemingly species-poor compared to the fish fauna of the Amazon River and Southeast Asia, nevertheless has representatives of most of the higher taxonomic groups. In marine and fresh waters in Canada there are representatives of about 190 families of the 480 or so that are recognized by ichthyologists. All nine of the major groups of related species recognized in the classification (at the ordinal level or higher) of freshwater bony fishes have representatives in Canada. Therefore, while the numbers of species in any one area may be relatively low, the overall diversity is impressive. The number of individuals per unit area in many waters is equal to that found in many other areas richer in species numbers. In high mountain lakes, prairie rivers, the Great Lakes, along the Arctic coastline, or in tide pools or offshore areas of the Atlantic and Pacific oceans, they bring a beauty and fascination to those of us willing to share some time with our aquatic relatives.

Lake, River and Sea-Run Fishes of Canada covers numerous topics in a way that is suited to a wide readership. The reader sees fishes through the eyes of an avid angler and a keen observer, who introduces their drama with considerable philosophical wisdom. It is almost impossible to make generalizations about fishes; their evolution has created an exception to almost every statement we might wish to make. Fortunately this book's author does not shy away from telling us of the many curiosities of fishes merely because he cannot mention all the exceptions. Nor does he shy away from introducing and explaining technical terms or using scientific names along with the common names of fishes. In addition, the reader is always aware that what we know about fishes comes from observation, studies and writings of many individuals.

We have much yet to learn about fishes, however, and all who enjoy them may contribute. Surprisingly, new species are still found in Canada. Most of these represent range extensions of known species, and an alert fisher may indeed be the first to identify a species previously unrecorded in Canadian waters (or in provincial or territorial waters, or in a river system). Rarely, a species new to science may be discovered and found to live only in Canadian waters, such as the whitefish found only in Nova Scotia and known as the Atlantic whitefish.

Despite the loss of a few species in the last hundred years, Canadian waters continue to be home to many important groups of commercial and sports fishes; some are in serious trouble, however. Most, if wisely managed by biologists with the help of politicians and the public, will continue to have healthy populations. The work of the Committee on the Status of Endangered Wildlife in Canada (COSEWIC) is important in identifying the status of various species, but it will take the collective actions of us all to ensure that no additional species are lost through our unthinking actions. We make changes to the environment and we harvest fish from the oceans, lakes and streams without knowing enough about them to be intelligent custodians and to ensure their survival for future generations, despite our follies. We worry about the effects of acid rain and climate change on fishes. These are things that seem beyond our individual control, but they are the result of our collective actions. If we fail to take remedial action we will see serious losses in our living resources. People tend to want to save only what they love or care about, and we may often love only that which we know well. Observant and caring anglers can play an important role in alerting authorities about problems, in protecting fishes and their habitat, and in being responsible for their own environmental actions. This book will surely bring much fascination about fishes to readers and thus it will serve a valuable role in keeping us in tune with nature whether or not we are anglers.

Despite the origin of the world's first fishes so long ago, these creatures are young in terms of the earth's history. Not surprisingly, regions of Canada are known to have had fishes almost back to when these aquatic animals first appear in the fossil record. This same area that we know as Canada, however, has undergone catastrophic changes—changes from inundation by ocean waters to appearance of desert-like conditions and high mountains. Finally, from the start of the past ice age and up to about only fourteen thousand years ago, most of Canada was covered by ice. This produced an inhospitable place not only for fishes but for most forms of life. In the strict sense, then, most of our fish populations have been in place for only about the last six thousand to twelve thousand years. So young, really—and how long will they last? Or will they outlast us, the masters of observation, documentation and alteration? As Fred Wooding believes, our mutual survival depends on our using our intelligence and custodial conscience.

I invite you to see Canadian fishes through this book and to let your readings become part of your wealth in understanding these fascinating creatures.

Introduction
THIS CREATURE CALLED A FISH

Fish are vertebrates. Like amphibians, reptiles, birds and mammals, they have a backbone. Most are cold-blooded; some, such as tuna, are warm-blooded.

Fish come in different shapes, sizes and colours; their anatomical characteristics, lifestyles and habitats are varied and complex. Some live only in fresh water, some live only in salt water, and some manage to survive in both. Some (salmon, for example) are born in fresh water, spend most of their lives in salt water and then return to fresh water to spawn. These are known as *anadromous* fish. Some are born in salt water (eels, for example), migrate great distances to spend most of their lives in fresh water, and then return to salt water to spawn. They are known as *catadromous* fish.

Most fish lay eggs to perpetuate their kind. A few, such as mosquito fish and coelacanths, hold their eggs in their bodies and give birth to live young.

Most fish take in oxygen through their gills, but some respire by other means. Lungfish have a swim bladder that serves as a lung. To survive they must move to the surface frequently to replenish oxygen needs.

Some fish can "fly" for short distances (Atlantic flying fish); some can walk on land (gobies and blennies). Some fish (Arctic charr) live in very cold waters of the northern polar regions; others do very well in desert pools where water temperatures reach 100°F (38°C). Some live in the deepest and blackest parts of the ocean's great depths, and are equipped with their own light-generating organs. Others live in tidepools, lakes and rivers at low and moderate elevations, some high up in mountains. Some even manage to exist in roadside ditches. Although lack of oxygen kills fish quickly, a few—such as the little banded killifish, often used as bait by anglers in eastern Canada—if kept moist can live for days out of water.

The smallest of all fish (and the smallest of all vertebrates) are the scaleless 0.31 inch to 0.39 (8 to 10 mm) long *Trimmatom nanus* of the Chagos Archipelago in the Indian Ocean, and the quarter-inch to half-inch (6 to 12 mm) freshwater *Pandaka pygmaea* of Luzon, Philippines. The largest of fish are the harmless whale sharks (*Rhincodon typus*), which grow up to lengths of 50 feet (15.24 m)!

Some freshwater fish, such as northern pike, pickerel, lamprey and eel, are long and slender; others, such as ocean sunfish, which have been known to reach lengths of nearly 11 feet (3.35 m), are almost oval in shape. Still others, such as flounder and halibut (which have both eyes on the same side of the head), are as flat as pancakes. Fish such as the saltwater oar fish and dragonfish are incredibly strange in appearance; others, such as butterfly fish and our own darters and sunfish, are stunningly beautiful. Nature has created a realm of fantastic extremes.

The basic components that make up the skeleton of a typical fish are the skull, vertebrae (or joined backbone, usually with ribs) and paired fins. These fins are known as the *ventrals* (or pelvics) and the pectorals. Unpaired fins on the midline of the body are the *dorsal, anal, adipose* and *caudal* (or tail fin), which are not as firmly linked to the skeleton as are the paired fins. A fish has no neck, the head being fused directly into the trunk.

To this structure are added other components which complete the creature's anatomy. Some of these are the *nervous, glandular, respiratory, muscular, digestive, reproductive* and *skin* systems.

The skin of fish is the tightest-fitting covering to be found on any of the backboned animals. Mucus (often improperly called slime) produced by glands in the skin covers it. This lubricant, in addition to enabling fish to move through water with a minimum

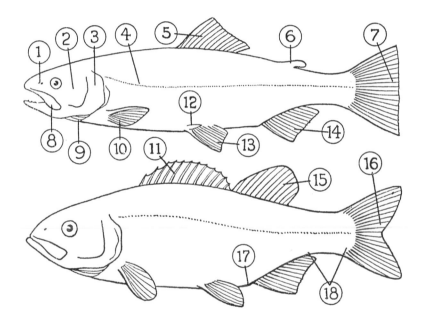

TWO HYPOTHETICAL FISH SHOWING MAIN EXTERNAL FEATURES:
1. Nostrils. 2. Preopercle or cheek. 3. Opercle or gill cover.
4. Lateral line. 5. Dorsal fin. 6. Adipose fin. 7. Caudal fin, square.
8. Maxillary. 9. Branchiostegals. 10. Pectoral fin.
11 Spiny, or first dorsal fin. 12. Fleshy appendage. 13. Pelvic fin.
14. Anal fin. 15. Soft, or second dorsal fin. 16. Caudal fin, forked.
17. Anus. 18. Caudal peduncle.

of friction, protects the body from attack by parasites, bacteria and other harmful organisms.

Anglers should always wet their hands when handling fish that are to be returned to the water, because dry hands remove so much of this mucus. Experiments have shown, however, that a fish sustains more injury from pressure on its internal organs when an angler tries to hold it still than from loss of the mucus. The safest practice is to wear wet gloves when handling a fish that is to be given a new lease on life, for the gloves permit a firmer grip with less pressure. Fishery workers always follow this practice when tagging, stripping spawn or milt at hatcheries, or removing scales for study.

Fish have two skin layers. The outer layer, the *epidermis*, is in most cases soft and transparent. The second layer of skin, the *dermis*, is thicker and made up of many living cells. Here are found the cells with pigments that create a fish's colouring; here, too, are strange crystals known as *guanine,* which can reflect light and thus produce the iridescent hues so noticeable in some species. The *lateral line,* which runs along the sides of a fish, is a sensory canal with a series of pore-like openings capable of picking up low-frequency vibrations. It also acts as a sort of thermometer, since it can detect changes in heat and cold.

The scales of a fish (only a few, such as catfish, lampreys, eels and leather carp, are scaleless) grow from the dermis and, in some cases, project through the epidermis. In some fish, such as trout, scales are so small that they are not readily apparent.

Most fish acquire scales after they hatch from their eggs and when still quite small. These appear in orderly, overlapping rows and, once established, remain constant in number and arrangement throughout the creature's life. In trout and salmon, however, extra diagonal rows of scales appear early in life after the original rows are laid down.

As fish grow, the scales increase in size to keep providing a protective covering. Rings of new scale substance are added around the edges. By means of these patterns trained fishery workers can determine the age of a fish in much the same way that we can determine the age of a tree. In an Atlantic salmon scale, for example, an experienced person can tell not only the particular fish's age, but also if it has spawned and how many times, and the number of years it has spent at sea. Knowledge of this kind is of vital importance in planning programs to ensure effective management of stocks.

Scales of freshwater fish are of three types. *Cycloid* scales are thin and more or less round, with smooth edges, and are found on the soft-rayed fish such as salmon, trout, charr and whitefish. *Ctenoid* scales have fine-toothed edges and are characteristic of spiny-rayed fish such as bass, perch and darters. *Ganoid* scales are thick and covered with an enamel-like substance known as *ganoine,* and are found on primitive fish such as gars and sturgeon. Scales can be regenerated or replaced when lost, but because the new scales do not show rings recording growth before regeneration, they cannot be used to determine age.

Like most living things, fish require oxygen to survive. In their environment this oxygen must come from the water. Some fish require more oxygen than others. Thus its abundance or scarcity can determine a suitable habitat. Carp, eels and most species of catfish can live in water where the oxygen content is low; in the same water, trout would soon die. Land vertebrates, including humans, take oxygen from the air they breathe through their nostrils and mouths and into their lungs. Fish, with some exceptions, breathe not through lungs but through gills.

Gills are located on each side of the head, and each is protected by a gill cover or *operculum*. When a fish breathes, it draws water in through the mouth. The closing of the mouth forces the water past the supporting arch and over the gills. The oxygen is absorbed into the blood vessels through very thin membranes, and unwanted carbon dioxide is discharged. The water is then ejected by opening the gill covers. The gill arch supports the gill rakers, which strain food and other solid objects from the water before it passes between the gills.

The digestive system begins with the mouth, which varies in size and position according to the feeding habits of each fish species. In some bottom feeders, such as suckers and sturgeon, the mouth is located under the head; in others, such as the surface-feeding banded killifish, it is upturned. In most freshwater fish the mouth is terminal or, to be less academic, up front.

Food passes through the mouth, into the throat, down the gullet and into the stomach. It is digested with the help of juices of the liver and pancreas and passes to the intestines, where nutritive parts are absorbed into the bloodstream and circulated throughout the body. The wastes then move farther along the intestines to be ejected through the anus. The kidneys, which hold urinary wastes, are on the roof of the body cavity immediately beneath the vertebral column; they are fleshy, dark red organs. Anglers should thoroughly scrape these out when a fish is cleaned, for they spoil rapidly.

Another form of excretion takes place through the gills, which give off waste gases, especially carbon dioxide. In some fish, waste materials are deposited in the skin; guanine, which causes the silvery or iridescent hues in certain fish, is actually waste material that is carried to the skin and forms into tiny crystals.

Teeth also vary greatly. In most predatory species they are found on the upper and lower jaws and the tongue. All members of the salmon family also have teeth on the roof of the mouth. In other fish such as minnows, which lack true teeth, structures known as pharyngeal teeth are present on bones on either side of the throat. In still other fish, such as whitefish species (with the exception of the Arctic inconnu), the jaws are toothless. The tongue of a fish is flat, gristly and immovable.

Fish have completely expressionless faces because they have no facial muscles. (Some, but not all, can change colour to show dominance, submissiveness or other conditions.) Unlike most animals, they do not express pain, anger or pleasure in ways we easily recognize. Yet fish experience both stress and pain. Anglers should remove hooks in fish to be returned to the water with care and as quickly as possible, and never rip them out. If the fish are to be kept for food, anglers should dispatch them as quickly and as humanely as possible.

Fish have muscles to open and close their mouths, move their eyes, swallow food and flex the body. But since they have no legs to help them move about, they must rely on their strong side muscles and to a lesser extent on their fins. Muscles enable the tail to serve as a rudder; the pectoral and ventral fins, when opened up, also act as brakes when a fish is stopping or making a turn. By flexing the body first on one side and then on the other, and by pushing against the water, a fish can move forward or backward (a rare few can apparently only go forward). This can produce slow, delicate movement or create extraordinary speed.

Most fish have *monocular* vision; both eyes cannot focus on the same object at once. Some, such as saltwater sea bass and seahorses, have *binocular* vision and can focus both eyes on the same object at once. Fish have no eyelids, although some sharks can drop a semi-transparent nictitating membrane over their eyes to help diffuse light. Lack of eyelids does not prevent fish from sleeping, however, even though they spend all of their lives with their eyes open.

Most fish species cannot see well beyond about a metre. Among the exceptions are the brown trout (*Salmo trutta*), whose vision is extraordinarily well developed. Its eyes have been likened to a combined microscope and telescope; they can focus simultaneously on near and distant objects. Another exception is the archerfish (*Toxotes jaculatrix*), a creature approximately 6 inches long (15.24 cm) inhabiting streams, swamps and brackish waters from India to the New Hebrides. This little fish cruises just under the surface; when its keen eyes spot an insect or spider, it pokes its head out of the water, takes precise aim and spits water at it with great force. The victim falls into the water and is consumed. Small archerfish are accurate up to 4 feet (1.22 m), larger archerfish up to 14 feet (4.27 m).

We now know that fish are not colour blind. Fish see and distinguish colours, as many scientific studies have proved. What the world really looks like through the eyes of a fish is more difficult to assess. Brian Curtis states that experiments have shown that bass (this also applies to trout) have "a strong preference for red over other colours, with yellow in second place."

The ocular faculties of fish give them capabilities which, endowed on humans, would prove hilarious: their eyes can be manipulated independently of each other, one eye looking forward and one backward, or one up and the other down.

There is no conclusive proof that fish have a highly developed sense of taste, although it is known that they can recognize the difference between bitter and sour. Some fish can recognize sweetness.

The tongue lies immobile on the floor of the mouth. It is rather poorly developed, but does have taste buds of a sort. Many species also have taste buds on the head, tail, chin, lips or snout. Catfish have additional sensory equipment—the barbels on their head have efficient taste buds.

In their natural habitat, often so cloudy as to be almost opaque, fish must rely heavily on their sense of smell; the olfactory organs in their nostrils are quite sensitive. The nostrils of most fish are unconnected with the mouth and are not used for breathing. Some fish, especially those with poor vision, are completely dependent on their sense of smell for locating food. Sharks are probably the best example. Brian Curtis suggests that "their complete dependence on smell may be the explanation of why sharks are apt to leave potential prey alone unless it is wounded. Their eyes are incapable of telling them that food is at hand, and they must wait until the odour of flesh reaches their nostrils." Whenever sharks attack humans—and not all do—it is because they have come close enough to detect human odours, especially blood.

Few species of fish display such highly developed olfactory faculties as the salmon. Although not all of their homing instincts are fully understood, it is believed that their extraordinary sense of smell enables them to return unfailingly after years at sea to the same rivers and streams where their lives began. Sometimes they even return to the very patch of gravel where they were spawned. Of all the miracles of nature, the completion of the salmon's homeward migration is one of the most astonishing.

Freshwater fish procreate their kind by the simultaneous release of eggs from the female and fertilizing sperm from the male. These are usually deposited in carefully prepared nests scooped out of gravel or other detritus, or released randomly over vegetation or other submerged objects to which they cling until hatched.

But not all follow these simple procedures. Yellow perch extrude eggs and sperm into long, gelatinous ribbons which attach to submerged objects or remain free-floating. Sticklebacks build elaborate nests out of grasses and other fibrous vegetation which they glue together with thread-like secretions from their kidneys. These tunnel-shaped nests have an opening at each end, and are designed so a female can enter, lay her eggs and swim out the other end. Once the eggs have been deposited the male swims through and, without stopping, fertilizes the eggs.

The number of eggs spawned by fish varies greatly. Often it depends on the size of the females as well as the size of their eggs. A northern pike may release as many as six hundred thousand eggs, a rainbow trout about four thousand and a madtom as few as fifty.

Longevity of fish is also variable. Pink salmon live for only two years, striped bass may live for thirty years and carp may live for sixty years.

Since the world's fresh and salt water holds some of the largest communities of living things, it seems unreasonable to think of them as silent places, even though their sounds and voices are beyond the human hearing range.

Can fish communicate with each other as do mammals such as whales, dolphins and porpoises? That question may yet produce surprising answers, for we know----as high-frequency microphones and other sophisticated detecting devices have proved—that many saltwater species are very noisy creatures indeed. This was dramatically demonstrated during the Second World War when a school of croakers passed through anti-submarine nets on the east coast of the United States. The racket they made brought about a full-scale enemy alert! Idyll writes that spiny lobsters make loud noises when they rub their long antennae against their horny armour, and that noise from large groups of snapping shrimps can be heard underwater "as far away as two and a half miles." Other first-class saltwater sound producers are sea trout, sea perch and weakfish. There are even singing fish called midshipmen, but I can't vouch for their talents.

How many species of living freshwater and saltwater fish are there? No one knows for certain. In his book *Fishes of the World* Professor Joseph Nelson, one of the leading authorities on species demographics, currently estimates their number at 24,618. He points out, however, that "since some groups are expanding with newly described species the eventual number may be closer to 28,500." Fish families with living species he estimates at 482. He estimates that about 40 percent of all fish occur in, or almost always in, fresh water. Fish, he also points out, constitute slightly more than half the total number of the 48,170 vertebrate species recognized.

Much more, of course, could be said to answer the question "What are fish?" Despite many masterful studies on the subject, science still faces many tantalizing unknowns. Planet Earth's waters are as much our last frontier as the cosmic abyss around us—and the challenges are as great.

1

Sockeye salmon
*(Oncorhynchus
nerka)*

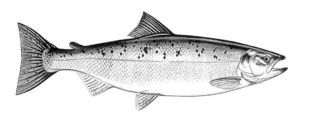

2

Chinook salmon
*(Oncorhynchus
tshawytscha)*

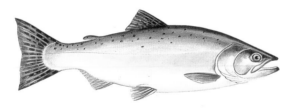

3

Pink salmon
*(Oncorhynchus
gorbuscha)*

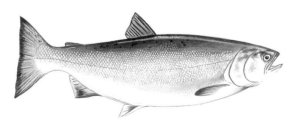

4

Coho salmon
*(Oncorhynchus
kisutch)*

5

Atlantic salmon
(Salmo salar)

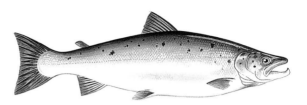

6

Rainbow trout
*(Oncorhynchus
mykiss)*

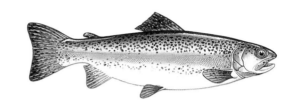

7

Brown trout
(Salmo trutta)

8

Splake
(wendigo)
*(Salvelinus
fontinalis x S
namaycush)*

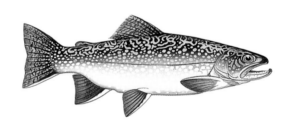

9

Arctic charr
*(Salvelinus
alpinus)*

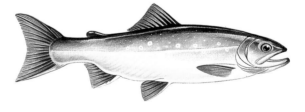

10

Brook trout
*(Salvelinus
fontinalis)*

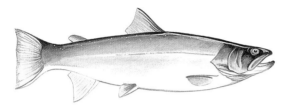

11

Dolly Varden
trout
*(Salvelinus
malma)*

12

Cutthroat trout
*(Oncorhynchus
clarki)*

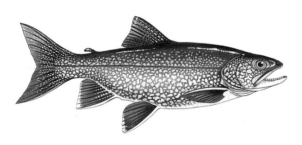

13

Lake trout
*(Salvelinus
namaycush)*

14

Arctic grayling
*(Thymallus
arcticus)*

15

Lake whitefish
*(Coregonus
clupeaformis)*

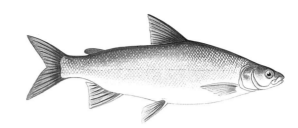

16

Mountain
whitefish
*(Prosopium
williamsoni)*

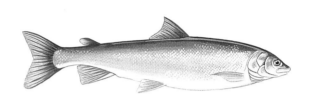

17

Rainbow smelt
*(Osmerus
mordax)*

18

Inconnu
*(Stenodus
leucichthys)*

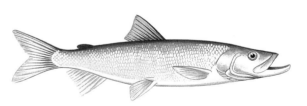

19

Northern pike
(Esox lucius)

20

Muskellunge
(*Esox
masquinongy*)

21

Largemouth
bass
(*Micropterus
salmoides*)

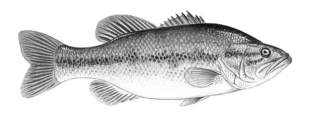

22

Smallmouth
bass
(*Micropterus
dolomieu*)

23

Bluegill
(*Lepomis
macrochirus*)

24

Pumpkinseed
*(Lepomis
gibbosus)*

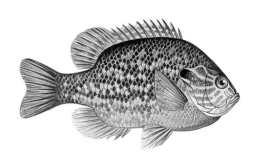

25

Black crappie
*(Poxomis
nigromaculatus)*

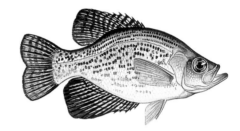

26

Yellow perch
*(Perca
flavescens)*

27

Walleye
*(Stizostedion
vitreum)*

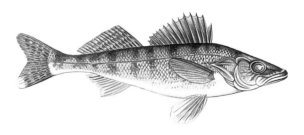

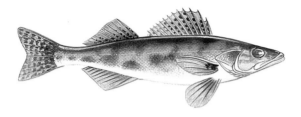

28

Sauger
*(Stizostedion
canadense)*

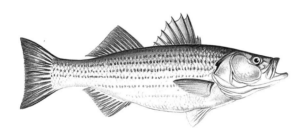

29

Striped bass
*(Morone
saxatilis)*

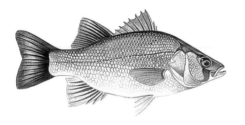

30

White perch
*(Morone
americana)*

31

Channel catfish
*(Ictalurus
punctatus)*

32

Brown bullhead
(*Ictalurus
nebulosus*)

33

Atlantic tomcod
(*Microgadus
tomcod*)

34

Burbot
(*Lota lota*)

35

Lake sturgeon
(*Acipenser
fulvescens*)

36

Goldeye
(*Hiodon
alosoides*)

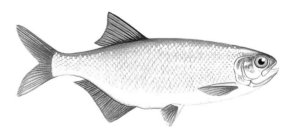

Salmon, Trout, Charr, Grayling & Whitefish

ORDER SALMONIFORMES

The Salmoniformes derive from primitive ancestors. Fossil evidence indicates that they existed more than one hundred million years ago. They are all members of the ancient Actinopterygii class that arose during the Devonian, the period that marked the evolution of the bony fishes.

The Salmoniformes order worldwide includes one family, eleven genera and about sixty-six species. All Salmoniformes spawn in fresh water.

The Salmoniformes are generally acknowledged to be one of the most interesting and—in the case of some species—the most commercially and recreationally valuable of all anadromous and freshwater fish.

Salmoniformes are diverse, but taxonomists have brought these species together because their anatomical characteristics leave little doubt about their close relationship. Anadromous and freshwater Salmoniformes of Canadian waters include all salmon, trout and charr; whitefish, inconnu, ciscoes and Arctic grayling

Not all Salmoniformes in Canadian waters are of interest to anglers, but there are enough species—particularly salmon, trout, charr, grayling, and the far-northern inconnu—to satisfy the piscatorial needs of fly-fishers and those who seek their prey by other means.

THE SALMONID FAMILY
Salmonidae

THE SALMON SUBFAMILY—Salmoninae

PACIFIC SALMON

There are eleven species of Pacific salmon: sockeye (including kokanee), chinook, coho, pink, chum, cutthroat trout, golden trout, Apache trout, rainbow trout (including steelhead), masu and amago, the latter two being indigenous to and found only in Asian waters. All eleven belong to the genus *Oncorhynchus*. The one Atlantic salmon species belongs to the genus *Salmo.*

Although salmon are among the best-known of fish, questions concerning both genera inspire continuing interest and debate among scientists:

- Did Pacific salmon and Atlantic salmon originate in fresh water or in salt water?
- Did both genera derive from a common ancestor, or did each genus evolve independently?

The theories now generally favoured are that salmon did originate in fresh water and that some form of genus *Salmo* was the progenitor of genus *Oncorhynchus*. But from what progenitor did they evolve? Was it a type of *Salmo* now long extinct, or was it *Salmo salar,* the Atlantic salmon as we know it today? Was it, rather, from an early trout-like species of *Salmo*? Could that

species have been a type of steelhead, the anadromous member of
the loosely defined rainbow trout group in the genus *Oncorhynchus*?
The answers lie far back in time and—despite important recent
research—may continue for many years to inspire research.

In 1958 Dr. Ferris Neave, FRSC, a scientist with what was then
the Fisheries Research Board of Canada, aroused the scientific
world with his paper "Origin and Speciation of *Oncorhynchus*,"
published in *Transactions of the Royal Society of Canada*. Dr. Neave
writes:

> In one of the farthest regions to which it penetrated, a large
> stock became isolated geographically and diverged mark-
> edly from the populations which continued to inhabit other
> coastal regions of the North Pacific. In due course the
> newly-evolved off-shoot spread back through the territories
> occupied by more conservative lines of ancestral stock. This
> process of reinvasion was facilitated by increased adaptation
> to ocean life and was accompanied or followed by a further
> splitting into several species.

Although Atlantic and Pacific salmon, and steelhead (the sea-
going rainbow type), are genetically and morphologically similar
in many ways, there is one major biological difference: Atlantic
salmon may live to spawn several times, whereas Pacific salmon
die after their first spawning. The steelhead is capable of several
spawnings.

The freshwater origin of salmon is a theory supported by a
number of distinguished scientists. In a personal communication
Dr. Lionel Johnson, a specialist in Arctic charr and an independent
scientific consultant who for many years was a senior member of
the Freshwater Fisheries Institute of the Department of Fisheries
and Oceans, writes:

> Many species within the family Salmonidae are anadro-
> mous, spawning in fresh water but migrating to the sea for

feeding, then returning to fresh water to reproduce. On the other hand, many Salmonidae species live out their lives entirely in fresh water. None of the family is completely marine, although a few populations of pink salmon reproduce in the coastal waters of British Columbia. Given this widespread habit of anadromy within the family, it is interesting to speculate on whether the salmonids are fish of marine or freshwater origin. Nevertheless, speculation it is, and likely remains so, unless some new and definitive evidence is brought to light.

The salmons, trouts and charrs are relatively unspecialized (primitive?), having characters such as extensive cartilage in the skeleton. This character is diagnostic of the presumed ancestors of more specialized modern fish, such as the cod, with its well-developed skeleton. The emphasis on cartilage, for some taxonomists, place the Salmonidae mid-way between the sharks and the modern teleost fish. Thus, if one goes far enough back, a marine origin to all fish might be indicated, for there are few freshwater sharks; however, to delve this far into history is rather like claiming direct descent from Adam and Eve.

More tangible evidence in support of my view that the Salmonidae have a freshwater origin, is that the 'core' members of the group—salmons, trouts and charrs—all spawn in fresh water. This habit seems to be rather a conservative one in general biological terms, therefore indicative of a freshwater origin. Supporting this is that none of the family is entirely marine and the closest relatives of the core group— fish such as the huchen (*Hucho hucho*) of the River Danube, the taimen (*Hucho taimen*) of Siberia as well as the whitefish (*Coregonus spp.*) [and] the grayling (*Thymallus spp.*)—are also freshwater spawners.

The second line of evidence comes from relationships within the Salmonidae. Within the salmonids, according to the eminent Canadian fish physiologist, Dr. Bill Hoar, there is a gradual increase in specialization with respect to living in the marine environment, from lake trout (*Salvelinus namaycush*), with very little saltwater tolerance, chinook salmon to pink salmon with the highest degree of specialization.

Arctic charr, which are relatively unspecialized with respect to a marine existence, unlike most other anadromous salmonids make an annual migration to the sea for feeding, returning to fresh water each fall, but not to spawn. Spawning is not annual, and in those years that spawning does not take place the individual charr does not, as a general rule, migrate to the ocean, but remains in fresh water over the preceding summer. There is also evidence to suggest that Arctic charr cannot spend an indefinite period of time in salt water, although the reverse is possible, as witnessed by the fact that many populations have lived in fresh water for thousands of years, having been isolated from the ocean during the retreat of the ice in the Post-Pleistocene.

These trends, Dr. Johnson pointed out, can be interpreted in the opposite way, but the absence of any fully marine species tends to argue against a marine origin for the family as a whole.

In his chapter "The Life History of Chum Salmon" in *Pacific Salmon Life Histories*, the late Dr. Ernest D. Salo, another eminent authority on salmonid biology, writes that "the arguments presented so far in the literature appear to favour a freshwater origin of Pacific salmon . . ."

Also supporting the freshwater origin theory is the existence of a permanently freshwater form of each of the two Asian species, *Oncorhynchus masou* and *Oncorhynchus rhodurus,* the permanently freshwater form (kokanee) of the North American sockeye *Oncorhynchus nerka*, and a permanently freshwater form (landlocked salmon) of the Atlantic salmon, *Salmo salar*. Also, transplantations of salmon to freshwater habitats in Europe, South America, Chile and New Zealand have been successful and in some instances—such as the establishment in the Great Lakes system of chinook, pink and coho—spectacular.

Dr. John E. Thorpe, a scientist based at the Freshwater Fisheries Laboratory (Pitlochry) of the Department of Agriculture and Fisheries for Scotland, however, writes in the winter 1988 issue of *The Atlantic Salmon Journal*:

> Recent comparative studies have led to a revival of the view held by most nineteenth-century biologists that salmon are marine fish. Not only have they been around for about one million years, their construction and shape suggest that they are derived from relatively simple predators—which probably spawned by scattering their eggs on the sea-bed of the beach, rather like their modern relative the capelin does.
>
> It is not a long step, in evolutionary terms, for that behaviour to have been transferred along the shore and into the most protected estuarine habitat (where some Pacific pink salmon spawn today), or further upriver. The riverine phase of some salmonids, then, can be viewed as a protective nursery stage for a fish whose principal home is in the surface layers of the open seas.

The editor of *The Atlantic Salmon Journal* adds a footnote to Dr. Thorpe's article: "It is a truism in science, however, that the more we think we know about a subject, the more we realize how little we really understand."

The streams and lakes of the salmon's birth and early growth and the oceans in which they reach maturity remain under intensive study. In laboratories, in field stations frequently located in remote wilderness areas, in estuarine and coastal waters and on ships far out at sea, specialists in a range of scientific disciplines are probing the lives and habitat of salmon and are seeking to replace the many intriguing unknowns with new knowledge.

Coincident with research is the vitally important work carried

SOME YOUNG OF THE SALMONIDAE FAMILY:
Sockeye salmon, coho salmon, chum salmon, chinook salmon,
pink salmon, Atlantic salmon and brook trout. Pink salmon
young are readily identified by their complete absence of parr marks.

#

out under the federal-provincial Salmonid Enhancement Program whose goal is to restore the Pacific salmon, as well the anadromous steelhead and cutthroat trout, to their historic levels of abundance. New hatcheries have been built, as have fishways to assist upstream and downstream migrants over natural and manmade barriers. New spawning channels have been constructed and huge numbers of additional fry and smolts are being released each year into wild waters. As a result, significant steps have been made in reaching the restorative goals. In addition private citizens' groups, many of them involving the enthusiastic help of schoolchildren, are supporting the Salmonid Enhancement Program in important areas such as stream clearance and embankment stabilization. Educational programs for both adults and children also raise public awareness of the importance of the salmon resource.

Scientists in this century have learned much about the salmon, including its migratory traits, reproduction, mortality and food habits. They are gradually bridging the gaps in their knowledge despite the difficulty of some questions, particularly those shrouded by the curtain of the sea.

A few years ago we believed the freshwater environment was the key to the survival of both Pacific and Atlantic salmon, and that in their saltwater wanderings they were not seriously at risk. This is no longer the case. Now one need only consider the horrendous oil spills in Alaskan and eastern North Atlantic waters, overfishing, pollution, the damages being done to freshwater habitats, and the awesome possibilities of global warming—all of which may require significant changes in present fisheries management strategies.

In a personal communication, Dr. Cornelis Groot, retired senior scientist of the Pacific Biological Station, and one of the world's leading authorities on salmon, said:

Present estimates of the impact of global warming on the marine climate off the west coast of Canada suggest that the average water temperature could rise by several degrees over the next fifty to a hundred years, and that the frequency and intensity of upwelling along the coast in summer could decrease. It is less clear how coastal salinity will change. The most important responses of the marine community to this change in climate will be in species compositions, due to extensions or contractions of present distributional ranges, and in an overall decrease in the production of traditional commercial species associated with the relaxation of upwelling.

Pacific salmon have a strong homing instinct and will be especially affected during freshwater life stages by the expected increase in temperatures and the accompanying changes in precipitation. Climatological zones and land biotypes are expected to shift northward by several hundred kilometres during this time. The expected changes in the freshwater environments may especially affect many sockeye and pink salmon stocks in British Columbia because these two species are at the southern end of their geographical range in the southern part of the province. The optimum distribution range of coho and chum salmon, which presently covers southern and central British Columbia and Washington State, may shift to northern British Columbia and southeastern Alaska. Chinook salmon are distributed farthest south and are expected to change their optimum range from the Columbia river basin to southern and central British Columbia.

The strong homing instinct of Pacific salmon will prevent populations from southern areas from moving northward with increasing temperature, when conditions become too severe for survival. Northern populations, on the other hand, will experience more favourable conditions for increased production. Higher temperatures and possibly lower salinities in west Vancouver Island coastal areas during the time that the juveniles reach salt water are generally correlated with lower return rates of adults for a number of Pacific salmon species. The expected temperature and winter precipitation increases may, therefore, negatively affect ocean survival. The biological mechanisms are not known, but it is assumed that changes in near-shore oceanic conditions modify food and predator composition and abundance.

Dr. Groot also suggests that migratory routes of returning adults could change in relation to oceanographic conditions. Since 1977, for example, Fraser River sockeye have increasingly approached the home stream via Johnstone Strait instead of Juan de Fuca Strait, and this may continue; Skeena and Nass river sockeye may make landfall farther north off southeastern Alaska when coastal temperatures become higher. As well, increasing temperatures in both fresh and salt water will increase parasite, viral and bacterial infestations.

Dr. Groot's forecast of the effects of global warming on North Pacific zones apply as well to the rest of the Northern Hemisphere, and it is inevitable that it would seriously influence Atlantic salmon and other Atlantic species. *Salmo salar* would also face an uncertain future.

The nine North American species of Pacific salmon run to some thirteen hundred rivers or lakes in British Columbia, and are native to scores of United States rivers or lakes from California to Alaska. In British Columbia they occur in their greatest numbers (depending on species) in the three major river systems—in the south the Fraser with its major tributaries the Nechako, Thompson and Chilko, and in the north the Skeena and Nass rivers.

Anadromous salmon, particularly those of the Pacific, return to their native waters on a delicately timed schedule; scientists can tell almost to the day when some runs will appear. But if their upstream migration is blocked by barriers, even where there are ladders, delays result. A minor barrier causing short delays is of little consequence; major barriers, or a series of them, can cause delays resulting in spawning failure and for all practical purposes the end of those races.

But even if the migration to the spawning grounds is successfully completed and a favourable seeding takes place, other problems face the new generations. Most serious are: areas of pollution where raw waste from domestic sewage systems and industrial plants are spewed into rivers for easy disposal; poisoning of waters through spraying of forests and other vegetation with insecticides; and removal of forest cover (sometimes to the water's edge) which destroys spawning beds by drying up streams, silting, causing flash floods or raising water temperatures to levels at which salmon cannot survive.

Effective freshwater management is complex and difficult, and calls for the management of the *whole* ecosystem, not merely a part of it. The problem is complicated by the fact that no two river systems are alike; each has its own peculiarities requiring its own special remedies.

Dr. Johnson, in his critical review of *Pacific Salmon Life Histories,* a comprehensive study published co-operatively in 1991 by the University of British Columbia and the Department of Fisheries and Oceans, writes:

> What is remarkable about the salmon as a genus is its luxuriousness or plenteousness, its burgeoning vitality as life is continually renewed in one of the most extravagant and abundant forms known, only to end in death when the short allotted life-span runs out.
>
> Many of the facets distinguishing individual species are variations on a theme with considerable overlap in detail, and the genus as a whole seems to be well fitted to the job of vacuuming up as much as possible of the annual production of small creatures such as copepods, shrimps, and shrimp-like organisms, squids, swimming shell-less molluscs and small fishes. Coho, for example, feed preferentially on fish but also eat invertebrates, whereas in pinks and sockeye

the reverse is true. Throughout the North Pacific the species intermingle in their migrations as they comb the vast area of ocean north of 40° N latitude leaving no swirl or gyre unexplored. Then they segregate to their individual birthing streams with undeviating precision, where again the various species, each with somewhat different requirements, explore the potential . . .

The other great enigmas of the genus are the great fluctuations in abundance, as for example, between odd and even years in pinks, or the four-year cycle of the sockeye, and secondly, the death of all species following a fixed life-span. We can only stand in awe of the sheer profligacy of a nature which destroys her handiwork at the peak of its abundance. Only the may-flies and cicadas work on a similar fixed schedule of increasing biomass, mass reproduction and then death. Why? Is such a fluctuating and determinant life history geared to maximizing production in an open system? Such a life history may be contrasted with the trend toward equilibrium shown by fish in more confined waters with their long indeterminant life-span and high, relatively constant biomass.

Could it be that lessons for our growth-oriented industrial society nestle within the basic biology of ecological systems?

Pacific salmon species are too often given a monetary value based only on their worth to the commercial fisheries. This assessment is misleading. All species contribute to the multi-million dollar income annually derived from the sports fishery, and from tourists who journey inland to see marvels such as the Hell's Gate fish ladders or the sockeye salmon spawning in the Adams River.

But economic value is not necessarily of the greatest significance; what the salmon offer in enjoyment and relaxation has a value beyond all computation. Coastal and estuarine fishing for salmon, as well as for sea-going trout, is as available to the fisher with a small skiff and faltering kicker as it is to the fisher with a triple-decker yacht. This pursuit is carried out in surroundings among the most beautiful in the world.

A lavish nature has created a paradise without equal: the Inside Passage from the Gulf Islands north through the Strait of Georgia and Johnstone Strait, thence to the Alaska Panhandle and beyond. There, in a setting of spruce-studded islands protected from the heavy roll of the Pacific, with the sometimes overwhelming Coast Range as a backdrop, anglers enjoy their sport, while commercial fishers in their efficient and colourful purse seiners, trollers and gill-netters go about the business of catching fish for market.

Sockeye salmon
(Oncorhynchus nerka)

No single species of anadromous fish has been the object of as much scientific research as has *Oncorhynchus nerka,* the sockeye salmon.

These remarkable creatures, often described by canners as the "wonder fish," are native to many rivers from the Columbia River north through British Columbia, west through the Aleutians, along the Kamchatka Peninsula and south to the Sea of Okhotsk. Sockeye have been reported in the Yukon River and in other Arctic waters as far east as Bathurst Inlet and the west coast of Victoria Island. Random runs have been reported as far south as the Sacramento River in California. The major North American stocks originate in waters tributary to the Columbia River (which serves as the Washington-Oregon state line), in the Fraser, Nass and Skeena rivers in British Columbia, and in streams entering Bristol Bay, Alaska.

The sockeye has a slender, somewhat compressed body, is greenish blue on the back and metallic green on the head. Its teeth are small and weak except at spawning, when they become strongly developed and hooked. Toward the end of its life the body of the male turns brilliant red with a grass green head, while the female becomes dark red with green and yellow blotches. At that time the male develops a pronounced *kype* or hook on the upper jaw, and a humped back. Weight at maturity is 4 to 5 pounds (1.81 to 2.26 kg), although some mature individuals have weighed up to 15.5 pounds (7.03 kg).

Sockeye spawn from August to November in rivers and streams tributary to lakes, with some exceptions: a few spawn in rivers not associated with lakes, as well as along the shores of lakes where the gravel is permeated by underground springs. The females excavate nests and deposit hundreds of orange-pink eggs, which are simultaneously fertilized by the sperm of the males. When the first nests are seeded, the females move upstream to excavate other nests, and spawning and fertilizing are repeated. This continues until each female has released all of her three thousand to four thousand eggs.

For the next few days the sockeye guard these *redds*, or series of nests, but finally, exhausted and grossly disfigured, females and males submit to the current and are carried downstream to die.

The eggs hatch the following spring. The young, known as *alevins*, remain within the nests for several months before emerging as free-swimming fry. Then, with the aid of the currents, they move to the nursery lakes. Sockeye fry and chum fry are quite similar in shape and pigmentation pattern, although at this stage sockeye are generally smaller.

Young sockeye remain in the lakes from one to two years, occasionally three, and then as *smolts* migrate to salt water. A few go directly to sea as fry. Migration to the sea is mainly during March, April and May.

The ocean life of sockeye is still not well known. Most juveniles, when leaving fresh water, apparently travel northward 6 to 10 miles (9.65 to 16.09 km) off the British Columbia coast until they reach central Alaska or Kodiak Island. During their maturing years they are found in enormous numbers in a huge area of the Pacific

Top: SOCKEYE SALMON
Centre: COHO SALMON
Bottom: CHUM SALMON

west to the Aleutian Islands, north to the Gulf of Alaska and south to about 40° N. Fraser River sockeye tend to be distributed more to the south and west than more northerly British Columbia stocks. Throughout their life at sea, sockeye feed heavily on *euphasiids*—high-protein shrimp-like crustaceans which are the major source of the sockeye's attractive, deep red flesh colour.

Sockeye returning to spawn enter their rivers of origin from May to October; the southern stocks generally arrive later than the northern. Most southern sockeye reach maturity after two or three winters in the ocean, but a small number come back to spawn after one year of saltwater life. Sockeye in far northern waters such as the Nass River in British Columbia and the Karluk in Alaska, however, may take as long as eight years to mature.

Each year sockeye return to their native rivers and lakes. The most celebrated Canadian race returns in even-numbered four-year cycles to the Adams River, one of the major arteries of the Fraser River system. In this spectacular event as many as one and a half million spawners struggle for space in the river's seven-mile length, while an additional half a million wait their turn to spawn in the adjacent 2.5 mile (4 km) Little River.

Sockeye are taken commercially in both inshore and offshore waters by purse seiners, gill-netters and trollers. Although they do not respond as readily to artificial lures as do other salmon, both anglers and commercial fishers are successfully using newly developed lures designed to resemble euphasiids. One highly regarded lure is a hook wound with red cotton to resemble a squid.

Angling for sockeye in Canadian fresh waters is prohibited, but there is an important sports fishery for them in northern areas such as Brooks River, Alaska.

Kokanee

Kokanee are sockeye salmon that spend their whole lives in fresh water although, as Scott and Crossman write in *Freshwater Fishes of Canada,* some individuals "can and will migrate and return with anadromous sockeye under certain circumstances." The rarity of these migrants, however, justifies describing the kokanee habitat as permanently freshwater.

There have been arguments for recognizing the two as different species or subspecies, but as Professor Joseph Nelson (in a 1968 article in the *Journal of the Fisheries Research Board of Canada*) observes, "the probable phenotypic basis of the partial isolating mechanisms between kokanee and sockeye, the ability of one form to produce offspring which can take up the life-history of the other, and the presumed multiple origins of kokanee from sockeye, make it advisable to designate both forms as '*Oncorhynchus nerka.*'"

In the same article Professor Nelson points out that "sockeye have presumably become extinct in many lakes which now have kokanee, due to the formation of falls resulting from landform changes and the rising coastal area."

Except for their much smaller size, kokanee are similar in most respects to the anadromous sockeye. This is evident in their shape and colouring, particularly at maturity, and in their spawning behaviour. Most kokanee have a lifespan of four years, but some live as long as eight years. They die after spawning.

Kokanee occur naturally throughout much of the freshwater range of the anadromous sockeye. In North America they are native to waters from Oregon north to Alaska and the Yukon, and in Asia from Russia to Japan. Stocking of kokanee in other waters has been widespread, however, both within and beyond their native ranges. In Canada plantings have been successful in Saskatchewan and Manitoba. In Ontario they are well established in lakes Huron, Michigan and Superior. Efforts to introduce them into Alberta lakes and into Lake Ontario have been unsuccessful. They are most numerous in British Columbia, where they may either occur with sockeye, or in some headwater lakes no longer accessible from the sea, in the absence of sockeye.

Kokanee, like young anadromous sockeye, live mainly on

plankton and aquatic insects. They in turn become food for larger fish such as Dolly Varden, rainbow and cutthroat trout, squawfish and coho salmon. Spawning occurs at different times in different areas: in British Columbia from September to October, in Ontario from November to December, and in other areas (depending on temperatures) from August to February.

Kokanee are excellent game fish, especially when they are feeding near the surface and can be taken on wet or dry artificial flies. Because they live primarily at intermediate depths, most are caught with sinking lures or with hooks carrying salmon eggs, maggots, worms and similar bait.

Kokanee average about a pound, but individuals of 3 pounds (1.36 kg) or more are common in some lakes. According to the International Game Fish Association, a 9 pound 6 ounce (4.25 kg) kokanee was taken in 1988 from Okanagan Lake, BC. Scientists are watching with interest and concern, however, the decrease of kokanee populations and the increase in size of individual kokanee in some British Columbia lakes. One 9 pound (4.08 kg) kokanee was taken from Kootenay Lake in 1990.

Kokanee have excellent table qualities, and like anadromous sockeye (sold mainly canned), are especially delicious smoked.

Chinook salmon
(Oncorhynchus tshawytscha)

Chinook salmon are the largest of the nine North American species. They are known in Canada by a number of names, but most popularly as *tyee* (when they exceed 30 pounds or 13.6 kg in weight), *white spring* or *red spring* (depending on flesh colour) and *jack salmon* or *jack spring* (small precocious males). They are significant in the Indian fishery and, like sockeye, have traditionally been a major part of native peoples' diet. Chinooks are eagerly sought by saltwater anglers; not only do they have superb eating qualities, they also fight hard and long when hooked.

The chinook's body is slender, deep and somewhat compressed. Its colouring is greenish blue to black on the back and upper sides (which sometimes show a faint reddish to rusty hue), and silvery on the belly. The head is a dark slate colour. The lower gums are black. Numerous large black spots show prominently on the back and dorsal fin and in both lobes of the caudal fin. As the fish approach the spawning grounds their colouring becomes dull red along the back and sides and greyish on the belly. In the advanced spawning stages the upper jaw of the male develops a *kype*, a pronounced downward protuberance or hook.

Chinooks occur in West Coast waters from central California north to Kotzebue Sound, Alaska, thence along the coast of Asia south to the Japanese island of Hokkaido. Although chinooks are native to more than one thousand rivers and streams in North America, only about two hundred rivers support large runs. Most important are the Sacramento, Columbia, Fraser, Skeena, Nushagvat and Yukon rivers. Small numbers of chinooks have become established in the Coppermine and Mackenzie rivers of the western Canadian Arctic, 1000 miles (1609.3 km) west of Point Barrow, Alaska. Stocks introduced into New Zealand, Chile and—in recent years—the Great Lakes, are now well established.

Like all salmon in their native ranges, chinooks are anadromous. Born in fresh water, they migrate as juveniles to the ocean where they mature; then they return to fresh water (usually to the same river system where their own lives began) to spawn. There they lay and fertilize their eggs, then die.

In his "Life History of Chinook Salmon" (*Pacific Salmon Life Histories*), Dr. M.S. Healey describes another pattern of chinook behaviour:

The species occurs in two behavioral forms. One form, which has been designated 'stream-type' (Gilbert 1913), is typical of Asian populations and of northern populations and headwater tributaries of southern populations in North America. Stream-type chinooks spend one or more years as fry or parr in fresh water before migrating to sea, perform extensive

51

offshore oceanic migrations and return to their natal river in the spring or summer, several months prior to spawning. Occasionally males of this form mature precociously without ever going to sea. The second form, which has been designated 'ocean-type' ('sea-type' in Gilbert, 1913) is typical of populations on the North American coast south of 56° N. Ocean-type chinook migrate to sea during their first year of life, normally within three months after emergence from the spawning gravel, spend most of their ocean life in coastal waters, and return to their natal river in the fall, a few days or weeks before spawning.

Chinook salmon inhabit coastal waters throughout the year. Runs—generally including more than one race, each heading for a different spawning ground—enter fresh water at different seasons. In general, more seasonal runs occur in southern than in northern waters. California's Sacramento River has spring, summer and fall runs; the Skeena and Yukon rivers have only one run each.

Chinook spawning grounds may be just above tidal water or many miles inland. By far the longest journey known is to the tributaries of Teslin Lake in the upper reaches of the Yukon River—a distance of nearly 2000 miles (3218.6 km).

Chinooks require deeper water for spawning than do other salmon. To ensure proper irrigation of their eggs they seek out areas where the flow of the current is stronger along the bottom than along the surface. Ideal conditions are generally found below logs jammed in the gravel, and between pools and riffles. The females excavate the nests.

The number of eggs spawned ranges from about twenty-five hundred to five thousand. Examination of one female, however, revealed the presence of an astonishing twenty thousand eggs. In places with a fast current, retention of eggs in the nest is often difficult and losses are sometimes heavy.

Young salmon hatch in the spring and remain in the nests for about two months, until the large yolk sac has been absorbed. When this occurs they wriggle up through the gravel to the surface to gulp air and become free-swimming. Some juveniles proceed directly to the ocean; others may remain in fresh water for up to three months or a year before starting downstream. At all stages of their journey to the sea, predatory fish, diving water birds and small mammals take a heavy toll.

In their saltwater wanderings the juveniles feed heavily on various small fish and crustaceans. The adults feed on invertebrates such as squids and shrimps, and on other fish, particularly herring. All in turn are preyed upon by larger fish and by marine mammals such as seals and killer whales. Young ocean-type chinooks spend their ocean life in coastal waters. Stream-type chinooks are long-distance travellers; they go as far as mid-Pacific where they are found, usually at considerable depths, with other salmon from North American and Asian waters.

Whether far at sea or in coastal waters, they feed voraciously and grow to great sizes. When they return they are in prime condition, solid and streamlined, and in their livery of iridescent green and silvery white they are beautiful to behold. Perhaps they will proceed upstream without delay or perhaps they will linger offshore or in estuarine waters, cruising in and out with the tide until instinct tells them to move on.

The way ahead may be smooth and uneventful, or they may face many of the same dangers they overcame in their journey downstream as juveniles. Eventually many reach their spawning grounds. The nests are excavated, and females and males pair off to release and fertilize their eggs. Most females die within two weeks, but males often survive longer.

Chinook salmon are caught commercially by purse seiners, gill-netters and trollers. Troll-caught chinooks are usually sold as fresh fish, while those taken by purse seiners and gill-netters are sold for canning or the frozen fish market. Anglers catch chinooks mainly by trolling with whole or strip herring, or artificial lures such as hootchies (squid imitations), plugs or spoons rigged with metal flashers. Chinooks also respond to lead Buzz Bombs and Stingsildas jigged close to the bottom. Favourite angling spots are riptides and rivermouths, especially at daybreak.

At maturity, most chinooks average 10 to 20 pounds (4.54 to 9.07 kg), although chinooks of 50 to 60 pounds (22.68 to 27.22 kg) are frequently caught. In and above that range they are called *tyees*. The largest chinook yet recorded weighed 126 pounds (57.15 kg) and was taken in a trap off Port Colpays in southeastern Alaska. There have been a number of rod-caught record breakers, however, such as the 82-pounder (37.19 kg) caught in 1951 in Rivers Inlet, British Columbia, and the 97.5-pounder (44.23 kg) caught in 1985 in the Kenai River, Alaska.

Other British Columbia waters in more recent years have yielded exceptional catches: the 85.5-pounder (38.78 kg) caught in Hakai Passage, the 61.5-pounder (28.89 kg) caught off Campbell River, the 61.5-pounder (27.9 kg) caught in Juan de Fuca Strait near Sooke, and the 64-pounder (29.03 kg) caught off Flower Island near Telegraph Cove on northern Vancouver Island. In eastern waters hatchery-reared chinooks, such as the 40-pounder (18.14 kg) taken from Lake Ontario, have also grown to prodigious sizes.

Pink salmon
(Oncorhynchus gorbuscha)

Pinks, also commonly known as *humpbacks* or *humpies* for the prominent bony hump that males develop before spawning, are the smallest and most abundant of all Pacific salmon. Primarily plankton eaters rather than fish eaters, they do not readily respond to anglers' lures. Occasionally, when returning to their natal rivers with coho or other homeward-bound species, they will attack artificial flies. A hooked pink will generally head for deep water, where it will work vigorously to free itself. Pinks, unlike coho, do not normally break water.

This species occurs from north-central California (as occasional

Top: CHINOOK SALMON
Bottom: PINK SALMON

strays) to the Bering Strait and Chukchi Sea, east along the Arctic coast near to—but not in—the Mackenzie River. On the Asian side of the Pacific, it occurs as far south as the Sea of Okhotsk and the Sea of Japan. Its major North American spawning grounds are more than one thousand West Coast streams between Puget Sound in Washington and Bristol Bay, Alaska.

Dr. William R. Heard, in his chapter on pink salmon in *Pacific Salmon Life Histories*, identifies six major population groups:

1. Puget Sound and British Columbia stocks
2. southeastern Alaska, central Alaska, and Alaska Peninsula stocks
3. Bristol Bay and western Alaska stocks
4. eastern Kamchatka and Anadyr stocks
5. western Kamchatka, Sea of Okhotsk and eastern Sakhalin stocks
6. western Sakhalin, Amur and Primore stocks (Sea of Japan)

In their prime, pinks are slender and somewhat compressed. They are handsome fish—silvery on the sides, steely blue or greenish blue on the back, and white on the belly. Numerous large, oval black spots are prominent on the tail and upper body. Their teeth are well developed. Scales are small and deeply embedded. Young pink salmon are easily identified by the complete absence of the parr marks that characterize other juvenile salmon.

When pinks return from their ocean migration to begin their journey upstream to spawn, their colour changes quickly. Males become quite dark on the head and back. A subdued reddish cast, with irregular brown and greenish blotches, appears on the sides below the lateral line. The fish turn greyish white on the belly. Males develop a large bony bump on the back, a hooked upper jaw and noticeably large teeth. Females, whose body shape remains relatively unchanged, become olive green on the sides with dusky stripes below the lateral line, and greyish white on the belly.

Most efforts to establish self-perpetuating runs of pink salmon, not only within the species' own traditional Pacific ranges but in waters well beyond such ranges, have succeeded only partially. In British Columbia, selected streams of the mainland, Vancouver Island and the Queen Charlottes were planted at various times with millions of eggs and fry. First responses were encouraging, but returns of spawning adults from the sea steadily declined and eventually ended. The only successes in establishing new runs on the West Coast have been introductions into southeastern Alaska and Washington's Puget Sound.

Attempts to establish pink salmon in Atlantic waters were made in 1958 when eggs were released in the North Harbour River of St. Mary's Bay, Newfoundland, at the south end of the Avalon Peninsula. These prospered at first, and progeny from them spawned elsewhere on Newfoundland's east coast and in Labrador, Nova Scotia and Quebec. Despite these initial successes, however, all of the runs have since declined and there is now doubt that any have survived.

A similar effort to establish runs of both pink and chum salmon into Hudson Bay was unsuccessful—but from that effort arose a bizarre accident that rates as one of the best of fish stories. And this one is true!

In 1956 fishery workers accidentally dumped several hundred Skeena River pinks en route to Goose Creek, a tributary of Hudson Bay, into Lake Superior at Thunder Bay. They survived, and today pinks are thriving in all of the Great Lakes. They are, with the possible exception of a small population in Fraser Lake on Alaska's Kodiak Island, the only known self-perpetuating species of Pacific salmon in fresh water. The irony is that the stocks planted in Goose Creek failed to survive! Pink salmon have a fixed two-year cycle and, like all Pacific salmon, die after spawning. The Great Lakes pinks are commonly much smaller than their Pacific counterparts.

Pink salmon in their native waters do not migrate far inland to spawn. Most spawning areas are within about 40 miles (64.37

km) of coastal waters. Nevertheless, some runs swim as much as 70 miles (112.65 km) into the interior, and some travel as far as the Babine River of the Skeena River watershed, a distance of nearly 400 miles (643.72 km).

Spawning takes place from mid-July to the end of October. Females deposit from eight hundred to two thousand eggs in nests excavated in gravel beds, and these are fertilized by one, or sometimes several, males. Most females prepare and spawn in more than one nest, and most males may release their sperm with more than one female. Adult fish die soon after spawning. The alevins hatch from late December to February, depending on water temperature. Not until April or May, when their yolk sac has been absorbed, do the fry emerge from the protective gravel and become free-swimming. They are less than 2 inches (5.08 cm) in length.

Almost immediately, often with migrating young salmon of other species, they make their way downstream to coastal waters. If they have only a few miles to travel they move at night, but if the journey is long they may also move during the day. At this time they seldom feed; when they do, they feed mostly on larvae, nymphs, stoneflies, mayflies, caddis flies and tiny crustaceans. The young fry in turn are eaten by predators such as cutthroat trout, Dolly Varden, coho smolts, kingfishers, mergansers and mammals.

They begin their journey toward the open sea toward the end of August, often in company of young chum and sockeye. Some schools of juvenile pinks, if late in migrating, do not linger in coastal waters but proceed directly to the open sea. The pinks' ocean sojourn lasts until the following spring when, in their second year, they begin the return journey to their natal streams. Their upstream migration occurs from July to October, and spawning takes place soon after their arrival at their spawning grounds.

At maturity pinks weigh from 3 to 5 pounds (1.36 to 2.27 kg), although fish of up to 10 pounds (4.54 kg) are occasionally caught. A rod-caught pink salmon that won notice on the West Coast weighed 15 pounds (6.8 kg), although this was nearly equalled by an Ontario hatchery-reared fish of 11 pounds (4.99 kg) taken in a Lake Huron tributary stream.

Commercial fishing for pinks takes place from July to October, mainly within territorial waters, especially around Vancouver Island and northward throughout the Inside Passage to Alaska. Good catches are made as far seaward as 50 miles (80.46 km), however. Purse seiners and gill-netters supply most of the pinks that are canned, while trollers supply the fresh fish market.

Chum salmon
(Oncorhynchus keta)

Chum salmon have the least consumer prestige of all Pacific salmon, mostly because they do not equal the high epicurean reputation of the other North American species. Their flesh, generally white or pale pink, comes fourth in protein content and fifth in fat after other salmon species. Chum are tasty fish, nevertheless, and their abundance gives them great importance to the commercial fishery and to native peoples.

The chum has a slender, somewhat compressed body, with strongly developed cone-shaped teeth. It is metallic blue on the back, with no distinct black spots, and silvery on the undersides. The tips of the pectoral, anal and caudal fins, especially in the male, are often white. In its prime it closely resembles the sockeye.

The maturing male chum, once it enters fresh water on its way to the spawning grounds, quickly becomes less streamlined. Its colour changes to brick red on the sides with irregular dusky streaks. The tips of the pelvic and anal fins turn white and the teeth become more strongly developed than those of other salmon. Its enlarged teeth led to its naming as *dog salmon*.

Juvenile chum are slender fish. They are dark-mottled, irides-cent on the back and silvery on the sides and belly. Oval parr marks, generally from six to fourteen in number, are prominent mainly above the lateral line. Mature fish have dark bars across their red sides; some have large grey blotches.

Chum salmon are the most widely dispersed of all Pacific salmon. They occur from California northward to the Bering and Chukchi seas, and east along the Arctic Ocean to the Beaufort Sea. They are indigenous to about eight hundred British Columbia streams and the Mackenzie River system of the Northwest Territories; chum have been noted in the Slave River as far inland as Fort Smith. In Asian waters they occur from Korea north to Siberia, and in the Arctic Ocean west to the Laptev Sea.

Chum are early and late run fish. Some arrive as early as the beginning of August; others arrive in October and November, even as late as January. Chum favour spawning grounds in the lower reaches of coastal streams, but there are exceptions—some ascend the Yukon River and travel to Teslin Lake in British Columbia, a distance of nearly 2000 miles (3218.6 km).

Females lay two to four thousand eggs. Soon after hatching the following spring, the young go to sea. The peak of the migration to salt water is reached about May. The juveniles usually remain in coastal waters during the summer and migrate toward the open sea in September. They wander about the oceans for three or four years, sometimes even seven years, before returning to the river systems where they were born. At sea they feed heavily on various marine invertebrates and other fish, and grow quickly.

Chum salmon are caught commercially by purse seiners and gill-netters. Although not avidly sought by anglers, they will respond to trolled metal lures and occasionally to artificial flies. Most commercial catches are made during August and September in inshore waters as the fish approach their native streams to spawn.

Mature chum average around 11 pounds (4.99 kg), although some individuals have reached more than 45 pounds (20.41 kg). Efforts to establish populations of this species in fresh water areas have been minimal and to date unsuccessful. Chum salmon hybridize with pink salmon.

Coho salmon
(Oncorhynchus kisutch)

Coho, along with chinook, are the Pacific salmon most eagerly sought by anglers. They are fish of great beauty and high courage. Surface fighters which are capable of long, swift runs, they provide the angler with demonstrations of acrobatic skills that leave the heart pulsating long after they have been netted.

One of their strongest manoeuvres is to sound to 30 feet (9.14 m) or more, skyrocket to the surface, tail-walk like a sailfish, and then make jump after jump, often changing direction in midair in their frenzied efforts to free themselves. Roderick Haig-Brown, in his classic *The Western Angler,* describes these jumps as "clean, far out of the water, beautiful to watch and splendidly exciting." A typical coho will make several runs and break water repeatedly before submitting exhausted to the angler's hold.

The coho has an elongated body, a conical head and firmly set needle-like teeth. The back is metallic blue and the belly silvery. There are numerous irregular black spots on the sides above the lateral line, at the base of the dorsal fin and on the upper lobe of the caudal fin. Although the average length of this fish is about 30 inches (76.2 cm), and its average weight between 5 and 12 pounds (2.27 to 5.44 kg), some specimens as heavy as 26.5 pounds (12.02 kg) have been caught; in fact a coho of 31 pounds (14.06 kg) was taken in Cowichan Bay on Vancouver Island, BC, in 1947.

Coho salmon inhabit waters from Monterey Bay in California to Alaska, west to Siberia and south to the Japanese island of Hokkaido. In their North American range they occur in greatest numbers in Washington, British Columbia and central Alaska waters.

More than a hundred years ago efforts were made to establish coho in the Great Lakes, but without success; later efforts also failed. In 1966 an effort succeeded because of better fish culture procedures. Coho are now present in all of the Great Lakes and provide a good commercial and sports fishery. In fact, in 1989 a hatchery-reared coho of 33 pounds, 4 ounces (15.08 kg) was rod-caught in Salmon River, New York—ironically beating out the wild, anadromous Cowichan Bay 31-pounder. Although coho in the Great Lakes are now somewhat self-perpetuating, the stocks mainly come from hatcheries. Great Lakes coho spawn from September to early October.

Coho salmon in their natural Pacific ranges hatch in the spring from eggs spawned the previous November or December (or sometimes January) in the gravel beds of freshwater streams, generally near the sea. There are nearly a thousand spawning streams in British Columbia alone. The fry—active little fish with bluish green backs, silvery sides and eight to twelve narrow parr marks—swim in schools close to the banks. As they grow older the schools disperse and the young move about independently.

Some juveniles migrate immediately to the sea, but most spend their first and often their second year in their parent stream or in adjoining lakes. There they live mainly on insect larvae and tiny crustaceans, and as they grow older, on small fish and mature insects. The following spring, in their hundreds of thousands, they respond to their migratory urge and swim downstream to estuarine waters. This exodus to the ocean generally occurs at night and when the streams are in flood. But, as with all juvenile salmon, only a relatively small number survive the journey to the sea. Predatory fish, birds and pollution may kill up to 30 percent of the young migrants. During their early life at sea they grow at a phenomenally rapid rate, doubling or tripling their size in two to three weeks.

Most Pacific coho remain well within coastal waters for their entire eighteen months of ocean life; the largest number wander the rich feeding areas of the Strait of Georgia and the west coast of Vancouver Island. Coho that migrate seaward travel as far north as Alaska, where they remain until late fall or early winter. There they feed heavily, first on crustaceans and then on herring.

Winter's cold sends the coho south—some as far as California— in a journey they complete in the spring. Then once again they migrate north, many sweeping widely seaward before heading into coastal waters. In late fall and early winter, generally after the pink and sockeye runs have reached their destinations, the mature coho enter fresh water to journey upstream to their spawning grounds—sometimes to the exact area of gravel where they themselves were born.

Mature coho are strong and beautifully formed when anglers and commercial fishers first encounter them, but sexual development brings remarkable changes. From sparkling metallic blue on the back, silvery on the sides and white on the belly, the males turn green on the back, bright red on the sides and dark red on the belly. They also develop grotesquely hooked snouts and large, sharp teeth. The spawning appearance of females is generally similar but less pronounced. At their spawning grounds they pair off. In depressions scooped in the gravel, each female deposits one thousand to six thousand eggs. After fertilization by the males, the eggs are covered with gravel. The adults die after spawning.

Coho are superb game fish. They respond to a variety of lures, among the most popular being streamer flies and fly-and-spinner combinations trolled unweighted behind a fairly fast-moving boat. The lure skipping in and out of the boat's wake imitates the action of small fish (herring or candlefish, for example, in Pacific waters) trying to elude a larger fish. Hooking a coho by this method, especially on a light rod, is a thrilling experience. When a good run is on, fly-casting without weights is also productive.

Coho flesh deteriorates quickly after capture, and anglers should keep their catch cool and well-covered. This quality control measure, of course, applies to all fish.

Masu
(Oncorhynchus masou)

Amago
(Oncorhynchus rhodurus)

Two Pacific salmon forms occur in Japan and Russian waters: masu (*Oncorhynchus masou*) and amago (*Oncorhynchus rhodurus*).

In Japan, masu salmon are also known as *sakura-masu*, meaning cherry trout—so named because the maturing anadromous adults return to the spawning grounds at cherry blossom time. A strictly freshwater form of masu is known colloquially as *yamame* or *yamabe*.

The life history of amago salmon is not yet fully documented. Normally they spend most of their lives in fresh water, although some populations are anadromous; most migrating amago salmon are females. The river-dwelling types are known as *amago*; lake-dwelling types are known as *biwamasu*.

As an interesting matter of taxonomy, Japanese scientist Dr. Kinji Imanishi believes that amago and masu are a single species. Debate continues on whether they are one or two species.

In his paper *Origin and Speciation of Oncorhynchus*, Dr. Ferris Neave writes that, of all species of *Oncorhynchus*, masu are most clearly related to an ancestor resembling the rainbow trout.

ATLANTIC SALMON

Atlantic salmon historically have been recreational and commercial fish of immense value. But these beautiful creatures continue to live a fragile existence, for only a few years ago the North American stocks were thought to be in danger of extinction. That, had it happened, would have been a tragedy of major proportion. Now, however, as a result of enhancement programs and severe restrictions placed on the commercial fishing of the species, there are encouraging signs that some of the great runs are being restored. Successful spawnings are taking place. The tragedy, it appears, is being avoided.

Atlantic salmon have occupied an honoured place in human affairs since the Paleolithic. This was borne out by a discovery made many years ago by archaeologists digging in the Pyrenees of Southern France. There they unearthed a reindeer bone on which was carved the likeness of a salmon. Discovery of the bone was important in itself, but what was equally important was the fact that it had been carved about 12,000 years before the birth of Christ!

Centuries after the Paleolithic artist made the carving, Julius Ceasar led his victorious armies into Gaul. As they spread over the countryside they saw great throngs of fish leaping in the rivers. These fish were new to the Romans and so enthralled were they by their grace and beauty that they gave them the name *salmo,* related to the Latin word *salire* which means "to leap."

Salmo salar, as it became known in scientific nomenclature, appears and reappears throughout the history and literature of the past several hundred years. Reference to the fish are common in the literature and mythology of Scotland, Ireland, England and Wales. Many books, now considered classics, deal solely with the species. To possess an original work—such as Eric Taverner's *Salmon Fishing,* Henry Williamson's *Salar the Salmon,* Agar Adamson's *Salmon Fishing in Canada,* Richard Nettle's *The Salmon Fisheries of the St. Lawrence,* Dean Sage's rare *The Restigouche and its Salmon Fishing,* or Lee Wulff's *Leaping Silver*—is to possess a treasure of lasting value.

Canadian literature has its own notable works, among them Anthony Netby's *The Atlantic Salmon,* Roderick Haig-Brown's *Silver,* and Robert Dunfield's *The Atlantic Salmon in the History of North America.*

Atlantic salmon have been reported in more than thirteen hundred streams in eastern North America. In Canada today they are native to at least five hundred rivers of Quebec, New Brunswick, Nova Scotia, Newfoundland and Labrador. Perhaps the most famous are Quebec's Madapedia and Grand Cascapedia, and New Brunswick's Restigouche and Miramachi, lovely rivers that meander symphoniously through beautiful countryside. Others include Nova Scotia's St. Mary's and Margaree, Newfoundland's Humber and Gander, and Labrador's Eagle and Foreteau, each in its own picturesque setting of wilderness splendour. Managing the fish population of approximately five hundred rivers in widely scattered—in many cases almost inaccessible—areas is obviously an enormous and costly undertaking.

Before European settlement in North America, salmon were abundant in rivers and streams flowing into the Atlantic Ocean from Ungava Bay as far south as Long Island Sound. In Labrador and Newfoundland, all of the Maritime provinces, and the states of Maine and Connecticut, these fish were a seemingly inexhaustible resource. Salmon were also common as far inland as Lake Ontario. Some of these may have been historically freshwater strains, however; migration of anadromous stocks so far inland would be amazing. Their journeys would take them from the ocean, up the entire St. Lawrence River, past the site of Montreal, through the turbulent waters of the Lachine Rapids (removed when the St. Lawrence Seaway was built), through the placid waters of the Thousand Islands into Lake Ontario, and finally to the point where they could go no further—Niagara Falls. Salmon spawned in Canadian rivers such as the Don, Credit and Humber, now almost within the shadow of Toronto's skyscrapers.

As settlements sprang up and expanded throughout this whole inland range, however, the status of the salmon underwent radical changes. Industrial plants, especially sawmills, spewed toxic and other wastes into the rivers for easy disposal. Dams often prevented the fish from reaching their spawning grounds. There was short-sighted overfishing.

A few years ago scientists decided that *Salmo salar* could be reintroduced into the Great Lakes as a self-perpetuating freshwater form. The Ontario Ministry of Natural Resources has shown notable faith in the species' ability to adapt to a freshwater environment. In 1988 the ministry's restocking program planted sixty-three thousand smolts, raised from eggs hatched in its fish culture station near Simcoe, into the Credit River and Wilmot Creek. Results have been encouraging, and scientists expect progeny from these salmon, some weighing up to 20 pounds (9.07 kg), to return annually from Lake Ontario to the spawning grounds. Working alongside Canadian authorities, the State of New York has also released many thousands of smolts into its own selected rivers.

We are now aware of the urgency to rebuild the Atlantic salmon resource. Federal and provincial governments, supported by some of the world's most distinguished fishery scientists—in co-operation with agencies such as the North Atlantic Salmon Conservation Organization (NASCO) and the salmon anglers' own Atlantic Salmon Federation (ASF)—are tackling the problem with renewed determination.

Establishing a strictly freshwater salmon fishery will be a great achievement. But fully restoring the naturally wild *Salmo salar* of the North Atlantic will be even greater.

Salmo salar, the Atlantic salmon, is a priceless resource and heritage that belongs not just to us, but to generations of the future. We merely retain it in trust.

Atlantic salmon
(Salmo salar)

"It has been said that anyone who has not seen a salmon has not seen what a fish should be—a statement which perhaps encompasses more pure and simple truth about the species than any other description," writes Robert Dunfield in his treatise, *The Atlantic Salmon in the History of North America*.

His assessment of *Salmo salar* will bring hearty agreement from anglers everywhere. In his words, this species is indeed a "sublime example of creation." This fish magnificently serves a dual purpose: as food *par excellence* and as an adversary that many find without equal in the world of freshwater angling.

The Atlantic salmon, like its Pacific cousins (coho and steelhead especially), is a courageous, determined fighter in defence of its freedom. Its vigour shows itself to the full when it is hooked; its graceful rises, long rushes and acrobatic leaps out of water generally give the angler everything he could ask for in the way of thrills. Often the skill of the salmon outdoes the skill of the angler, especially if the angler is giving the fish a sporting chance by using a light rod and fine leader. And, like all of its Pacific cousins, it shows the same determination and courage in overcoming obstacles to its return journey to its natal spawning grounds.

Atlantic salmon are strictly northern fish, native to waters on both sides of the Atlantic Ocean. On the North American side they occur in Ungava Bay, Hudson and Davis straits, southern Greenland, Labrador, Newfoundland, the Maritime provinces and Quebec. There are many landlocked populations, particularly in Quebec, Newfoundland, Nova Scotia, New Brunswick and northeastern New England.

At one time they were abundant throughout the St. Lawrence River as far inland as Lake Ontario. Those stocks, like anadromous and landlocked stocks in a number of eastern states, fell victim to industrialization, pollution and overfishing. Efforts to restore wild salmon in United States waters, particularly in Maine and Connecticut, are meeting with success, however; in time Maine's Penobscot River may again become a major producer. Although anadromous salmon still return to some rivers in the lower St. Lawrence (the Quelle River is now the western limit), they have been absent for many years from the St. Lawrence River above Quebec City and from the Great Lakes area.

Atlantic salmon represent more than a source of recreation: they have become a way of life. This species has a mysterious influence on human hearts and minds. Spend an evening or two in an outfitter's camp and listen to the talk of anglers who know their rivers and the ways of salmon. Walk in the company of those who cast their delicate Rusty Rats or Black Bears—or those Victorian classics, the Jock Scots, Durham Rangers, and March Browns—into clear, lovely pools. Or, better still, experience even once the great power and cunning of a salmon on a light rod. Then you may sense the magic spell of the sport and the species.

ATLANTIC SALMON

Atlantic salmon are known by various names that relate primarily to age groups and to mature fish that return to the ocean after spawning. Newly hatched fish still within the nest, with their yolk sac still attached, are known as *alevins;* those that have emerged to become free-swimming are called *underyearlings.* When they increase in size and carry distinctive vertical bars and red spots on their sides they are known as *parr.* When they are ready to go to sea, their bars and red spots have disappeared, they have become more silvery and their body shape has changed, they are known as *smolts*. Salmon returning to home waters after spending one winter at sea are known as *grilse* (*grilt* in some Maritime communities); those returning after an absence of a year or more may be called *multi-sea winter salmon*. Those going back to sea after spawning are referred to as *spent, black* or *kelt*.

A typical Atlantic salmon has a long, moderately stout, trout-like body and a short head. When fresh from the sea, its colour is bright steely blue above the lateral line and silvery below. Numerous black X-like spots on the head, upper body and fins may be prominent. After a period in fresh water its steely blue is superseded by a brownish red cast. By the time the fish have spawned, the overall colouring of both male and female becomes quite dark. Their spawning garb is more in tune with the sombre woodland colours that follow the brilliant hues of autumn, and they blend in with the mottled bottom of the riverbed. Males, especially, are creatures of changing form. Sleek and beautiful when first they entered the rivers, as spawning approaches they tarnish rapidly, and their lower jaw develops a pronounced hook.

At spawning time, males and females in pairs excavate their nests in the gravel of the riverbed. As the male guards against competing males, the female turns on her side and scoops out a hollow 12 to 18 inches (30.48 to 45.72 cm) deep. This hollow is made by the current she creates through the powerful fanning of her tail. When she has accomplished this, both fish settle over the depression. The female expels six hundred to eight hundred amber or pale orange eggs for every pound (about 1320 to 1760 for every kg) of her weight. These are then covered by the whitish sperm of the male. Small sexually mature parr may move alongside the male and join in fertilizing. When the fertilized eggs have settled into the cavities of the bed, the female moves forward. Powerfully fanning her tail, she forces enough gravel downstream to cover the nest. The pair may make and seed a number of nests in this way, and may take several days to complete spawning.

Spawning is a physical ordeal for the salmon and mortality in both sexes is often high. Fish that survive return to the sea either almost immediately or not until the following spring. Meanwhile, in the eggs that were spawned in the fall, rapid growth takes place. The vivified embryos within grow large as they assume the distorted but certain shapes of small fish. Early in the spring the eggs hatch and the alevins (or *fry*), each with a yolk or food sac attached, emerge. For about a month the tiny creatures depend for nourishment on this sac, but eventually they absorb it. At that time, as free-swimming underyearlings, they move away from the protection of the nests to find food from microscopic life in the stream.

Growth is much slower now. By the time they are ready to leave fresh water to begin their sea wanderings, they may be two to eight years old, but may weigh only a few ounces. Their length is about 3.5 to 7 inches (9 to 18 cm).

These young salmon (or *smolts*) begin their journey to the sea in the spring. As they head for brackish water at the river mouths, their bodies take on a silvery hue. Their tails lengthen noticeably and become less forked. Full of the exuberance of youth, they seem to sense the great adventure before them. Now there is no lingering. Often it takes but one rise and fall of the tide to carry thousands of them into the obscurity of the sea that will be their home until they respond to the call of their own spawning.

At sea young salmon grow quickly, gorging themselves on small creatures such as fish, sand eels and various kinds of marine worms and crustaceans. As the months pass they turn to fare such as herring, a highly nourishing fish which contributes most to their rapid growth.

But as the salmon prey upon others, so too are they preyed upon. In fresh water they had to contend with enemies such as kingfishers, mergansers, eels and trout; in salt water they meet new predators including sharks, tuna, swordfish and seals.

The sea life of Atlantic salmon averages one to two years, sometimes as long as five years. They may remain close to home waters, or they may journey up to 1500 miles (2413.95 km) to the great marine pastures in Davis Strait, between Baffin Island and Greenland, where they mingle with salmon from European rivers. During that time they grow anywhere from 3 pounds (1.36 kg) to 60 or 70 pounds (27.22 or 31.75 kg).

The average weight of mature salmon is about 15 pounds (6.8 kg), although individuals of 30 to 40 pounds (13.6 to 18.14 kg) are not uncommon. The largest rod-caught salmon, weighing 79 pounds 2 ounces (35.89 kg), was taken in the Tana River in Norway in 1928. A salmon weighing 47 pounds (21.32 kg) was taken in 1982 from the Grand Cascapedia River, Quebec; another taken from the same river (year unknown) weighed 55 pounds (24.94 kg).

Salmon return to the rivers in the peak of condition, but once in fresh water they practically cease feeding; for energy they draw almost entirely on their stored fat. Why they respond so eagerly to artificial flies during their river fasting is baffling. Is it inspired by their saltwater feeding habits? Do they have vague memories of their eager feeding on nymphs and terrestrial insects while still youngsters in their native streams? Do they seize flies out of curiosity or irritation? No one knows for sure; on examination, their stomachs contain little or no recognizable food.

Like Pacific salmon, Atlantic salmon return not only to their natal river, but often to the very stretch of gravel where they were spawned. The journey may be long or short, depending on water conditions and the distance the fish have to travel. Salmon that spawn in the lower reaches may arrive at their destination within a few days, there to remain for the rest of the summer and fall before spawning. Other fish, with longer journeys, may travel for weeks and have only a short time to rest before their seeding begins. Sometimes a late-run fish, perhaps still carrying sea-lice, occupies a pool with fish that came in earlier and have become blackened by their long stay in fresh water.

By winter the last spawning salmon reach their destination. Save for an occasional latecomer, most of the lower pools are now empty. But throughout the rivers, often at the very headwaters deep in the forest, schools of salmon—the males hook-jawed, both sexes bearing the scars of long journeys—complete their ultimate task. New life comes from old in many thousands of eggs—the salmon of the future—that are seeded in the gravel beds. Wearily the parent fish slip back to still waters to live or die; a few go back to sea and return to spawn again.

Angling for Atlantic salmon in Canadian waters is restricted to fly-fishing. Open seasons and catch limits vary from province to province.

How are Atlantic salmon caught? To do justice to a subject as broad and as esoteric as this would require a book in itself. Indeed, a vast literature deals with the history, biology and capture of this species; some of the most sought-after volumes go back hundreds of years.

For a study of the techniques of salmon angling, I suggest Lee Wulff's *The Atlantic Salmon.* An old but favourite book is Eric Taverner's *Salmon Fishing,* and a comprehensive overall study of this fish is Anthony Netby's *The Atlantic Salmon—A Vanishing Species?* And every salmon angler, novice or expert, would benefit greatly by subscribing to the *Atlantic Salmon Journal,* the official publication of the Atlantic Salmon Federation.

As for equipment—rods, reels, line, wet and dry flies, and all the other engaging paraphernalia required to become skilled in the sport—a whole angling fellowship awaits to advise you on the correct approaches to the art.

Landlocked salmon

Similar to the anadromous Atlantic salmon and also known as *Salmo salar* is the so-called landlocked, Sebago or ouananiche salmon. The name does not accurately describe these fish; in many waters they have ready access to the sea. For reasons not fully understood, however, most do not take advantage of this freedom to migrate, but remain throughout their lives in their home lakes and rivers.

Landlocked salmon, a highly respected game fish, are in most respects identical to their sea-going kin both anatomically and taxonomically. Minor differences include larger eyes and scales, and slightly longer fins. Coloration varies under the influence of different environments but is essentially the same as in anadromous types. Migration and spawning patterns are also similar to those of the anadromous salmon; mature fish leave the lakes in the fall to journey upriver to their spawning grounds. Males mature at about three or four years; females at four or five years. Nest building, egg laying and fertilization (even the assistance of sexually mature young parr) follow similar patterns. The young hatch the following spring and remain in the streams for a year or two before moving into the lakes. There they feed mainly on other fish such as perch, smelt, minnows and the like. Nymphs, as well as newly-hatched terrestrial insects, often send these fish (as they do trout) into a frenzy of activity. At that time they provide fly-fishers, especially, with heart-pounding sport.

Landlocked salmon occur naturally in Canadian waters, mainly in the Lake St. John district of northern Quebec, as well as in Labrador, Nova Scotia and New Brunswick. They are also well established in some areas of Northern Ontario. Their major natural range in the United States is Maine, where they are rated as the state's most important freshwater game fish. Landlocked salmon have been introduced successfully into many US eastern waters, particularly in Lake Memphremagog and Lake Champlain. Restocking has also been done in some rivers running into Lake Ontario.

Although very large salmon are occasionally caught, such as the 18-pounder (8.16 kg) taken from New York's Oswego River in 1978, the average size of these fish is 2 to 8 pounds (0.91 to 3.63 kg). The largest rod-caught landlocked salmon on record, weighing 35.5 pounds (16.1 kg), was taken in 1907 from Sebago Lake, Maine. It was about a yard (0.91 m) long!

TROUT AND CHARR

Trout and charr fishing is one of the most esoteric of all arts. Hundreds of books have been written about these fish, graceful and genteel techniques have been developed for their capture, and a great and sometimes mysterious legend has been built around them. With the possible exception of the Atlantic salmon, they have probably caused more anglers to become amateur ichthyologists, entomologists and limnologists than has any other species of fish; their capture by means of artificial wet or dry flies depends on sensitive developments of the aquatic and terrestrial insect world. A serious trout or charr angler cannot help but become, at least to some extent, a naturalist.

Trout and charr (also spelled char) have been the subject of intensive investigation by scientists for many years. Perhaps the most harried have been the taxonomists who classify and name the many species in our waters. Several decades ago some authorities recognized thirty-three species in North America. Today, although there is still debate, the American Fisheries Society recognizes twelve native species.

The major taxonomic differences in simple terms between trout and charr:

- Charr have a small patch of teeth in the centre of the vomerine bone in the front of the roof of the mouth; in trout the teeth in the vomerine bone form a zig-zag pattern and extend farther back.
- Charr scales are much smaller and brighter than those of trout.
- The spots on charr are grey, yellow, orange or red—never black or dark brown as on trout.

The charr are:

- lake trout (*Salvelinus namaycush*)

- brook or speckled trout (*Salvelinus fontinalis*)
- Arctic charr (*Salvelinus alpinus*)
- Dolly Varden trout (*Salvelinus malma*)
- bull trout (*Salvelinus confluentus*)

Charr are also predominately fall spawners; trout generally spawn in the spring.

The rumblings that may be heard in the background probably come from some anglers who are loath to abandon traditional usage for the sake of scientific accuracy. To most of them, these fish will remain what they always have been—trout! And so in this book, at whatever risk, trout they remain.

Until recently rainbow, Kamloops and steelhead trout were all classified as Salmo gairdneri. They are now classified as Oncorhynchus mykiss, since new research shows they are closer to species in genus *Oncorhynchus* (Pacific salmon) than they are to those in genus *Salmo* (Atlantic salmon and brown trout).* They also are of the same species as East Asian trout. But why do they have three officially recognized common names? All three are rainbows, but they have differences:

Steelhead are rainbows that—like salmon and some forms of cutthroat, brook and brown trout—are anadromous; they are born in fresh water, spend part of their time at sea, and then return to fresh water. Like all salmonids, they spawn in fresh water.

Kamloops are freshwater rainbows native to southern interior British Columbia lakes including Kamloops, Okana-

---

* Although rainbow (including the steelhead form) and cutthroat trout are now classified as Pacific salmon, they are listed for readers' convenience with the trout species.

gan, Kootenay, Adams, Shuswap and Paul lakes, among many others.

Rainbow is the generic name for both Kamloops and steelhead freshwater variants.

Both freshwater and anadromous rainbows, depending on geographic location, may differ in body shape and coloration. They are commonly known by a number of regional names. Identification can be a challenge, for rainbow and cutthroat trout often hybridize, and their progeny can be difficult to classify. Broadly speaking, trout in fresh water with a pinkish or reddish band along their sides may be some type of rainbow.

The saltwater coloration of anadromous trout is distinct from their freshwater coloration. When brook and brown trout spend time at sea, for example, they lose much of their brilliant colouring and become more silvery; when they return to fresh water they regain their freshwater markings and colouring. Pronounced colour changes also occur in Pacific and Atlantic salmon when they re-enter fresh water travelling toward their spawning grounds.

Trout in high-altitude lakes commonly have finer scales than those in low-altitude lakes; they also differ in markings and colour. How different a trout must be to be regarded as a different species and given a different scientific name, however, taxonomists have not yet agreed. Thus some authorities list more kinds of rainbow trout than do others. As Dr. Robert Campbell suggests in a personal communication, "Perhaps newer advanced techniques such as DNA 'fingerprinting' may provide the definitive answers."

Artificial rearing of trout and charr to supplement wild populations and cross-fertilization of some species to develop new strains have for many years been important in Canada's federal and provincial fish culture programs. In fact Canada has operated hatcheries to rear fish from artificially fertilized eggs since 1858.

This activity is now nation-wide. Early cross-fertilization failed to develop new and better game fish, however. The crossing of Atlantic salmon with brown trout, for example, produced a fertile form little better than either of the parents; the work was abandoned. In later years efforts to cross brown trout with brook trout, rainbow trout and landlocked salmon also failed to originate new and self-perpetuating forms. Efforts to cross rainbow trout with brook trout and landlocked salmon also failed.

About a century ago, however, scientists in the United States attempted to bring about a marriage between brook and lake trout. Interest in the project lapsed, but in 1946 J.E. Stenton— then park warden at Banff National Park—revived the experiment in Canada. He succeeded. So great was the interest in this hybrid that a contest was held to name the resulting trout. Three favourite names emerged, *wendigo, splake* (speckled trout and lake trout) and *moulac,* from the French *truite mouchette* and *truite du lac. Splake* won out and is now most commonly used.

As governments began to recognize the value of trout, widespread transplantation of species began. Brook trout (speckled charr), originally eastern fish, were planted in many selected waters in the Prairies and British Columbia. Kamloops and steelhead rainbows, originally western fish, were established in eastern Canada.

Trout propagation has since been extensive in all provinces, but British Columbia has undertaken especially interesting work. The rivers and lakes of BC's west slope were stocked and now support large populations of fish—particularly of anadromous species such as salmon, steelhead and cutthroat trout—but less than seventy-five years ago most high-elevation lakes were barren of fish. A successful sports fishery now flourishes there.

No fish are more avidly sought than the trout and charr. On the West Coast, anglers favour steelhead and freshwater rainbows, anadromous and freshwater cutthroats, Dolly Varden, introduced brook trout, and the less abundant introduced brown trout. In the far north they prefer Arctic charr, Arctic grayling and lake trout. In East Coast estuaries many anglers avidly pursue sea-run brook and sea-run brown trout. Elsewhere in Canada brook, rainbow, lake and brown trout are favourites.

Char or charr? The choice of usage has long provoked spirited debate within the scientific community, though few anglers in this country give a hoot one way or another. The American Fisheries Society and the International Game Fish Association, interestingly, use char in their common names lists.

Yet few would question the judgment of Dr. Eugene K. Balon, editor of the scholarly *Charrs: Salmonid Fishes of the Genus Salvelinus*, described as "an anthology of reviews and original studies by the world's leading experts of current knowledge about charrs . . ."

In a lighter vein, American scientist William Markham Norton defends the double *rs*: "When this term is spelled with two r's, it has only one connotation, i.e., 'a fish belonging to the genus *Salvelinus*'! In America we frequently note signboards with the word 'char-broiler' displayed over eating places—meaning the meats are broiled over briquets or charcoal. If you ever see one labelled *charr-broiler* (as I did in Sweden), it means that the cooks specialize in one of the most delightful delicacies yet to be discovered in America—broiled charr!"

A Canadian scientist, Dr. Don McAllister, also defends the double *rs*—"in deference to the pronunciation of those anglers who habitually pursue it in Scotland, the word should be spelled *charrr*."

Rainbow trout
Kamloops trout
Steelhead trout
(Oncorhynchus mykiss)

When Roderick Haig-Brown in *Fisherman's Spring* posed the question "When to call a fish a rainbow?" he gave this answer: "I wouldn't know. When he isn't a steelhead, I guess. When he isn't a mountain Kamloops or a golden trout. When he's caught landlocked in coastal waters. When he weighs less than five pounds in a stream open to salt water. Or maybe just the way we've always done it—when it seems like he's a rainbow."

Haig-Brown knew a great deal more about these fish than he let on, and he also knew that the answers to the question were many and often perplexing. But anglers, most of whom would rather catch fish than bother with the complexities of taxonomy and speciation, understood his philosophical humour and were glad of company in their bewilderment. Most anglers find the change in scientific name from *Salmo gairdneri* to *Oncorhynchus mykiss* less than exciting. They're still rainbows, whether sea-run or freshwater, and they're among the finest game fish anywhere.

Even though rainbow, Kamloops and steelhead are all one species, their life histories are extremely variable. One constant is that steelhead in their native Pacific habitat are anadromous— born in fresh water, they migrate to and inhabit salt water before returning to fresh water to spawn.

Steelhead have been widely and successfully introduced into freshwater lakes and streams, particularly those with access to larger bodies of water such as the Great Lakes. Typically for ocean-going fish, freshwater steelhead spend most of their lives in larger waters and return to their home stream only to spawn. Since anadromous really implies journeys from fresh to salt to fresh water, fish that make long freshwater journeys are more properly described as migratory.

Scott and Crossman record an amazing freshwater migration. "One fish, taken in the Bay of Quinte, Lake Ontario, in January, 1958, had been part of a tagged group released in Great Lakes rivers in Michigan. From release to capture, a period of eight months, it had travelled about 600 miles, survived a descent of Niagara Falls (unless it negotiated the Welland Ship Canal) and grew 10 inches (25.4 cm) in length."

Rainbow, Kamloops and steelhead trout are silvery overall.

They are identifiable by their many black spots on the back and on the adipose, dorsal and caudal fins, and by an iridescent pink to reddish band along the lateral line. The spots on the caudal fin readily distinguish rainbow from brown trout, which have virtually unspotted tails, and from cutthroat trout, which may not have the lateral line colouring but which have orange or red slash marks on the lower jaw. (Cutthroat at spawning time frequently do show a pinkish tinge along the sides.)

The number and size of spots on rainbows depend on whether the fish are living in big waters such as the sea, estuarine waters and large lakes, or in small lakes and streams. Differences may be due to light intensity: the more light, the more and larger the spots. Colour is also influenced by environment. As with other trout, clear water produces fish that are more brightly hued than does dark or murky water. Rainbows living in rivers are usually darker than lake-dwelling or sea-run fish.

The head of the rainbow is small. Well-developed teeth are found on the paired bones on the roof of the mouth, on the front bone on the roof of the mouth, and on the tongue. The tail is slightly forked. Juvenile rainbows, with noticeably forked tails, carry eight to thirteen widely-spaced parr marks on the lateral line, and from five to ten dark marks on the back between the head and the dorsal fin; the tips of the dorsal and anal fins are white or orange.

There is much variation in the spawning times of rainbow trout, although most in lower latitudes spawn in the spring. Rainbows generally choose sites with fine gravel and well-aerated water, such as a riffle at the head of a pool tailout, and spawn by day and night. Two males will sometimes service one female. The eggs hatch four to seven weeks later, depending on temperature; three to seven days after hatching, the alevins become free-swimming. They immediately face life-threatening problems including disease and predatory fish, birds and animals. Trout are strongly territorial; mortality can be significant when a large population of fry in a small stream must compete for limited food. Because of this, Roger Barnhart writes that up to 50 percent of the fry may perish during their first month.

Juvenile steelhead remain in fresh water for one to five years, but most in warmer streams make the journey as smolts, during their second and third year. Biologist Ron Ptolemy notes that in colder northern streams, the growing season may be less than one hundred days a year, and the young do not reach the smolt stage until their fifth year. This occurs in tributaries of the Upper Skeena, for example. The stay at sea of these fish varies but is normally two to three years. In their northern ranges, however, they may remain in salt water for three to four years before their first return to fresh water.

Although steelhead may return during every month, there are two main runs—the winter runs of November to April, and the summer runs of May to October. Winter-run fish normally spawn during April and May of the year they return, but summer-run fish do not spawn until spring of the following year.

After spawning the spent fish make their way downstream. They may either continue seaward or remain in estuarine pools for a time before beginning their outward migration. We know little of their ocean wanderings, but most Canadian runs of juvenile steelhead are believed to journey far seaward, even as far as Japan, and many are caught in Alaskan and Aleutian waters. At sea they feed mainly on greenling, squid and amphipods, and attain their greatest—sometimes prodigious—growth. They fall prey in turn to other fish and marine mammals.

Most steelhead return to spawn in their natal streams. Unlike salmon they do not necessarily die, but may live to make other sea journeys. According to Ptolemy, some streams have a high percentage of spawning steelhead, and as much as 20 percent of them may be repeat spawners.

The original native ranges of rainbow, Kamloops and steelhead are the waters of the Pacific slope extending from the Kuskokwim River in Alaska, south along the coasts of British Columbia and the United States, to the Tropic of Cancer in Mexico. In Asia they

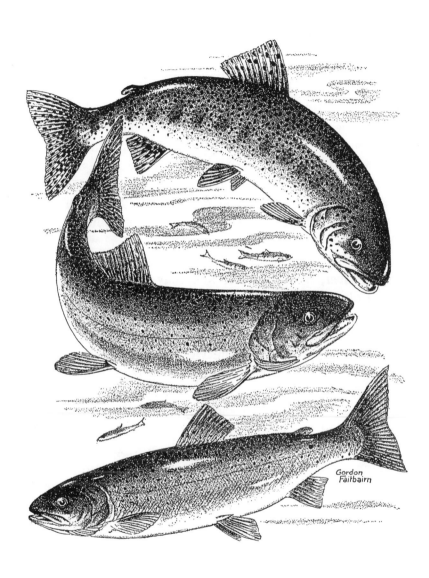

Top: CUTTHROAT TROUT
Centre: STEELHEAD TROUT
Bottom: KAMLOOPS TROUT

are native to Pacific waters from the Kamchatka Peninsula south to the rivers draining the Okhotsk Sea. Most populations are in lakes and rivers west of the Rocky Mountains; some are native to waters on the east slope of the Continental Divide in the Peace River drainage of British Columbia and the Athabasca drainage of Alberta.

Rainbows are bottom feeders and live on invertebrates, crustaceans, insects and the eggs of other fish, particularly salmon. During hatches of terrestrial insects they are ready surface feeders and respond well to both dry and wet artificial flies. Rainbows grow to amazing sizes; the largest steelhead recorded was taken in Alaska and weighed 42 pounds, 2 ounces (19.11 kg). Freshwater rainbows are much smaller, averaging 3 to 4 pounds (1.36 to 1.81 kg).

A remarkable strain of rainbow trout, however, spawns in Lardeau River, a tributary of Kootenay Lake in southeastern British Columbia. These fish, which share ranges with standard Kamloops trout, are known most commonly as Gerrard trout after a small community on Trout Lake, the headwaters of the Lardeau River. They are considered the world's largest rainbow trout, averaging 15 to 20 pounds (about 6.8 to 9.07 kg), and fish up to 52 pounds (23.6 kg) have been recorded. Unlike the standard Kamloops, whose diet consists mainly of invertebrates and whose average weight is 3 to 4 pounds (1.36 to 1.81 kg), the Gerrard strain feeds mainly on kokanee (landlocked sockeye salmon). This, along with unusually favourable spawning conditions in the Lardeau River at Gerrard, largely accounts for their immense size. The standard Kamloops trout have a lifespan of five to six years, but the Gerrard strain may live for as long as eight years.

Attempts to establish Gerrard rainbow populations elsewhere in Canada and the United States earlier in this century nearly ended in disaster. The demand for eggs was so great that eventually only about fifty of the fish were left to perpetuate the native stocks. Few of the transplants succeeded. Two notable exceptions were Jewel Lake in south-central British Columbia, where individuals weighing more than 50 pounds (22.68 kg) have been recorded, and Lake Pend Oreille in Idaho, where a fish weighing 37 pounds (16.78 kg) was caught. According to Steve Raymond a 56 pound Kamloops (25.4 kg) was troll-caught in Jewel Lake in 1932; this was never authenticated, nor was the capture in the same lake of a Gerrard rainbow said to have weighed 48 pounds (21.77 kg) three days after it was caught!

The near-collapse of the Gerrard strain brought changes including revised management techniques, habitat protection, regulated fishing and other protective measures. The Lardeau River spawning run has now been restored to its original size of about one thousand fish. Gerrards are once again considered vulnerable, however, largely because of the serious depletion in Kootenay Lake of kokanees, their main source of food.

Rainbow, Kamloops and steelhead trout are among the most highly respected and eagerly sought of all Canadian game fish. Whether they rate higher in the esteem of anglers than do brook, brown, or cutthroat trout is debatable. What is known is that when hooked they fight with amazing vigour to free themselves.

The conservation of these remarkable creatures, however, deeply concerns scientists, resource managers, anglers, and all others who value fish as a vital part of our wildlife heritage. This is especially true of steelhead. Waters that sheltered dependable runs of these great creatures a few years ago are now virtually barren; in some rivers scientists fear that they face extinction. The reasons for the declines are generally well defined, but the solutions are many and complex.

Anglers understandably share a deep concern for the welfare of this species. Through local fish and game clubs, influential agencies such as the Steelhead Society of BC, the Pacific Salmon Foundation, the Sports Fishing Institute of BC, and the BC Fish and Wildlife Federation, they support efforts to restore the resource to its former greatness. The loss of the steelhead rainbow would be a major tragedy, and one that must never be allowed to happen.

Rainbow trout—steelhead, Kamloops, or rainbow by any other name—make superb eating. Their flesh may be bright red, pink or even white, depending on their food source. It is tender and sweet, and when smoke-cured is more than the equal of smoked salmon.

ADDITIONAL NOTE: The golden trout (*Oncorhynchus aguabonita*) which Haig-Brown mentions are native only to high-elevation waters of the Kern River drainage of California's Sierra Nevada Mountains. They have been introduced with varying success into high lakes in other western states.

Golden trout are similar to rainbow trout but, as described by Nelson and Paetz, are usually more colourful. They have more and smaller scales, larger but fewer body spots and fins with brighter orange or white tips. Also, the adults have more pronounced parr marks. These scientists state that they are "more closely related to rainbow trout than to cutthroat and some recent workers consider the two to be conspecific" (of the same species).

In Canada, golden trout occur only in Alberta, which introduced them to enhance the province's sports fishery. Although not considered as vigorous combatants as rainbow or cutthroat, they perform well when taken on a light fly-rod. The largest golden trout taken from Alberta waters was a 4 pound (1.81 kg) trout caught in South Fort Lakes. In United States waters, golden trout weighing 16 pounds (7.26 kg) have been recorded. The flesh of this species is pinkish red and has an excellent flavour.

Cutthroat trout
(Oncorhynchus clarki)

If taxonomists suffer from insomnia, these remarkable trout have probably caused them more sleepless nights than any other salmonid. So complex is the species' family tree, with its subspecies, hybrids and variants, and so vast and disparate is its geographical range, that for some taxonomists it continues to be an icthyological jigsaw puzzle.

Cutthroats, until recently classified as *Salmo clarki,* are called a polytypic group—which simply means they exist in various types or forms, although Nelson and Paetz point out that even "their status and relationships are uncertain."

Dr. R.J. Behnke recognizes fourteen subspecies, four major and ten minor. All but one inhabit exclusively lakes, rivers and streams. The exception is the coastal cutthroat, which occurs in two forms, one strictly freshwater and the other anadromous. Canadian waters are home to only two indigenous forms of cutthroat, both rated as major, the coastal cutthroat (*Oncorhynchus clarki clarki*) and the west slope cutthroat (*Oncorhynchus clarki lewisi*). A third major subspecies, the Yellowstone cutthroat (*Oncorhynchus clarki bouvieri*), has been introduced into Canada through hatchery operations but has a limited presence. The fourth major subspecies, the Lahontan cutthroat (*Oncorhynchus clarki henshawi*), occurs only in the United States.

The cutthroat clan is extremely complex. Many factors may influence the trout's size, coloration, scale counts, number of gill rakers and other characteristics. Among these factors are interbreeding within different strains, hybridization with rainbow trout, and environmental conditions such as habitat—rivers, lakes, large or small streams, salt water—diet, water temperature and even latitude.

One can but generalize about the coloration of a typical cutthroat of either interior or anadromous type. Scott and Crossman observe, "This species shows a bewildering array of colours and pigment patterns from watershed to watershed and between the anadromous and inland stocks. This has been further complicated by cross-transplantation of the two main stocks in British Columbia and elsewhere on the Pacific Coast. One of the main colour characteristics usually used to distinguish this species from other black-spotted trout are two yellow or orange to red lines in the skin fold of each side of the lower jaw, from which the common name is derived. These are variable in size and intensity, faint in young, and faint to absent in individuals in the sea or recently migrated from the sea."

Ted Burns, in a paper published by the British Columbia Fish and Wildlife Branch, writes: "Immature species at sea are green to metallic blue on the dorsal surface and upper sides, grading to silver on the lower flanks and snow white on the belly. As spawning approaches, they take on a lemon yellow to brownish tinge and the characteristic paired slash marks on the lower jaw become a vivid orange or red. Maturing sea-run cutthroats are often called 'yellowbellies.' Coastal cutthroat are generally more heavily spotted than steelhead, resident rainbows or the Yellowstone cutthroat of the Kootenays."

Distinguishing cutthroats from rainbow trout is sometimes a challenge to even the most knowledgeable angler. The first, usually most obvious, difference is the red or orange slash marks on each side of the cutthroat's lower jaw. These marks may not be apparent in anadromous cutthroats when they are in salt water. The second difference is the cutthroat's basibranchial or hyoid teeth on the plate behind the tongue. These are usually not present in rainbows.

Also, the cutthroat's jaw is longer than the rainbow's, the upper portion being more than half the length of the head, and the cutthroat's eye is well forward of the back of the upper jaw. The rainbow's upper jaw is less than half the length of the head, and the eye is usually in line with the back of the upper jaw.

Dymond writes that studies he made of cutthroats in a stream near Revelstoke, however, showed that the fish there differed structurally from the coast form. They had shorter heads, deeper and wider bodies, deeper caudal peduncles, longer pectoral and ventral fins, and larger eyes. They were, he observes, reminiscent of Kamloops rainbows.

Most cutthroat trout are spring spawners, although some rare populations spawn in the fall. When water temperature in streams or lakes reaches about 50° F (10° C), the female seeks out a gravelly area. There she vigorously thrashes her tail, making a depression about a foot (30.48 cm) in diameter and four to five inches (10.16 to 12.7 cm) deep. When she has settled into the depression a male swims to her side, and the trout simultaneously release eggs and sperm. The fertilized eggs then fall slowly into pockets in the gravel. After this the female swims ahead and thrashes her tail again to cover it with as much as 8 inches (20.32 cm) of gravel. Each female may make more than one nest, and more than one male may move in to release additional sperm. An average female releases an estimated eleven hundred eggs over the spawning period. Six or seven weeks later the eggs hatch, and in about another week the fry leave the nest to become free-swimming. When they reach the parr stage they are difficult to distinguish from young rainbow trout.

Of the three cutthroat subspecies in Canadian waters, perhaps anglers most eagerly seek the coastal form. Its popularity lies in its greater availability, especially to those living close to salt water, even to those living in the shadow of city skyscrapers. During April or May, under cover of darkness, the young smolts migrate from their parent stream to the estuaries. For the next three to seven months they travel in schools through estuary shoals, along beaches and in bays. Their movements seldom take them far from their home streams.

During their wandering they feed on smaller creatures including shrimp, smelt, stickleback, herring, sand worms, squid and many marine larvae. They grow rapidly. In the late fall and early winter they return to ascend their home stream where they may overwinter. The following spring their seaward journey begins again and continues each year thereafter. Although some anadromous cutthroats spawn after spending one or two summers in salt water, some may not spawn until their fifth year. Often very small streams have sufficient flow for brief periods to enable some sea-runs to spawn successfully. Those fish that complete the spawning cycle in such waters return a few days later to the ocean. The interior forms of cutthroat—the west slope and Yellowstone—may follow similar life patterns. In some areas they leave their natal streams in the spring, migrate to lakes where they spend the summer, and in the fall and early winter return to their streams to spawn.

Cutthroats of various species occupy an extensive range from southeastern Alaska to northern California. They are present in at least ten of the western states. In Canada the native coastal cutthroat is present in most British Columbia waters with historic access to the sea, and in some landlocked waters. The native west slope cutthroat occurs in freshwater lakes and streams in southeastern British Columbia and southwestern Alberta. The introduced Yellowstone cutthroat is found mainly in southeastern British Columbia.

Cutthroat trout, whether sea-run or freshwater, are among the gamest of western sports fish. Although they seldom exceed 4 pounds (1.81 kg), some interior forms have been caught weighing as much as 10 pounds (4.54 kg). Freshwater populations in Cowichan, Great Central and Buttle lakes on Vancouver Island have produced cutthroats weighing 15 pounds (6.8 kg). Some anadromous cutthroats have weighed 10 pounds (4.54 kg). The International Game Fish Association notes that a 20-pounder (9.07 kg) was captured in Pyramid Lake, Nevada, in 1986. The same lake produced a 41 pound (18.59 kg) cutthroat in 1925. The life expectancy of all cutthroats is four to seven years, but Scott and Crossman write that some may live as long as ten years.

Freshwater cutthroats respond readily to dry or wet flies and small spinning or wobbling lures. Ted Davis, a Victoria angler widely noted for the perfection of his hand-tied flies, favours a well-hackled Grizzly Wulff for dry-fly fishing, and the Mickey Finn, Rolled Muddler and California Coachman for wet-fly fishing. He suggests the Mallard and Silver or any similar silver-bodied fly will also do a good job of imitating sticklebacks and herring, both important cutthroat feed. Any fly that resembles migrating salmon fry is also productive.

Cutthroats are fine game fish. They are spirited fighters, al-

Top: BROOK TROUT
Centre: RAINBOW TROUT, Steelhead type
Bottom: BROWN TROUT

though they do not perform as acrobatically as rainbows. A fly-rod will whip hard when the fish rush to, and try to hole up in, deeper water. As food they are superior, for their orange-red flesh is rich and flavoursome.

In Canada the welfare of the species, especially the sea-run forms, is being monitored. The preservation of this remarkable natural resource has become a matter of concern to many anglers. For them the use of barbless hooks and the practice of "catch and release" is now commonplace. Like most forms of wildlife forced out of their natural habitats by human intrusions, some interior cutthroat populations in the United States have been decimated. Some have simply vanished. Every effort is being made to prevent this from happening in Canada.

Brown trout
(Salmo trutta)

"Salmo trutta," writes the eminent Ernest Schwiebert, "is a gentleman." His anthropomorphic assessment may stretch things a bit, but there is no denying the brown trout's remarkable influence on humans almost since the beginning of recorded history.

The brown trout is the fish whose apparent likeness was painted on tomb walls in the ancient Egyptian city of Thebes about 1500 BC. This is the fish, along with the grayling, that the Roman writer Aeolian (AD 170–230) writes about in his *De Natura Animalium*. The brown trout was a central character in Dame Juliana Berners's *The Treatyse Of Fysshynge wyth an Angle* (1496), was highly esteemed by Izaak Walton and Charles Cotton in *The Compleat Angler* (1676), and was the focus of Franz Schubert's *Quintet in A, The Trout*. It prompted Canada's own angler essayist Roderick Haig-Brown to rate it as "the finest trout from a fly-fisherman's point of view."

The brown trout—in both freshwater and sea-run forms—predominates in angling literature. During the past five hundred years, but especially since the later nineteenth century, its worth as a sports fish has inspired scores of books that have brought their authors literary immortality. First editions of such classics as *Chalk Stream Studies* by Charles Kingsley (1858), *Fly Fishing* by Sir Edward Grey (1899), *Trout Fishing from All Angles* by Eric Taverner (1929), *The Way of a Trout with a Fly* by E.M. Skues (1949), Schwiebert's monumental two-volume *Trout* (1978) or the 1991 classic *Trout* (in Stackpole Press's "Wildlife Series") remain treasured possessions.

But *Salmo trutta,* "gentleman" though it might be, is not unblemished in reputation. In its Old World waters it reigned by right of ancient citizenship and was appropriately honoured; when introduced to North America it was quickly labelled an intruder that established itself at the expense of our native salmonids, especially *Salvelinus fontinalus,* the brook trout.

Yet anglers recognized it as a worthy fish: pleasing to look at, interesting in its behaviour, strong to resist capture and good to eat. It won acceptance on the understanding that it should not be introduced to too many waters where native trout are doing well. The brown trout can thrive in waters too warm or environmentally unsuitable for other trout, however, making propagation of the species in such places a worthwhile contribution to a good sports fishery.

Brown trout are known by common names including Lochleven trout, *Salmo trutta levenensis* (the loch was made famous by Sir Walter Scott's poem *Lady of the Lake),* Von Behr's trout, English brown trout, German brown trout and European brown trout. The names commonly used today are brown trout and brownie.

Brown trout, both freshwater and sea-run, are indigenous to Iceland, the British Isles, and most other countries of Europe and Asia. They are now well established as introduced species in many parts of North and South America, Africa and New Zealand. The species is one of the most widely transplanted of all salmonids.

Salmo trutta first came to North America in the winter of 1883. Under an arrangement with Baron Lucius von Behr of the German Fisheries Society, eighty thousand eggs were taken to a hatchery at Northville, Michigan. The fry were released the following spring in Michigan's Père Marquette River. They (along with later shipments of German brown trout and Scottish Lochleven trout) were the progenitors of populations now well established in all US states and territories.

In 1884 the colony of Newfoundland first introduced the Lochleven variety to North America when a hundred thousand eggs arrived from the Howietoun hatchery in Scotland. Five years later the Von Behr variety was introduced to Canadian waters when fry from the Caledonia Hatchery in New York were successfully planted in Lac Brûlé, Quebec. Today the brown trout provides excellent angling in Newfoundland, Nova Scotia, New Brunswick (where there are both freshwater and sea-run forms), Quebec, Ontario, Saskatchewan, Alberta and British Columbia.

The British Columbia stock, from Wisconsin and Montana hatchery eggs, have produced some sea-run forms. Progeny from these stocks are long-time residents of the Cowichan River and the Cameron Lake-Little Qualicum drainage of Vancouver Island. In the early 1980s brown trout were stocked into a few other Vancouver Island lakes and into Adorm River near Kelsey Bay. There are no brown trout populations in Prince Edward Island, Manitoba, the Yukon or the Northwest Territories.

The stockily built brown trout more closely resembles the Atlantic salmon than any other trout; this is most noticeable in its much thicker caudal peduncle and larger adipose fin. As a trout rather than a charr, it has larger scales and strong sharp teeth on the entire length of the vomer (the bone at the front of the roof of the mouth).

"Elegant" best describes its appearance. The 4-pounder (1.81 kg) that took the outdoor writer Les Leacock's White Ghost one afternoon from BC's Cowichan River was nature's artistry at its best: light brown on the back and sides, whitish along the lateral line, fading to golden below and white on the belly. Many large and small black and rusty red spots adorned the head, back and sides to slightly below the lateral line, from the cheeks to the almost square caudal fin. A halo surrounded some spots. All of the fins were yellowish brown with light spots; the pelvic and anal fins were edged in white.

A typical brown? Who's to say? Colour markings in fish can be extremely variable, usually depending on habitat. Browns returning to fresh water from the sea, for example, are generally silvery in colour, black or deep blue on the back, with only a few large black spots above the lateral line and near the head. In Newfoundland and the Maritime provinces they are often mistaken for Atlantic salmon. After adjusting to fresh water their colouring changes to become more like the fish that Les Leacock took (and dutifully released) in the Cowichan. Juvenile browns have narrow parr marks and a few rusty red spots along the lateral line. Paetz and Nelson in *The Fishes of Alberta* note, interestingly, that the brown trout is "our only salmonid with light and black spots on the body."

Most brown trout mature at three or more years. Spawning takes place during the day in the fall and early winter, depending on locality; it may be as late as early January in BC's warmer coastal climates. Browns spawn in streams or sometimes near rocky lakeshore reefs. Females lay their amber eggs (an estimated fifteen hundred to two thousand) in shallow depressions they have scooped in sand or gravel, and males immediately fertilize them. Brown trout may make several redds and cover them with detritus before they finish spawning. The eggs hatch in six to eight weeks, and the alevins emerge from the nests in April or May. Growth, which is dependent on temperature and food availability, can be fairly rapid. A yearling may reach nearly 6 inches (15.24 cm); a five-year-old may grow as long as 19 inches (48.26 cm). Some browns live for more than ten years.

Brown trout are inherently timorous. They react warily to any unfamiliar disturbance from leaving their nests to old age. Opinions differ about the brown's eating habits, but it appears that older fish hole up in sheltered places near the bottom or in deep pools to feed on organisms such as crustaceans, molluscs, worms, salamanders, aquatic insects and—in shallower water—minnows and small trout. These veterans will rise avidly to the surface, however, when a hatch, especially of mayflies, is in progress. Young and less cautious browns are more commonly surface feeders, with aquatic and terrestrial insects making up the bulk of their diet.

As most anglers will attest, *Salmo trutta* is also one of the wariest and most difficult of the salmonids to catch. Wet and dry flies are not the only productive lures, however. Live bait such as worms, minnows, frogs and crayfish, as well as small spoons and spinners, will often spring the browns into action, even big ones hiding in pools. Although the average size of resident brown trout is 2 pounds (0.91 kg), individuals of 10 pounds (4.54 kg) or more are frequently caught. Sea-run browns grow larger; the Canadian record is still the 28 pound 8 ounce (12.93 kg) fish caught in Witless Bay, Newfoundland. The so-far uncontested world record is the 39 pound 4 ounce (17.8 kg) veteran caught in 1866 in Loch Awe, Scotland.

Brown trout and brook trout sometimes naturally hybridize, producing a form known as tiger trout, and browns have also been artificially crossbred with rainbow trout. The results in both instances have contributed more to scientific knowledge than to the sports fishery.

Arctic charr
(Salvelinus alpinus)

Arctic charr, as the name suggests, are primarily northern residents—occurring in both landlocked and anadromous forms throughout circumpolar regions, continuous except for the expanse of the North Atlantic ocean between Greenland and western Siberia.

One almost feels a sense of betrayal in revealing too much about these remarkable creatures. Many are still relatively secure within their natural arctic ranges, but commercial and angling pressure on Arctic charr has been heavy in recent years. In addition, they have traditionally been a dietary staple for northern peoples and their dogs.

Throughout their North American, European and Asiatic ranges, Arctic charr vary greatly in conformation and coloration—so much that twenty-six species, anadromous and nonanadromous, were once identified. Most are so closely related to *Salvelinus alpinus* that separate species are no longer warranted, and the number is now lower. As long as Arctic charr exist, however, they no doubt will continue to be a taxonomic challenge.

A typical Arctic charr is trout-like in appearance, having a long, somewhat rounded body, forked tail and small pointed head. The eyes are large and the cycloid scales are so fine and deeply embedded that they are almost imperceptible to the touch. Teeth are present on the upper and lower jaws, on the anterior bone in the roof of the mouth and on the tongue. As spawning time arrives the lower jaw of some male populations develop a noticeable upward hook. A similar but smaller protuberance sometimes develops on mature females.

Dr. Lionel Johnson, a noted authority on Arctic charr, describes the species' coloration:

> It is extremely variable, ranging from dark blue or dark green to brown on the back and sides, changing to silver or a dull white on the belly. Intense blues and greens with white/silvery bellies are characteristic of fish returning from the sea, whereas non-migratory stocks within a single lake range from dark blue to brown, with frequently a red, orange or yellow coloration on the paired fins and belly. Red spots may be present along the flanks and in some populations these may be surrounded by a bluish halo.
>
> No description, however, does full justice to the vivid coloration of many stocks. In the spawning season, males—particularly in anadromous populations—may develop an

intense red coloration over the whole body except for the leading edges of the fins and tail, which are an iridescent white. This white leading edge may be retained through the non-breeding period, but loses its iridescence. In the females a similar situation develops, but the red coloration is less intense and is confined to the flanks and belly, the back retaining its blue or bluish green colour.

The life cycle of the far northern Arctic charr is especially variable and complex. As with other salmonids (notably Atlantic salmon and Pacific sockeye) there are two distinct types: those that remain exclusively in fresh water and those that spend significant periods of their lives at sea. All reach maturity in fresh water, however, and choose either lakes or streams in which to excavate their nests and lay their eggs.

Times of maturity vary widely in anadromous Arctic charr. Some, including charr homing to rivers in Alaska and Yukon, are believed to reach maturity between four and six years; others, such as those in the Eastern Arctic, specifically the Baffin Island region, mature between seven and seventeen years.

Spawning times vary, but spawning usually takes place in September and October. Arctic charr choose sites in water 6 to 16 feet (1.83 to 4.88 m) deep, with a coarse sand and gravel bottom scattered with moderately large stones. These may be in rivers, often in pools below rapids or falls, or in lakes. The female chooses the site, and by turning on her side and beating her tail vigorously, creates a flow of water strong enough to excavate a depression. Into this she deposits approximately twenty-seven hundred to seven thousand eggs. She may make as many as eight or more nests before spawning and fertilization of the eggs have been completed.

Males, which often fertilize the eggs of more than one female, generally remain in the area throughout the spawning period; females tend to move away from the redds when they have finished spawning. Females spawn every second or third year.

The eggs hatch the following spring, at about the time the parent fish begin their migration back to sea. The young charr do not become fully anadromous, however, until their fifth to seventh year.

Unlike salmon (with the exception of coho) migrating charr remain mainly in inshore waters during their ocean sojourn. All anadromous Arctic charr, mature and immature, leave the sea in the fall to overwinter in freshwater rivers and lakes. Not all returning mature fish are spawners, however, for some go back and forth several times before they spawn.

Nonanadromous charr, which tend to reach maturity when smaller and younger, follow the same lifestyles and require the same habitat and upstream spawning conditions as sea-going charr. They share the same kinds of food: aquatic insects, molluscs, small fish and a variety of bottom organisms. In the far north ninespine sticklebacks are especially important in their diet.

Arctic charr, both freshwater and anadromous, are among the most widely distributed of the salmonids. They also occupy the most northerly ranges. Dr. Johnson, in his scholarly study in *Charrs: Salmonid Fishes of the Genus Salvelinus,* writes that there appears to be no northern limit to anadromous and landlocked stocks of Arctic charr. To support this he points to a 1963 report by Dr. H.B. Bigelow that charr have been noted on the northern coast of Discovery Harbour, Ellesmere Island—at 82' 34"° N— about eight hundred kilometres south of the North Pole! Arctic charr, he adds, are also the only freshwater fish north of Lancaster Sound on Melville Strait.

Charr are present in Alaska and throughout the Canadian Arctic mainland and islands, and in a southerly range which includes Labrador, Newfoundland and northern Quebec. Populations are also present in Maine and New Hampshire. These southern relic forms (most commonly known as *blueback* and *Quebec red*) were once considered subspecies (*Salvelinus aureolus, Salvelinus oquassa,* and *Salvelinus marstoni*), but were reclassified in 1974 as a single species, *Salvelinus alpinus.*

As juveniles or young adults Arctic charr are the prey of fish-eating birds such as gulls, terns, and yellow-billed and red-throated loons. Sea-going charr are sometimes taken by seals, but such predation is believed to be minor. During the spawning season, however, northern pike often attack both resident and anadromous charr.

Johnson writes of Nettilling (Seal) Lake on Baffin Island, which he describes as the only freshwater body in Canada known to contain a permanent winter population of ringed seals. Since no other food is available, the seals subsist solely on charr. In Alaska, his report also says, grizzly bears and wolves have been seen feeding on charr.

Arctic charr are a primary food source in the far north, particularly for native peoples and their dogs. In Labrador the charr fishery has been economically important for more than two hundred years, and in Newfoundland the species also sustains an important commercial fishery. Most of the catch is taken in gill-nets.

As sport fish, Arctic charr are considered by many anglers to be the equal of Atlantic salmon. They share many of *Salmo salar*'s fighting characteristics: long runs, acrobatic leaps and furious head-twisting. High-water fishing calls for spoons, plugs, spinners or heavily dressed flies with enough weight to reach bottom levels. When low, fast water prevails these charr are said to respond to nearly any pattern of brightly coloured wet flies. When insect hatches are on, dry flies are generally productive.

Anadromous charr are schooling fish. During summer—before their upstream journey to their natal lakes and rivers, where they will remain icebound until spring—they range along shorelines and in estuaries. There the fishing is at its best.

Depending on their feed, the Arctic charr's flesh may be deep orange-red or almost white. In prime condition they are an acknowledged delicacy.

Brook trout
(Salvelinus fontinalis)

The English interpretation of the name *Salvelinus fontinalis* is as attractive as the fish itself: little salmon living in a spring. It suits this beautiful freshwater and sea-going creature. Small wonder that North American angling literature features the brook trout more than any other species.

Visual artists have been less attentive, unfortunately, although the steel engravings in The Naturalist's Library *Ichthyology* in 1843 portrayed fish with great precision. The exception was the now highly-prized Currier and Ives lithograph series. The most celebrated of the Currier and Ives pieces shows Massachusetts Senator Daniel Webster and the great trout he caught in a Long Island river in 1832. The best version of the event appears in Ernest Schwiebert's remarkable two-volume *Trout.*

It seems that the senator, while attending morning service at the Presbyterian church in the hamlet of Brookhaven on the Nissequoque River, received a whispered message. The trout, one that for years had evaded capture, had just been seen in a nearby millrace. Webster, unable to resist temptation, slipped out of his pew with some friends during the singing of—as Schwiebert relates it— "Shall we gather at the river," and hurried to the millrace. The battle was still in progress long after the service had ended and much of the congregation gathered along the bank to cheer him on. Eventually, to loud applause, he landed the creature. Schwiebert suggests that the fish may have weighed 9 to 10 pounds (4.08 to 4.54 kg); A.J. McClane, in *Game and Fish of North America,* suggested that the trout portrayed in the Currier and Ives lithograph was nearer 3 pounds (1.36 kg).

All good fish stories, however, survive both great elaboration and the passing of time. Senator Webster's exploit became so famous that in 1854 it was entered into the United States congressional record!

Salvelinus fontinalis—like the lake trout, bull trout and Dolly

Varden—is not a trout but a charr. It is generally the smallest of its family. It is outclassed in coloration by the brown trout, and is a less spectacular rod-bender pound for pound than the brown or rainbow. Its culinary qualities, however, "take the gold" from the brown or rainbow.

Salvelinus fontinalis has a mystique. Perhaps its habitat helps to endear it to anglers. The brookie is a wilderness-dweller with a compelling need for the clean, cool water of a river, lake, pond, or even a tiny meadow stream you can step across. One associates brook trout with canoe trips or fly-ins to remote lakes like the one that inspired Canadian poet Wallace Havelock Robb to write:

> *The lone loon calls and rocky walls*
> *Resound the mournful sound.*
> *It grieves away the dying day*
> *And darkness falls around . . .*

Since it is the nature of brook trout to be wanderers, it is not surprising that some living in streams with access to the sea leave their freshwater habitats and spend two to three months in salt water before returning to spawn. These are known as *coasters* (in some areas as *slobs!*). They provide good sport for anglers working estuarine and inshore waters throughout much of eastern Canada, particularly from late April to early June and from October to December, depending on the area.

The brook trout does well in low-altitude habitats but thrives at alpine heights. There are as many trophy-sized brookies in the mountains of Chile and Argentina (derived from stocks originally planted there from North American hatcheries) as within the species' native ranges in eastern North America. Brook trout, because of their unblemished reputation, endearing characteristics and adaptability to foreign waters, are among our most successful piscatorial goodwill ambassadors.

Nature was in a bountiful mood when she created *Salvelinus fontinalis,* so handsome in form and coloration that it moved the late Vadim Vladykov, a highly respected Canadian scientist, to write of it lyrically as the "queen of our lakes and rivers in a sparkling array, vigorous as the rapids of brooks where it abounds, savoury and delightful as a breeze over the shady pools it frequents." Scientists are generally a pragmatic lot, but Dr. Vladykov obviously had a special affection for the brookie.

We can understand why the brook trout—the most extensively studied of all the charr, according to Dr. Geoffrey Power—commands such a large degree of respect from anglers and scientists alike. Scientists have done a vast amount of research and culturing on the species and have produced substantial scientific literature. It may be less generally known that this has led to its widespread use in physiological, toxicological, pharmacological and bioassay work. The brook trout, Dr. Power writes, "has become the white rat of aquatic science."

Salvelinus fontinalis is similar in conformation to the brown trout. It is a robust, elongated fish with a relatively large head, large terminal mouth, and strong teeth on the jaws, tongue and front part of the mouth. The maxilla reaches beyond the eye (a similar feature helps distinguish largemouth from smallmouth bass). The small cycloid scales are virtually imperceptible to the touch. The caudal fin in mature trout is square or slightly forked, but in juveniles (distinguished by eight to nine steely blue vertical parr marks on the sides) the fin is forked.

Geographical location and habitat influence the brook trout's coloration, which consequently varies greatly. Colour generally ranges from olive green to dark brown, occasionally almost black, on the back and sides. There are olive-coloured worm-like markings on the back and roundish markings on the sides; the sides also have numerous red spots, each surrounded by a bluish circle, mainly below the lateral line. The dorsal and tail fins are prominently marked with small black dots. The pectoral, pelvic and anal fins are pink or red, and edged with white; above the white is a band of black. Before spawning season their bellies are whitish, but as spawning season approaches the colouring of both male and female brookies become more pronounced. In males, especially, the belly becomes bright red and the lower jaw develops a hook or *kype*.

Sea-run brook trout turn silvery in salt water but resume much of their brilliant colouring on re-entering fresh water. At that stage they cannot be distinguished from the freshwater populations. The anadromous fish undergo a strange body transformation at sea, however; studies have shown that when they first re-enter fresh water their heads are smaller, their bodies are almost cylindrical and their fins are shorter. As sexual maturity approaches, their body features regain the robust forms typical of freshwater brook trout.

Brook trout are native to northeastern North America, from Labrador southward throughout the Hudson Bay watershed (including Belcher and Akimisi islands) to Newfoundland, the Maritime provinces, Quebec and Ontario and numerous offshore islands including Anticosti and Grand Manan. In the United States they are native to waters throughout the Appalachians, Georgia, Iowa and the headwaters of the Mississippi. Transplantation beyond their original northeastern range has been extensive; they are now present in all provinces, as well as in many mountain regions of the western United States. The species has been successfully introduced into streams and lakes in South America, New Zealand, Asia and several European countries.

Brook trout spawn during daylight hours between late August and early December in shallow, well-oxygenated water with gravel bottoms. Spawning grounds may be in lakes or streams, sometimes far upstream. An average female lays two thousand to three thousand eggs for each pound (4400 to 6600 per kg) of her weight.

The young hatch in the spring but remain in the gravel, drawing nourishment from the nutrients in their tiny yolk sac. When these have been absorbed, they leave the protection of the gravel to become free-swimming. At first they feed on the microscopic life in the water. As they grow, their diet includes terrestrial and aquatic insects and their larvae, molluscs, crayfish, worms, other fish, frogs, and sometimes small mammals such as field mice, voles and shrews. Sea-going brook trout feed on marine creatures including smelts, silversides, mummichogs, small eels and invertebrates such as amphipods, isopods and sandworms. Brook trout are in turn preyed upon by kingfishers, mergansers, great blue herons and other raptors, perch, pickerel, and—to a lesser extent—mink and other mammals.

Wild brook trout mature at about three years, occasionally at two. Their average lifespan is four to six years, the shortest of all the charr. Some live a year or two longer, however, and there are records of stunted brook trout more than twenty years old living in Bunny Lake, California.

One of the most notable achievements of fish culturists has been their success in fertilizing brook trout eggs with lake trout sperm. This hybrid, known as *splake,* is not self-perpetuating and stocks must be produced in hatcheries. It grows to considerable size, however, with some fish weighing as much as 16 pounds (7.26 kg). Splake are excellent sport fish.

Brook trout in streams or lakes feed throughout the day, but more heavily in the evening and early morning when terrestrial insects are more active. Anglers working streams should look for holding stations where rocks create backeddies; there trout can lie in wait for passing surface or subsurface feed. Stream-dwelling trout also feed on the bottom, where they consume more substantial fare such as crustaceans. Lake-dwelling trout cruise near the surface, particularly when terrestrial hatches are taking place, but also cruise at lower depths in search of emerging aquatic insect larvae and small fish. Young brook trout in lakes feed heavily on zooplankton. Brook trout in salt water eat mainly fish.

Anglers developed the artificial fly, believed to have been invented by Macedonians about 1000 BC, into extremely convincing lures that trout and other salmonids would strike at in preference to their natural foods. From primitive beginnings evolved hundreds of imitations—and countless imitations that really don't imitate anything but still manage to fool trout. A mere mention of Parmachene Belle, White Wulff, Alexandra or Royal Coachman will stir the adrenalin in any angler.

Brook trout are superb game fish. Even young fish hooked on either artificial flies or metal lures will put up a spirited fight. A trout weighing 3 to 4 pounds (1.36 to 1.81 kg) is considered a large fish. The International Game Fish Association still recognizes the 14.5 pound trout (6.58 kg) that Dr. J.W. Cook took in 1915 from the Nipigon River in Ontario as the largest on record; the highly respected Joe Brooks, however, writes in his book *Trout Fishing* that in 1969 Fred Shaw of Boston took a brook trout weighing 15.2 pounds (6.89 kg) from the Tusiask River in Labrador.

The flesh of the brook trout is firm, delicately flavoured, and usually pink or salmon in colour. It is an especially superb delicacy when medium-smoked.

ADDITIONAL NOTE: Scientists are still trying to establish the true status of the aurora trout, at present called *Salvelinus fontinalis timagamiensis,* native to several lakes in the Timiskaming district of northeastern Ontario. Acid rain is thought to have decimated these natural stocks, and by 1971 they had disappeared.

Prior to their disappearance, however, brook trout *(Salvelinus fontinalis)* were apparently introduced into the lakes. The resulting hybrids are similar to brook trout apart from their extremely variable markings, described by Scott and Crossman as "non-speckled and non-spotted." Efforts to produce self-perpetuating populations have not succeeded, but stocks are being rehabilitated through hatchery operations of the Ontario Ministry of Natural Resources. There are differences of opinion as to whether *Salvelinus fontinalis timagamiensis* is a valid subspecies of *Salvelinus fontinalis,* or just a form of that species.

The aurora trout is considered unique and, because of its fragile numbers, COSEWIC lists it as endangered.

Bull trout
(Salvelinus confluentus)

For many years scientists strove to agree on the correct classification of what is commonly called the bull trout or, more correctly, the bull charr.

This fish, a strictly western species, is so similar to the Dolly Varden that the two were originally grouped under one scientific name, *Salvelinus malma.* Painstaking study by taxonomists has now revealed enough differences in head and cranial skeleton characters to prove that the two are distinct species.

Anglers as well as scientists find this interesting, although sensitive anglers may well ask why *Salvelinus confluentus* must retain its common name. Could bull trout not have been simultaneously changed to something like the lovely appellation Dolly Varden? Since it belongs to a group favoured with attractive names, does "bull" not seem a little inappropriate?

A taxonomist's expertise is often needed to accurately establish the differences between bull trout and Dolly Varden. Three exterior characteristics of bull trout help to set them apart: their broader and more laterally compressed head, larger mouth and more slender body.

Dolly Varden seldom exceed 7 or 8 pounds (3.17 or 3.63 kg) in weight, whereas bull trout often grow to much greater sizes. The record-breaking bull trout weighing 32 pounds (14.52 kg) was taken on rod and reel by N.L. Higgins in 1949 from Lake Pend Oreille, Idaho. It was 40.5 inches (102.87 cm) in length and had a girth of 29.75 inches (75.57 cm).

Bull trout are native to northwestern North America throughout the coastal and interior range extending from California to Alaska, and in lakes and rivers of the Rocky Mountains and Cascade Range, and on both sides of the Continental Divide. The status of this species is being monitored, however. Bjornn writes that in many streams of their original range they are now absent and in some cases virtually eliminated; Nelson and Paetz also strike a warning note, pointing out that "there has been a significant reduction in the range of this species . . . especially in the eastern portion of their range in Alberta." They also warn that perhaps the Prairies' last bull trout, a downstream population in the Oldman River, "is also certain to disappear if its migration path continues to be blocked by the recently constructed Three Rivers Dam." This was predicted in 1991 by W.E. Roberts. Bjornn says "relatively viable" populations still exist in some drainages of the Fraser and Columbia rivers, some coastal rivers and some Montana streams east of the Continental Divide.

Bull trout, unlike some populations of anadromous Dolly Varden, dwell only in fresh water throughout their known range. Their preferred habitats are cold streams and lakes, especially those fed by glaciers and snowfields. They eat primarily fish and other bottom feed, especially insects.

Bull trout mature during their fourth to tenth year. Like many other salmonids they spawn in the fall; adults return afterward to the river or lake where they spend their maturing years. The eggs hatch about four months later. Bjornn writes that for the first one to four years they remain in their natal streams, then migrate to a larger lake or stream where they remain for another two to four years. They do not return to their natal streams again until they are ready to spawn.

The gastronomical qualities of bull trout (or any other fish) are only as good as their cook, but they give even an amateur chef a fair start. The flesh is usually pinkish, firm and flavoursome. As game fish bull trout, like Dolly Varden, are generally considered inferior to other trout. They will respond to artificial flies, but most anglers take them on metal lures by casting or trolling.

Dolly Varden trout
(Salvelinus malma)

Those unfamiliar with the Dolly Varden may believe the name of this species is more attractive than the fish itself. It is a beautiful creature, but as one writer observed, it lacks "the dash and zip of other trout."

Different stories account for the Dolly's name. One version is that during Charles Dickens' tour of the United States in 1867 his historical novel, *Barnaby Rudge,* was at the height of its popularity. A favourite character in the book was the coquettish Dolly Varden, well known for her love of colourful, gaily spotted clothes. Dickens' public readings from *Barnaby Rudge* sparked a craze among women for similar hats and calicos. One young lady of influence, seeing the spotted trout for the first time, jokingly declared that it must be a Dolly Varden trout.

Scientists have questioned the accuracy of this story, among them Professor Joseph Nelson of the University of Alberta. Although Dickens did make Dolly Varden a major character in the book, he nowhere described a colourful, spotted dress!

The fictitious Dolly did become a popular subject for English painters, however, and a canvas depicting her colourful dress may have inspired fashion designers. Dresses named after Dolly then quickly became popular. Subsequently, a woman angler in California reputedly admired the trout she was watching and named it a Dolly Varden. Professor Nelson also notes that, according to scientists Cavender and Behnke, the name may originally have described a related salmonid, the bull trout (*Salvelinus confluentus*).

Unfortunately some fishers do not welcome the Dolly Varden. In many areas sports and commercial fishers dislike its allegedly heavy predation of the eggs and young of the most valuable salmon species, the sockeye. Years ago Alaska briefly paid a bounty of two and a half to five cents for each Dolly Varden caudal fin turned in. The Dolly's status improved somewhat when in at least one lake an even greater predator of sockeye eggs and fry was the sockeyes' own relatives, young coho!

The bounty program was "one of the greatest boondoggles in the history of Alaska fisheries," writes Professor Robert H. Armstrong of the University of Alaska in his treatise on Dolly Varden in Stackpole's *Trout*. Many tails turned in were actually from rainbow trout and salmon, the species Alaska authorities sought to protect!

Studies of Dolly Varden food consumption have shown that, despite their insatiable appetite for most forms of aquatic life, they probably consume no more sockeye eggs and young than do steelhead and cutthroat trout. The Dolly has been maligned.

There are two types of Dolly Varden. The southern form occurs from Puget Sound in Washington north around the Alaska Peninsula; the northern form occurs from the Alaska Peninsula east to the Beaufort Sea and Mackenzie River. Armstrong writes that Dollies are particularly abundant in Alaska. In British Columbia the Dolly Varden is the most widely distributed salmonid, with populations in both Vancouver Island and the Queen Charlottes.

The Dolly Varden is typically trout-like in appearance. The freshwater type is generally dark blue to olive green on the back and upper sides, and white or dusky on the undersides and belly. Yellow, orange or red spots (nearly as large as the pupil of the fish's eye) are especially numerous along the lateral line. The pectoral, pelvic and anal fins are white or creamish; the dorsal and caudal fins are dusky with sometimes a few pale spots. (McPhail and Lindsey write of a freshwater population in Summit Lake, Kenai Peninsula, Alaska, whose sides are always bright red.)

Some Dolly Varden live permanently in inshore salt water. The sea-run Dolly is normally dark blue on the upper part of the head and on the back and upper sides, silvery on the lower sides, and silvery or white on the belly. This coloration is apparently inconsistent; in *The Trout and Other Game Fishes of British Columbia* Dymond writes that "in the sea the Dolly Varden is almost plain silvery." Spawning males are more vividly coloured than spawning females—red on the belly, olive brown on the sides and back, and black on the lower jaw, gill covers and parts of the head. As spawning approaches the spots become more pronounced and the fins turn reddish-black with creamy leading edges. In both sexes the lower jaw develops an upward hook or *kype*.

The Dolly Varden's spawning procedure is complex. Simply stated, both forms remain in fresh water for their first three or four years, spending most of that time in the area where they were born. Sometime during those years anadromous southern Dolly Varden make their first migration to sea, remaining in coastal waters until the coming of winter. Then they find a stream leading to a lake, where they overwinter. In the spring they return to the sea. This back and forth migration, perhaps involving several rivers and lakes, continues for the next two or three years, until they search out their natal river and return to spawn. These sexually mature fish average only 1 to 2 pounds (0.45 to 0.91 kg).

Dolly Varden in the northernmost areas of Alaska and Canada face different challenges, for lakes and rivers with access to the sea freeze solid in the winter. Suitable overwintering and spawning sites are, Armstrong notes, "probably without exception, associated with major springs in the larger rivers." Northern Arctic populations do not make the sea-to-lake migrations characteristic of southern stocks. Nonanadromous Dolly Varden are migratory only in spending the first two to four years in the area where they were born, then mostly moving to larger waters such as lakes and rivers, then returning to their natal streams to spawn.

Both anadromous and freshwater Dolly Varden become sexually mature in their fourth or fifth year. Spawning takes place throughout September and October, mainly by daylight, in rivers with a moderate current. The female scoops each nest out of the sand and gravel. Then the female and male lie side by side—mouths agape, backs arched and bodies quivering—expelling eggs and sperm. More than one male may accompany each female during spawning. The orange-red eggs drop into the protection of sand and gravel and hatch the following spring. The young fish, both anadromous and freshwater, remain in the rivers for two to four years before moving into the lakes. The migration downstream of sea-going forms occurs in May and early June.

Dolly Varden feed on many freshwater and saltwater aquatic vertebrates and invertebrates, as well as the eggs and young of salmon and other fish such as smelt, stickleback, kokanee and whitefish. Dymond writes that "they do not confine themselves to fish, for mice, frogs and even birds have been found in their stomachs. . . . Their food was found to be practically identical to that of the cutthroat, indicating that the abundance of these fish in the streams is a serious drain on the food supply which supports the trout."

Most anglers give the Dolly Varden only passing marks compared to cutthroat or brook trout. They are relatively easy to catch and respond readily to most types of artificial lures, including wet and dry flies. They rarely break water in their efforts to free themselves, a trait that lessens their sporting appeal. The sea-run forms are generally small, weighing 1 to 3 pounds (0.45 to 1.36 kg). The freshwater form seldom exceeds 7 or 8 pounds (3.18 or 3.63 kg). The flesh is pink and of good flavour.

Lake trout
(Salvelinus namaycush)

Two things about these splendid creatures may come as a surprise to some anglers. First, although commonly called trout they are scientifically classified as charr. Second, they are the second largest of all the salmonids. Only the great chinook salmon of the Pacific are larger.

But how would you like to land a lake trout that was 52 inches (132.08 cm) long, with a girth of 38 inches (96.52 cm), and that shot the scales around to 65 pounds (29.48 kg)? That's what Larry Daunis did in 1970 at Great Bear Lake, NWT. It was small compared to the 102-pounder (46.27 kg) net-caught in Lake Athabasca, NWT, in 1961 by Orton Flett. Legend has it that in 1818 a 120-pounder (54.43 kg) was taken from the Great Lakes!

Lake trout, first described in 1792, were originally classified as *Salmo namaycush*. Later the scientific name was changed to *Cristivomer namaycush*. In 1948 the species was returned to its original genus and is now officially recognized as *Salvelinus namaycush.* Over their extensive range they are known by various popular names including *salmon trout, landlocked salmon, grey trout, Great Lakes charr, forktail trout, mountain trout* and *mackinaw trout.*

A typical lake trout has a long, somewhat slender body with a deeply forked caudal fin. Its head, eyes and mouth are large. In older fish the upper jaw extends well behind the eye. There are well-developed teeth on the jaws, tongue and roof of the mouth, and a row of teeth in the middle of the palate. A distinguishing characteristic is the slender caudal peduncle.

Lake trout coloration varies greatly, but generally speaking the fish has an overall darkish appearance ranging from grey to green, dark brown or even nearly black. The body is almost completely covered with light grey or white spots, but there are none of the red spots so characteristic of other charr. Scott and Crossman write that lake trout in some large lakes can be so silvery that the spots are difficult to see. Some fish carry traces of orange on their pelvic, anal, pectoral and, occasionally, on their caudal fins. As in all charr, the scales of the lake trout are fine and deeply embedded.

This species is indigenous to and occurs through much of northern North America, but as Scott and Crossman point out, "even within the general range distribution patterns exhibit peculiar clustering in certain regions and complete absence from others that appear equally suitable." They occur in all provinces and territories except Newfoundland. They are also well established in Alaska and in Arctic islands including Baffin, Southampton, King William, Victoria and Banks. They occur in some upper New England states as well as in Montana and Idaho. This species has also been successfully introduced into South America, New Zealand, Sweden, Switzerland and France.

Lake trout are cold water fish. Except for fall and early winter, when they move into the shallows to spawn, they dwell mainly in the depths. In more northern waters some stocks inhabit relatively shallow lakes and their connecting rivers. Spawning usually takes place every second year from August to December depending on geographical location, when water temperature reaches about 57°F (13.88°C) in the south to 48°F (8.88°C) in the north. The trout choose sites in water from 5 to 40 feet deep (1.52 to 12.19 m)—sometimes as deep as 100 feet (30.48 m)—with a bottom of honeycombed rocks, boulders, ledges or coarse gravel. Unlike other salmonids, lake trout do not make nests, although they usually sweep the sites clean of silt and detritus with their tails. The spawning female is accompanied by one or more males, which fertilize her eggs as she randomly releases them. Spawning takes place in lakes at night, or during the day if it is dark and windy; some spawning may also take place in rivers. The female may release up to eighteen thousand eggs, four hundred to twelve hundred for each pound (880 to 2640 per kg) of her weight.

Opinions differ as to whether they wander significant distances; most authorities suggest that some fish return year after year to spawn in their natal lakes or streams. But the homing pattern is inconsistent. Lake trout are also slow to mature. In southern waters they mature at about six years, and in far northern waters at twelve to sixteen years or more.

Lake trout are omnivorous feeders with seemingly insatiable appetites. During their early lives they consume large quantities of larvae, insects, small crustaceans, worms and the like. As they grow they feed on almost anything that moves, including other fish such as smelt, sculpins, perch, whitefish, ciscoes and alewives, and even small mammals. McClane writes of one 8 pound (3.62 kg) laker so full of black fly larvae that it had nothing else in its stomach. In return for eliminating these pests, perhaps we should declare a temporary closed season on lake trout!

Lake trout spend most of their time among ledges and scattered boulders and rocks, so avoid angling for them in places with smooth bottoms. In addition, lake trout seem to bite more readily under an overcast sky and a good breeze. In southern waters, especially during the warm months of summer, they usually

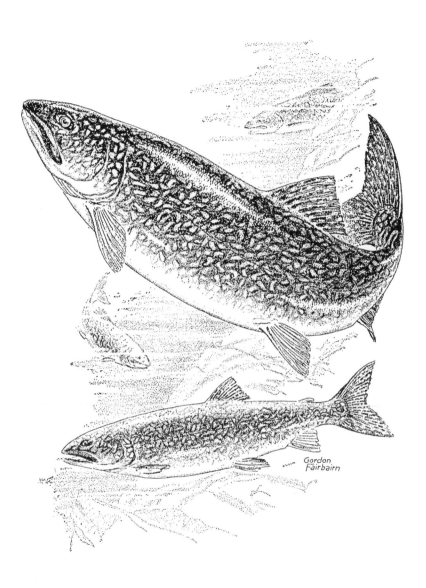

LAKE TROUT

115

retreat to the deep parts of lakes; trolling with metal lures or live bait should be effective. In the fall, when the fish may move to shallower waters, fly-casting or spin-casting can succeed. In winter, anglers jig for them through holes in the ice; in many areas (such as Lake Simcoe, Ontario) ice-fishing is a popular sport. The same methods are used in the far north, although some lake trout there inhabit shallow water year-round.

Commercially this species has great value. The sea lamprey, water pollution and overfishing, however, have now reduced the once huge Great Lakes fishery to lakes Superior and Huron and adjacent waters. The Northwest Territories commercial fishery centres mainly around Great Bear Lake and Great Slave Lake. Lake trout is marketed fresh or frozen, occasionally canned or smoked, and is popular with consumers. The flesh is firm and delicately flavoured, and ranges from white to deep orange-red.

ADDITIONAL NOTE: In 1970 scientists gave the name *Salvelinus siscoet* to a form of lake trout called *siscoet,* but better known to fishers as *fat* because of its extremely oily flesh. They inhabit, and are believed to spawn in, deep water of Lake Superior. They have no sporting or commercial value and are said to be palatable only when smoked. Similar in appearance is another form of lake trout called the *bumper, paperbelly* or *bank trout,* often found near offshore banks and reefs.

THE GRAYLING SUBFAMILY—Thymallinae

Grayling are closely related to the salmon, trout, charr and whitefish families. They are considered as intermediate between trout and whitefish. Until recently they were considered a separate family, Thymallidae, but under a new systematic arrangement they are now classified as a subfamily, Thymallinae.

The one genus (*Thymallus*) consists of four species, all inhabiting mostly arctic and subarctic ranges. They are *Thymallus brevirostris* (Mongolia), *Thymallus thymallus* (Britain to central

Europe), *Thymallus nigrescens* (Lake Kosogol, Mongolia) and *Thymallus arcticus* (western Siberia and North America). There are also numerous subspecies.

The North American grayling, *Thymallus arcticus,* is much sought-after as a game fish. There is much controversy about its coloration, its alleged odour of wild thyme, and its sporting and table qualities.

Arctic grayling
(Thymallus arcticus)

The Denholm Angling Club, as I remember it, was hidden away beside a pristine, privately owned lake about forty kilometres north of Ottawa. Its handful of members were mainly senior civil servants who, when not involved in the affairs of state, spent as much of their spare time as possible in pursuit of the lake's lovingly propagated brook trout. When not on the lake (fly-fishing only!) they relaxed in conversation in the club's lounge (politics and business matters totally forbidden), and as well paid appropriate homage to Scotland's finest.

I remember Denholm with particular clarity because during one weekend there was an animated discussion between two members who had just returned from fishing trips to the Arctic, on the merits and demerits of Arctic grayling. One extolled their beauty, the other considered them drab; one enthused over their fighting spirit, the other was ambivalent. Both members denied that grayling smell of wild thyme. Grayling, they agreed, smell as fish normally smell, although there was cautious admittance to a temporary mild odour reminiscent of cucumber.

The Salmonidae family was part of ichthyological literature long before Dame Juliana Berners or Izaac Walton wrote their books. We are indebted to Howard T. Walden II for recording in *Familiar Freshwater Fishes of America* that the Roman writer Aeolian "mentioned the *thymallus,* a kind of grayling (of Macedonia) and its odour of a freshly gathered bunch of thyme."

Aeolian lived from AD 170 to 230, thirteen centuries before Berners and fourteen before Walton, and is credited as "the first in history to describe an artificial fly." Was Aeolian, then, the originator of the now controversial wild thyme theory?

Izaac Walton gave the theory credence in *The Compleat Angler*: "Some think he feeds on Water-time, and smells so at his taking out of the water; and they think so with good reason as we do, and that our Smelt smell like Violets at their first being caught, which I think is truth."

One suspects that many writers since Walton have simply repeated his claim without personal experience to back it up, however, for literature now tends to rate it as charming folklore. Yet one has to wonder why the grayling subfamily is scientifically classified as Thymallinae and why all graylings carry the Latin name *Thymallus,* referring to wild thyme.

The beauty of the grayling is also in question. One dissenter writes that the "gushing superlatives" some writers use to describe the grayling "are not only trite but highly inaccurate."

Roderick Haig-Brown, always a sensitive observer, in *Fisherman's Summer* describes this encounter and his reactions: "It was blue, a changing turquoise blue that showed in one moment and was lost in the next. When we got her on to the rocks the blue showed vividly along her back and the huge dorsal fin amazed me not only by its size and its scarlet border but by the iridescent turquoise of its heavy spots. In the Arctic fog, beside the mighty rush of the falls . . . the whole fish had a special beauty that has never failed in my memory; but there are degrees of vividness even in such a thing as this, and it was the splendour of the blues that dazzled my mind's eye in its many moments of recall during the next several years."

Grayling have other defenders, most of them scientists who have studied the species at first hand. McPhail and Lindsey write in *Freshwater Fishes of Northwestern Canada and Alaska* that "the Arctic grayling is a uniquely attractive fish, beautiful to look at, sporting to catch, and quite palatable." Scott and Crossman in

Freshwater Fishes of Canada describe grayling as "strikingly coloured fish . . . a joy to behold."

At times such as spawning there are pronounced coloration
variations; habitat, diet and perhaps even water temperature
could affect pigmentation. Brook trout taken from muddy waters,
for example, almost always lack the brilliant colours of trout taken
from clear waters. I recall a recently published photograph of a
"typical" grayling that made the fish look almost black, even its
normally spectacular dorsal fin.

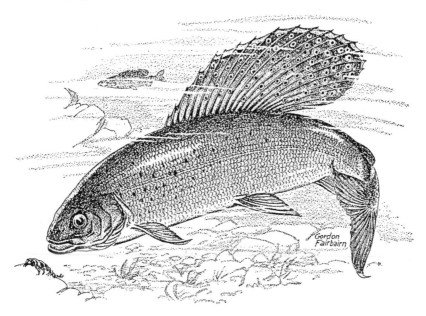

ARCTIC GRAYLING

Grayling are trout-like in appearance, apart from their dispro-
portionately large dorsal fin, large cycloid scales, smaller head
and mouth, and more noticeably forked tail. They have the trout's
typically long, laterally compressed body. The back is dark blue
or purple, the sides purple to grey with scattered black spots
(more numerous on juveniles) on the forward part. The ventral
fins are striped with pink and white, and a dark stripe runs from

below the pectoral fins to the pelvic fins. Small teeth are present on the jaws, head of the vomer, palatines (paired bones on the roof of the mouth) and generally the tongue. The snout is pointed. The mouth, when opened, is somewhat square.

But the magnificent fan-shaped dorsal fin, with its scattering of orange and green spots, and its edging of red or orange, sets grayling apart from all other North American freshwater fish.

The range of *Thymallus arcticus* extends from the Kara and Orb rivers of northern Eurasia, south to Mongolia and the upper Yalu river in Asia. It begins again in Alaska, and continues throughout the Yukon and the Northwest Territories to the west coast of Hudson Bay. The only Arctic islands whose lakes contain grayling are believed to be St. Lawrence Island in the Bering Sea and Vansittart Island off Melville Peninsula in the Eastern Arctic.

Grayling in North America were originally of three subspecies; Arctic grayling, Montana grayling and Michigan grayling. Montana grayling are secure in the headwaters of the Missouri River in Yellowstone National Park, but Michigan grayling are now extinct. Grayling have been introduced successfully into mountainous areas of Vermont, Utah and Colorado. Populations in some rivers flowing into lakes Michigan, Huron and Superior disappeared more than half a century ago. Subsequent restocking efforts failed. A population of grayling, which spread northward from stocks planted in western Montana, is also present in southeastern British Columbia.

Arctic grayling are spring spawners, but spring arrives at different times throughout the vast Arctic and subarctic expanse of the Canadian north. As soon as the ice breaks up in the rivers and lakes (usually from April in subarctic regions to June in the High Arctic), grayling move to shallow tributaries with gravel or rocky bottoms and a good flow of water. Spawning takes place only during the day and is demonstrably emotional. Grayling do not make nests or redds.

Scott and Crossman write: "During spawning the male curves the extended dorsal fin over the female almost like a clasping organ, the female gapes, there is vigorous vibration, the male gapes, sex products are discharged and somewhat covered by the material stirred up by the vibration. The female may spawn only once, or several times in different areas."

No parental care is given to either the eggs or young, and after spawning the adults make their way back to the lakes and rivers.

The heavy, amber-coloured, slightly adhesive eggs, on average between four and seven thousand from each female, hatch in thirteen to eighteen days. The alevins absorb their yolk sac in about eight days. At that time they begin consuming zooplankton such as fish larvae and small crustaceans, then turn to larger aquatic and terrestrial insects. McPhail and Lindsey write that in northern lakes, terrestrial insects often make up over half of the grayling's summer diet. But, these scientists point out, grayling are opportunistic feeders and their stomachs may contain snails, small fish and even young lemmings.

The time of maturity and average lifespan of grayling depend on their habitat. In Great Slave Lake, according to Scott and Crossman, 93.5 percent spawn between six and nine years, although some males and females become sexually mature at four years. The maximum spawning age, they estimate, is eleven to twelve years. The grayling in Montana, on the other hand, mature and spawn much earlier. Most are believed to die after their fourth year.

The Denholm Angling Club member who was ambivalent about the grayling's fighting qualities was a devout Arctic charr and Atlantic salmon angler, and so can perhaps be forgiven his lack of enthusiasm for the species. But Arctic grayling, though smaller and perhaps less spirited than Arctic charr, are first-class combatants and well worth pursuing. They are relatively easy to catch, especially with artificial dry or wet flies, and fight strongly in and out of the water to defend their freedom. Their white, firm flesh is delicately flavoured.

My introduction to Arctic grayling took place one summer morning at Wrigley Landing on the Mackenzie River, where the river begins its long journey from Great Slave Lake to the Beaufort Sea. It was hot, and there were voracious mosquitoes and bulldog flies everywhere. Despite these discomforts, I couldn't ignore the great numbers of grayling in the cold, gin-clear waters over the sand and gravel bars. My companion and I rigged up our fly-rods and used 3x leaders, to which we attached Dark Cahills on #10 hooks. The first casts met with instant response. My fish, as soon as it felt the sting of the tiny barb, began a quick run with the current. A mild snub on the line set the hook and brought the fish to the surface with a strong, crosscurrent rush, followed by three good leaps out of the water. Then it was all over.

From then on it was much the same, although not all rises were alike. In some cases the grayling rose gracefully and gently sucked the fly into its mouth. In other cases the rise was decisive; the fish would leap clear of the water either with the fly already in its mouth or would take it on its downward plunge.

Since their diet is mainly terrestrial insects, grayling—sometimes in large schools—are most frequently seen cruising just below the water's surface. In such situations they respond well to artificial flies, although small metal lures are equally productive.

Grayling, like lake trout and Arctic charr, have long been important as a source of food for northern native peoples. They are not large fish, however. The average weight is between 1 and 2 pounds (0.45 and 0.91 kg), but much larger individuals are occasionally caught. A trophy grayling of 5 pounds, 15 ounces (2.69 kg) was taken from Katseyedie River, NWT, in 1967, and there are unconfirmed reports of a 6-pounder (2.72 kg) caught near Great Bear Lake in the mid-eighties.

THE WHITEFISH SUBFAMILY—Coregoninae

The whitefish subfamily, Coregoninae, inhabits waters in Europe, northern Asia and North America. Its three genera are *Coregonus*, *Prosopium* and *Stenodus*. The species are known more familiarly as lake whitefish, ciscoes, round whitefish and inconnu. All are related to salmon, trout, charr and graylings.

Until relatively recently, seventeen species inhabited Canadian waters: thirteen in the genus *Coregonus,* three in the genus *Prosopium,* and one in the genus *Stenodus.* This number, according to COSEWIC, has since been reduced by the extinction of the deepwater cisco (*Coregonus johannae*) in the Great Lakes. Three other coregonines—the spring cisco (*Coregonus* sp.), the Squanga whitefish (*Coregonus* sp.) and kiyi (*Coregonus kiyi) are rated as vulnerable. Three—blackfin cisco (Coregonus nigripinnis)*, shortnose cisco (*Coregonus reighardi*) and shortjaw cisco (*Coregonus zenithicus*)—are rated as threatened. The Atlantic whitefish (*Coregonus huntsmani*) is rated as endangered.

Coregonines remain under intensive study by scientists, who are still far from establishing a stable classification of the various species. The problems are tremendous because of the variations in their morphology. One apparent anomaly is that fish in lakes adjacent to or interconnected with each other may differ in characteristics such as shape, size, scale and gill raker counts.

Coregonines have probably inhabited the Northern Hemisphere since long before the Pleistocene, always preferring cold water. Many, even some of the smallest, remain deepwater inhabitants; some, such as the threatened blackfin cisco, frequent depths of 600 feet (182.88 m) or more. Some coregonines (inconnu, lake whitefish and least cisco, for example) have access to the sea and are anadromous, but in their saltwater migrations they do not stray far from the river mouths.

Classifying the different coregonines has long been a challenge to scientists, as McPhail and Lindsey explain in *Freshwater Fishes of Northwestern Canada and Alaska*:

> During each glaciation, whitefish populations were isolated in various melt-water lakes around the margin of the ice, some in the north and some in the south. Sometimes isolation was protracted enough for the evolution of separate

species in separate areas, so that when the new water connections formed during the withdrawal of the ice the two kinds of whitefish might invade each other's areas without inter-breeding. In other instances where divergence had not proceeded quite so far the removal of ice barriers resulted in two slightly different kinds of whitefish by hybridizing when their ranges rejoined. The characters of whitefish are highly subject to modification by conditions under which the young develop, so that the same species may appear quite different in different lakes. To further complicate their taxonomy, the same species may occur in North America, Russia and Europe and may have been given different names in different countries. Hence, the species names and descriptions . . . are only tentative, partly because much more information is required, and partly because whitefish do not always fall into categories that conform to our formal system of naming species.

A striking example of isolation resulting from ice withdrawal is the discontinuous distribution of the pygmy whitefish. This creature 4 to 5 inches (10.16 to 12.7 cm) long occurs in Montana, Alberta and Alaska. In 1952 it was also detected in deep areas of Lake Superior, and it occurs elsewhere only in British Columbia and Yukon. The lake whitefish, by contrast, is present in most provinces and occurs extensively throughout the Northwest Territories and Yukon. Its arctic range also includes Alaska.

Scott and Crossman recorded another example of restricted distribution. Four cisco species—the extinct deepwater cisco, the threatened shortnose cisco, the vulnerable kiyi and the bloater— once inhabited the Great Lakes basin alone. Here lies a zoogeographic mystery. Scientists identified the deepwater cisco only in lakes Huron, Superior and Michigan (it also occurs in Lake Nipigon, and in Winnipeg, Reindeer, Athabasca and Barrow lakes); the shortnose cisco in all lakes; the kiyi in lakes Ontario, Huron, Superior and Michigan (as well as Lake Nipigon); and the bloater in all Great Lakes except Erie.

Coregonines, except for some ciscoes known as *freshwater herring*, have smaller heads and mouths than do salmon and trout, but otherwise are similar to them in body shape. They have forked tails and an *auxiliary process* (or dagger-like projection) at the base of the pectoral or pelvic fins. Most are virtually toothless; any teeth present are small and weak.

The scales in all coregonines are cycloid and large. The inconnu of the Western Arctic is a taxonomic exception. It has a long, somewhat pike-like jaw, and a large mouth containing very short teeth on the jaws and on the paired bones on the roof of the mouth. It is also the only fish-eating coregonine. It is the largest coregonine and the sole representative of the genus *Stenodus*.

Coregonines are handsome creatures, but less brilliantly attired than salmon, trout and charr. Most have a clean, crisp appearance and an overall silvery colour which reflects a pink or purple iridescence. The back may be black or shades of blue, green or brown.

Some coregonines spawn in winter, some in the spring, and some during late summer or early fall. Some do not spawn every year. Spawning may occur in deep water, sandy or gravel shallows, or fast midstream waters over rocks. The fish deposit their eggs and then abandon them. Incubation time depends on water temperature. Lake whitefish spawn from November to December in southern waters, but from September to December in northern waters. Eggs hatch the following spring.

Most coregonines live in deep or midwater environments and are schooling fish. They feed on bottom invertebrates, plankton, and aquatic insects and their larvae. Some consume other fish and their eggs, however, and some rise to the surface of the water to feast on hatches of mayflies or caddis flies. Hybridization among coregonines is relatively common.

At one time coregonines were important commercial fish. Overexploitation, destruction of their environment, and depredation by sea lampreys has reduced their economic significance. Some less hardy species have vanished.

Whitefish and some species of ciscoes are still important commercially. Some become dog food in northern regions, and at least four—lake whitefish, lake herring (cisco), mountain whitefish and inconnu—are game fish. Most smaller species are important as feed for other fish.

Lake whitefish
(Coregonus clupeaformis)

Lake whitefish have the widest North American distribution of all coregonine species. They occur in every Canadian province and territory except Nova Scotia, Prince Edward Island and Newfoundland. They occur in some freshwater areas of Victoria Island (near Cambridge Bay, Northwest Territories) and are sometimes taken at sea. They are present in many lakes in Alaska.

This species has a deep, slightly compressed body and somewhat arched back. The head is small and short, and the short, blunt snout is characterized by a small overhanging mouth. Typically for this subfamily, the lake whitefish has large, smooth cycloid scales, the fins are soft-rayed and the tail is forked. The teeth are either weak or almost absent.

The coloration of this wide-ranging species varies greatly. Fish in northern waters may be dark brown or green on the back and silvery or yellowish on the belly. Fish in southern waters may have an overall silvery colour, or may be greenish brown or brown on the back. Some fish in southern inland lakes may be almost black on the back, shading to silver on the sides and white on the belly. Southern whitefish tend to have whitish fins; northern fish may have dark or dark-tipped fins.

Lake whitefish inhabit lakes and larger rivers; in some rivers having access to the sea they are anadromous. In northern waters they normally spawn from September to October, and in southern waters from November to December. They lay their eggs on shallow, sandy bottoms or on shoals. Each female lays ten to twelve thousand eggs for each pound (22,000 to 26,400 per kg)

Top: WHITEFISH
Centre: CISCO
Bottom: LAKE WHITEFISH

of her weight. Parent fish return to deep water after spawning. Hatching usually takes place after the water warms the following spring. During their first year the young live mainly on plankton and microscopic life, but as they grow older they move to deeper water. Then their diet changes to bottom invertebrates such as molluscs and shrimps, insect larvae, plankton, eggs of other fish, and sometimes smaller fish.

Angling for whitefish is a popular summer and winter sport; hook-and-line techniques are most productive. Many anglers anchor a buoy over water 60 to 80 feet (about 18.29 to 24.38 m) deep, and bait the area for several days with small cubes of perch or other fish. They then leave the spot unbaited for a day or two. After that they bait a hook with a cube of fish flesh, lower it to within a few inches of the bottom, and jig frequently to attract the fish's attention.

A whitefish bites delicately, not closing its jaws on food with a gulp but sucking it into the mouth. The seizure is sometimes much like a nibble, and it is wise to pause before setting the hook. Too quick a set can easily tear the hook loose from the fish's tender mouth. When whitefish are surface-feeding on mayflies or caddis flies they can be taken by fly-casting. Anglers sometimes deep-troll with several hundred feet of line in the hope of running into a hungry school. The lure, generally a metal spinner, is slowly drawn over the lake bed.

At one time the Great Lakes had the largest commercial whitefish fishery, but stocks there have been seriously depleted by overfishing, pollution and the ravages of sea lampreys. Today most whitefish come from Manitoba, Saskatchewan and the Northwest Territories. Lake whitefish are marketed fresh and frozen, and small quantities are smoked. Whitefish roe is made into a type of caviar, and the smoked liver makes a delicious paté.

Lake whitefish average 2 to 4 pounds (0.91 to 1.81 kg), but some reach weights of 30 to 40 pounds (13.61 to 18.14 kg). As a food fish they are excellent.

Mountain whitefish
(Prosopium williamsoni)

Mountain whitefish occur only in western North America. Their range extends from the interior drainages of Wyoming, Montana, Idaho, Oregon, Northern California and Washington, and north to the lakes and streams of British Columbia on both slopes of the Continental Divide. They occur in foothill and mountain waters of Alberta, and in the southern limits of the Mackenzie, Liard, Peace and Athabasca rivers.

The mountain whitefish is elongate, rounded in cross-section, greyish to light brown on the back, silvery on the sides and white on the belly. Its head is somewhat pointed and much smaller than a trout's head. Its mouth is small and overhangs the lower jaw. Except for a few inconspicuous teeth on the tongue, there are no teeth in the jaws or mouth. Typically for coregonines, the scales are cycloid.

Mountain whitefish inhabit clear, cold lakes and streams. Stream fish often favour fast-flowing cuts and riffles, while lake-dwellers prefer shallow water along gravel or rocky shorelines. The mountain whitefish feeds chiefly on bottom invertebrates such as insect larvae, molluscs, plankton and other fish. It will also consume its own eggs, and the eggs of trout and salmon. Normally a bottom feeder, it will feed at all levels or the surface in its search for food.

This species spawns from October to early February, depending on geography, over gravel or rubble in the shallows of lakes and streams. On average, the female lays five thousand eggs which hatch in early spring.

For most anglers this is a yet-to-be-discovered game fish. It not only puts up a spirited defence of its freedom but, taken by fly or spin-casting, responds with all the vigour and panache of trout. A whitefish characteristically never smashes at a lure, but sucks it in gently; it is best to pause (long enough to say "hang in there, buddy") before setting the hook. It rates as one of the tastiest fish, particularly when smoked. Mountain whitefish are sometimes erroneously called grayling.

Cisco
(Coregonus artedi)

The cisco, commonly known as *lake herring* or *tullibee*, is a North American species whose Canadian range extends from the Great Lakes north to Quebec and Labrador, and west to Manitoba, Saskatchewan and Alberta. They have recently been found in a lake in the Northwest Territories. Schooling fish, they generally prefer midwater depths in large lakes and rivers. Some rivers flowing into Hudson and James bays have populations that migrate to spend short periods in salt water.

The size of mature fish varies, depending on geography, but the average weight is 0.5 to 1.5 pounds (0.23 to 0.68 kg). Scott and Crossman write that the largest specimen known to them was caught in central Lake Erie in 1948. It weighed 8 pounds (3.63 kg).

This species, like the lake whitefish, has an elongate, laterally compressed body with large, cycloid scales. Its lower jaw, when closed, projects beyond the upper jaw. All ciscoes have teeth only in a narrow patch on the tongue, although some adult fish also have teeth in the lower jaw. Coloration varies from place to place, and even within populations living in the same lake. Some fish are steely blue with an emerald green overcast on the dorsal areas. Others are dark blue, or green to grey or light tan, on the back and sides. One constant is the silver or white of the lower sides and belly.

Ciscoes spawn, usually in shallow water, from November to December in southern areas and from September to October in northern areas. The eggs are scattered over gravel or sandy bottoms and hatch in the spring. Although primarily a plankton feeder the cisco also consumes crustaceans, insect larvae and other fish. In turn it is heavily preyed upon by northern pike, walleye, perch, rainbow trout and lake trout.

At one time the cisco or lake herring was a leading commercial species in the Great Lakes. Stocks have now declined drastically. An important commercial fishery remains, however, and considerable quantities are marketed fresh, frozen and smoked. In the north it is important to the diet of native peoples and their dogs.

The lake herring is a good springtime sports fish; where trout are not available it is a favourite of fly-fishers. It can also be taken by still-fishing, using live bait, or spin-fishing with metal lures. Its flesh, though somewhat bony, is firm and sweet. It is highly regarded in smoked form.

Inconnu
(Stenodus leucichthys)

This little-known coregonine—even its name means "unknown" in French—is found in the arctic watersheds of Europe from the White Sea to the Bering Strait, and south to the northern part of the Kamchatka Peninsula. In North America it occurs in Alaska, Yukon and the western Northwest Territories, inhabiting river systems such as the Yukon, Mackenzie, Liard and Slave.

The inconnu (also called *conny*) is the largest of the Coregonidae, occasionally reaching weights of 60 pounds (27.22 kg). It has an elongate and laterally compressed body with a forked tail. Its long head, with the lower jaw projecting beyond the upper, gives it a pike-like appearance. Its mouth is large, and the teeth on the upper and lower jaws are small. The scales, as in all coregonines, are cycloid. It has an adipose fin. Inconnu are usually dark green to light brown on the back and sides, and silvery on the belly.

Little is known of the biology of this fish, although it is generally believed that spawning takes place in late summer and early fall, the eggs being released randomly over gravel in riffle areas. Some populations of inconnu are anadromous.

Inconnu are caught commercially in gill-nets. Some are marketed in fresh and frozen forms, but the bulk of the catch is sold to United States markets and smoked. In the Far North dried inconnu are important as dog food. The freshly caught fish has white, oily, somewhat soft flesh, and cannot compete with other flavoursome northern species such as Arctic charr and grayling. Some anglers give the inconnu a high rating, and it may perform well when taken on light tackle. Most regard the inconnu as a "take it or leave it" species when other more popular game fish are available.

INCONNU

Pike, Muskellunge, Pickerel & Mudminnows
ORDER ESOCIFORMES

Two families—Esocidae and Umbridae—of the Esociformes order occur in Canadian waters. The Esocidae family consists of one genus, *Esox*, with five species:

- **Amur pike** (*Esox reicherti*)—occurs only in Siberia
- **Northern pike*** (*Esox lucius*)—has a large circumpolar distribution; a major sports fish in Canada
- **Muskellunge** (*Esox masquinongy*)—largest of the family; occurs in limited numbers only in eastern North America
- **Chain pickerel*** (*Esox niger*)—occurs only in eastern and south-central North America

---

* The names "pickerel" and "pike," confusingly, are also both often used to identify walleye (*Stizostedion vitreum*), a member of the perch family, Percidae.

- **Grass pickerel** (*Esox americanus vermiculatus*)—occurs only in eastern North America, more abundantly in United States than in Canada
- **Redfin pickerel** (*Esox americanus americanus*)—occurs only in eastern North America

THE PIKE FAMILY
Esocidae

Pike are a breed apart. Ancient humans, long before they invented writing, acquired a fear that some people retain to this day. Pike have long been the source of the tallest fish tales ever told.

Their appellations are many. In an eleventh-century Bavarian story they are described as "wolves among fish." Lacepède, the early nineteenth-century French naturalist, called them "freshwater sharks." Walton referred to them as "tyrants of fresh water." The gentle Roderick Haig-Brown, Walton's twentieth-century counterpart, called them "freshwater barracudas."

As for tall tales . . .

Pliny, the Roman naturalist whom Stephen Downes in *The New Compleat Angler* describes as the "father of lies and of popular encyclopaedias of natural history," claimed that pike can grow to 1000 pounds (453.6 kg)! Pliny, however fanciful, could not have meant pike. Until the Swedish botanist Linnaeus (AD 1707–78) originated the binominal method of naming plants and animals, Latin *Esox* referred not to pike but to various salmonids. Pliny must have been referring to a salmon. But up to 1000 pounds? Pike do grow large. A 78-pounder (35.38 kg) was said to have been captured some years ago in Ireland. But since the species' average weight in European waters is about 10 pounds (4.54 kg), perhaps Pliny had too much *vinum!*

Esox lucius in North America can be hefty as well. There are unofficial reports of a 55 pound (24.95 kg) fish taken from a New York state reservoir in 1940. But in *The Treasury of Angling* Larry

Koller writes that he has seen pike "far out-weighing that one hanging from drying racks in Alaskan Indian villages."

Truth be known, however, not many northern pike reach the great sizes often attributed to them. Although 40-pounders (18.14 kg) are occasionally caught and 20-pounders (9.07 kg) are not uncommon, average weights are 8 to 10 pounds (3.63 and 4.54 kg). Even so, that's 8 to 10 pounds of fighting fury!

Konrad von Gesner, the fifteenth-century Swiss biologist, retold a celebrated pike yarn about the Emperor's Pike taken from a lake in Wurttenberg in 1497. The story has been translated many times, but Koller says "This fish was reported to be 19 feet long and to bear an inscribed ring in his gills that gave his date of birth as AD 1230. The skeleton and identifying ring were preserved in the Mannheim Cathedral for many years, until some seeker after truth discovered that the skeleton had been considerably lengthened by the addition of extra vertebrae."

That's stretching things a bit, don't you think?

Cholmondeley-Pennell, who in 1865 published the now treasured *Book of the Pike*, relates this story: "The best authenticated instance of attempted manslaughter on the part of a Pike is one which occurred within a comparatively recent date in Surrey. A lad aged 15, named Longhurst, had gone into Inglemere Pond, near Ascot Heath, to bathe, and that, when he walked in to the depth of four feet a huge fish, supposed to be a Pike, suddenly rose to the surface and seized his hand. Finding himself resisted, however, he abandoned it, but still followed, and caught hold of the other hand which he bit severely. The lad, clenching the hand which had first been bitten, struck his assailant a heavy blow on the head, when the fish swam away. W. Barr Brown, Esq., surgeon, dressed the wounds, two of which were very deep, and which bled profusely."

But are pike really dangerous to humans? Downes staunchly defends their innocence. He claims that they show a good deal of cautious curiosity and, if approached, will depart in great haste. He does tell of one attack, but claims that it was a case of mistaken identity. A diver wore a dark suit in the murky waters of England's Norfolk Broads, but wore a gold watch over the suit's wrist. The pike took the flashing metal for prey and seized it in its mouth "not realizing that it was connected to the rest of the diver."

Some of the most intriguing pike mythology, however, is related by Professor Richard C. Hoffmann, of York University in Toronto. He writes in his scholarly introduction to *An Annotated Bibliography of the Pike, Esox lucius (Osteichthyes: Salmoniformes)*:

> Folk tales and popular practices that perhaps originated in assimilation of Christian notions by early medieval Europeans treated in mythic ways the pike and its attributes. In a widespread story, the markings on a pike's head were seen as displaying the instruments of Christ's passion: cross, ladder, hammer, nails, thorns, whip and sponge. The tale explained that as Christ carried his cross through a brook where the pike lived, the fish looked out and was forever marked by what he saw. One variant of Scandinavian provenance listed the pike among the most harmful things created by the devil to vex God. When angels captured these creatures and brought them before God, he saw on the pike's head a cross. So he blessed the fish and made it good and useful to mankind. A Latvian legend told how the pike grew very large, and forgetting in its pride God's command to eat only fish, caught and ate a fisherman. As a reminder, lest the pike again so err, the tale continued, God ordered the pike to carry on its head all the tools of the fisherman: the set-net as jaws, the spear as teeth, the hooks as gills. What enters the set-net is trapped, what the spear grasps is held firm; what reaches the hooks sticks tight.

"Perhaps," Professor Hoffmann added later in his treatise, "the idea of the pike as a fish of superior standing explains why in 1177 AD nobles in charge of a great knightly tournament held in Champagne offered a trophy pike to the champion."

There is no dearth of Canadian tall tales, and their making is a social preoccupation of most anglers. One from the far north, in several versions, concerns an old trapper who lived along the banks of the Yukon River. Devil lakes in that part of the country, he claimed, contain northern pike so monstrous in size that they can swallow not only an angler but his canoe as well! Efforts to authenticate this story failed, for it is believed one of the monster pike did the trapper in!

Esox lucius suffers shameful treatment in Canada, however. It is undisputedly fierce when hooked (many anglers claim that it fights for its freedom as well as its cousin, the muskellunge), and has very acceptable table qualities when taken from cold waters. Yet it is sometimes treated with contempt, and there have been numerous wasteful slaughters of pike. Incidents of small northerns and muskies being clubbed and thrown back are not uncommon. And some so-called sportsmen have barbarously forced the creature's jaws open with an upright stick and tossed it back into the water to face a slow and painful death. In some cases they have misidentified the fish, however, because juvenile northern pike look much like their smaller and less popular cousins, the pickerel.

Actually, northern pike and muskellunge deserve the angler's respect; in every sense they are big game. Anglers can almost always depend upon them to provide good sport even when other species are hard to get, as in the winter when they fish for northern pike through the ice. Their habits of smashing at a lure, making good runs, sounding, and suddenly rising to the surface to churn the water into a boil, are all the angler has a right to expect of any fish.

The big member of the pike family—*Esox masquinongy,* the muskellunge—is an individualist. It is to fresh water what the barracuda is to salt water—a solitary, powerful and (to some) terrifying creature.

Every serious angler has dreamed at some time of doing battle with one of these tackle-busters. To hook and capture a muskie is to reach one of the pinnacles of angling success. If achieved, it is an honour well earned and an experience never to be forgotten.

The smallest members of the pike family—the chain, grass and redfin pickerel—were once plentiful in eastern North American waters, but their numbers have greatly declined. COSEWIC rates their status in many Canadian waters as rare.

All pickerel are inhabitants of shallow, weedy ponds, streams and lakes. Like other members of the Esocidae family, they are nonschooling. They have no standing as game fish, but it would be a sad day if they were ever classified as exterminated.

Anglers are sometimes unable to identify different members of the pike family, especially when specimens are of uniform size. This confusion is understandable because of the similarity between all types, and because markings and coloration vary greatly even among individuals taken from the same waters.

There is one simple way of establishing identification. Remember that in the northern pike the cheeks are fully scaled, but only the upper half of the gill covers are scaled; in the muskellunge only the upper half of both cheeks and gill covers are scaled; and in pickerel both cheeks and gill covers are fully scaled. This method of identification may not always be reliable, however, because hybrids often occur in the pike family, especially from northern pike and muskellunge. In hybrids the cheeks and gill covers often carry unusual and confusing scale patterns.

An old wives' tale claims that pike won't bite during the hot days of summer because they are shedding teeth. Quite wrong! The teeth in these fish are constantly being replaced.

Northern pike
(Esox lucius)

Thoughts of northern pike conjure up visions of cool, crisp autumn days. This is a time that stands distinctly apart from all other seasons of the year: the ground is covered with the leaves of maples, aspens and birches, the air is filled with the nutty smell of their dying presence; the call of black-capped chickadees seems a little more urgent; the haunting cry of loons echoes and re-echoes across the hills; and the first wild geese pass overhead southward, unmistakably announcing the advent of winter. This, indeed, is northern pike time.

Although widespread throughout Canada, this species occurs in greatest numbers in eastern Canada, especially in Ontario and Quebec. It's a good fish, the northern, but probably more than others bears the brunt of the most unfair of descriptions—vicious, evil, solitary marauder, mean-looking and rapacious, rough guy. As one writer complained, "He's a devil if the lakes and rivers ever spawned one."

Join me in a defence of *Esox lucius*. This creature cannot be faulted for its ferocious face—that's the way Nature put it together, and in a sense it's a masterpiece of design. Nor can it be faulted for the way it seeks its livelihood by eating (for the most part) other fish—a practice followed by most species. It is, admittedly, the scourge of trout waters and has no place in them, but in habitats shared with bass, perch, sunfish and the like, it is a worthy although dominant citizen. The "poor man's salmon," as some call it rather patronizingly, in prime condition can fight for its freedom with as much vigour as a chinook. Done to a turn with the appropriate condiments, it is as tasty as lake trout. So a tip of the hat to *Esox lucius*. Long may it prosper!

The northern pike is a long, slender fish with a large, flat head and broad, paddle-like jaws containing many sharp, backward pointing teeth; there are also patches of teeth on the roof of the mouth. Small scales are present on the cheek and upper half of the gill covers, and there are five sensory pores on each side of the underside of the lower jaw. Its dorsal and anal fins are large and far back on the body, and the caudal fin is deeply forked; all of the fins may bear prominent dark spots.

The coloration of the northern pike is variable and influenced by its lake or river home. Generally it is dark green to olive or grey-green on the back, lighter green on the sides, and white or yellowish on the belly. The back and sides of adults carry irregular rows of oval-shaped light spots. The sides of juveniles carry light-coloured vertical bars which later are transformed into spots.

The northern pike shares with Arctic charr the distinction of having the most extensive range of all freshwater fish. It is well known throughout northern Europe and Asia as well as North America. It is present in all provinces and territories except mainland Newfoundland and the Maritimes (it does occur in Labrador). It also occurs in Alaska, but not in the arctic islands. In British Columbia it occurs only in the small northeastern corner.

Northern pike spawn in the spring before the ice leaves the lakes or rivers. The fish move in large numbers to the shallow waters of small inlet streams or to shallow bays and marshy areas where there is adequate water coverage. The female, accompanied by two or more males, usually of smaller size, deposits her spawn randomly over a soft weedy bottom. As the heavy, adhesive eggs settle, the males fertilize them. A female may lay more than a hundred thousand eggs, although the average is said to be about thirty-five thousand. The eggs, which are left unguarded, hatch in approximately two weeks. The young remain in the nursery area for a month or more feeding on aquatic life, and then migrate to deeper water. Young pike grow fairly rapidly and may reach about a foot (30 cm) by the time they are a year old. By the end of their fourth year, when most males and females reach sexual maturity, they have grown to 2 feet (61 cm) or longer. After their fourth year, pike lose their slender shape and become more full-bodied.

Northern pike, throughout their lives, are voracious feeders. They eat just about any moving creature that crosses their line of sight, but the bulk of their diet consists of other fish. They also eat muskrats, ducklings, frogs and crayfish. Pike themselves are preyed upon during their juvenile years; many wind up in the stomachs of herons, loons, mergansers and larger fish—including adult pike.

Northern pike are not roamers. They tend to stay quietly under weeds or other protective cover as they wait for passing prey. Most anglers take them on quickly moving, flashy affairs such as spoons, plugs, and spinner-fly combinations. Live bait is also effective, sometimes in still-fishing but more often for trolling. Ice-fishing for northern pike is a popular winter sport, especially in parts of Ontario. Pike bite best during the early morning and late afternoon and usually spend those hours in relatively shallow water. On hot days they tend to retire to deeper parts of the rivers or lakes. The flesh of this species is white, flaky and flavoursome. Skinning the fish before cooking, or washing it in hot water, will remove the surface mucus which can adhere to the flesh and lessen its delicacy.

Henry Van Dyke in his *Fisherman's Luck,* published nearly a century ago, writes glowingly of the pike: "Do you remember Martin Luther's reasoning on the subject of the 'excellent large pike'? He maintains that God would never have created them so good to the taste, if He had not meant them to be eaten."

Muskellunge
(Esox masquinongy)

Closely related to the northern pike and pickerel is the gargantuan of the family, the muskellunge, found only in a limited eastern North American range. *Esox masquinongy,* a solitary inhabitant of relatively shallow, weedy areas of lakes and rivers, is the largest of all Canadian freshwater fish. There is an authenticated record of one muskellunge weighing 69 pounds, 15 ounces (31.72 kg), rod-caught in the St. Lawrence River in 1957 by Arthur Lawton.

Although the Statutes of Canada give official recognition to the name *maskinonge* and the species is scientifically described as *Esox masquinongy,* the most commonly recognized name is muskellunge. Other regional designations include *muskie, northern muskellunge, lunge, tiger muskie, Great Lakes maskinonge, St.*

Lawrence muskellunge, Ohio muskellunge and *Wisconsin muskellunge.*

The muskellunge is similar in shape to the northern pike and bears a remarkable resemblance to the saltwater barracuda. Its long body has a duckbill-shaped head and a large mouth containing many sharp teeth. The dorsal and anal fins are set well back on the body near the forked tail. Scales on the head are present only on the upper half of the cheeks, and there are six to nine sensory pores on each side of the underpart of the lower jaw. (The cheeks of the northern pike are fully scaled and the underpart of the lower jaw usually has only about five sensory pores.)

Muskies' coloration varies considerably, but is generally dark slate grey to greenish brown on the back, silvery grey on the sides and white on the belly. Because of pronounced differences in markings and colour of fish taken from several locations, three subspecies were at one time recognized; *Esox masquinongy masquinongy* (St. Lawrence-Great Lakes muskellunge), *Esox masquinongy immaculatus* (the northern or tiger muskellunge), and *Esox masquinongy ohioensis* (the Ohio muskellunge). These subspecific classifications have been abandoned as minor variations within the species.

Most muskies taken from Ontario waters carry pronounced vertical dark bars on the sides from head to tail; most taken from Quebec waters are heavily marked with large round spots. Other markings, or lack of markings, have been noted in fish from both regions.

Muskellunge occur only in eastern North America. In Canada the range extends throughout the St. Lawrence River, in lakes St. Louis and St. Francis near Montreal, some sections of the Thousand Islands, all of the Great Lakes, and to many inland waters such as the Ottawa and Rideau river, the Rideau and Kawartha lakes, Lake Simcoe, Lake Nipissing, Lake Timagami, French River and Lake of the Woods, to name a few. It has a good foothold in Manitoba where it was introduced and is now reproducing naturally.

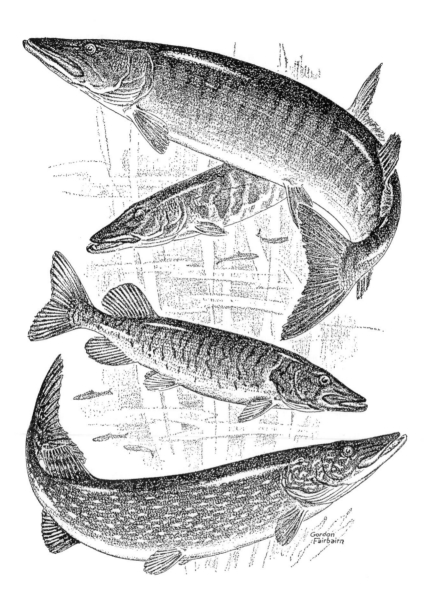

Top: MUSKELLUNGE with JUVENILE MUSKELLUNGE behind
Centre: GRASS PICKEREL
Bottom: NORTHERN PIKE

Muskellunge spawn in the spring soon after the ice disappears. Parent fish build no nests. Females scatter their eggs randomly in shallow water of tributary streams, inundated marshes and weedy bays; eggs are untended. If the water temperature stays above 50° F (10°C) the eggs hatch in about two weeks. The fry grow rapidly, taking nourishment from their yolk sacs, and in about a month and a half reach about 2 inches (5.08 cm). The young usually remain in the nursery area until late fall or early winter and then move off to deeper water.

From birth to death they feed heavily on other fish, especially the yellow perch. So voracious is their appetite that they will also consume ducklings, muskrats, mice, snakes and birds. The growth rate of muskellunge varies, but the average is believed to be about 8 inches (20.32 cm) after two years, about 23 inches (58.42 cm) after three years and about 32 inches (81.28 cm) after four years.

Many anglers go after muskies, but few succeed. Anglers accomplished in other types of fishing come back empty-handed season after season from the muskie grounds, yet amateurs sometimes catch near-record fish. It takes considerable good luck to find muskies, even in waters known to contain them.

Perfect weather, best time of year, best time of day, best equipment, even the best areas: these are no guarantee of success. The muskie is a moody, erratic nonconformist. At times it will sulk and ignore everything; at other times it will seize anything that comes in sight. Today's good lure may prove hopeless tomorrow. Ideal conditions may stir up nothing more than the weeds; poor conditions may result in smash after smash. The only way to hook a muskie is to keep on fishing for it!

Experience has shown that a stormy, cloudy or windy day when the water is ruffled is usually the most productive. Wind from the south or west is also desirable. Tackle should be solid; the rod must be sturdy enough to set the hook and withstand the strain of battle, but have enough flexibility to ensure good casts. What lure to use? Almost any plug or spoon will do. Although muskies may smash at an idle or barely moving lure, a fast-moving bait frequently gets a response.

A muskie hits with the force of an express train. What happens after that depends on the personality of the fish itself. A typical muskie will peel off yards of line in seconds in one of the most astounding runs you could experience. It will remain close to the surface and then, in a rage, leap clear of the water. Then it appears at its awesome best—gill covers wide open showing their serrated red layers, mouth agape with a display of fierce white teeth, and a long, powerful body gyrating in violent shakes before it splashes resoundingly back into the water. There may be several such acrobatic performances. Then the fish will dig deep, either to remain motionless or to cruise slowly about, while it decides its next move. Remember: it will be the muskie's move, not yours! About all you can do is remain calm, keep a taut line and call upon all your skills in rod handling.

Eventually the fish will tire, and you will get glimpses of its great white belly as it twists and turns in its last struggles. But reel it in cautiously and be prepared for the unexpected. Many a muskie has been lost in these final moments. A loose line or a careless motion with gaff or net can send it away in a powerful dash, or high in the air. Study your fish carefully before using gaff or net and be sure, very sure, that its strength is gone. Finally, before the fish is boated, dispatch it as quickly and humanely as possible.

Many anglers have discovered that in shallow water the big fish can be taken on fly-rods of the length and weight used for Atlantic salmon. Productive lures are streamer flies, popping bugs and small flashy metal lures. Although muskellunge are rated the largest of all strictly freshwater fish in Canada, the average weight taken by anglers is about 10 pounds (4.5 kg). Many big bruisers are in the 40 to 50 pound (18.14 to 22.68 kg) range. It's anyone's guess when someone will break Arthur Lawton's 1957 record.

The muskie's flesh is white and flavoursome, but as with all members of this family, it is wise to skin the fish or remove the mucus by rubbing it down with hot water.

Chain pickerel
(Esox niger)

Grass pickerel
(Esox americanus vermiculatus)

Redfin pickerel
(Esox americanus americanus)

Pickerel in Canadian waters have limited interest as game fish. They are more highly regarded in the United States, where their range is wider and more populous. This is especially true of the chain pickerel.

Like their big cousins the muskellunge and northern pike, the pickerel inhabit quiet, shallow, densely weeded streams, lakes and ponds. There, for hours at a time, they will remain virtually motionless until food—minnows, sunfish, bluegills, frogs—pass by. Then they will dart out, seize their prey and quietly return to their resting place to await the arrival of another meal. They are voracious and nonselective in their eating habits, and almost anything that moves is at risk.

The chain is the largest pickerel. Average weight at maturity is 1 to 2 pounds (0.45 to 0.91 kg), but larger specimens are sometimes reported, such as the record 9 pound, 6 ounce (4.25 kg) chain rod-caught in Georgia in 1961. Chain pickerel in Canada are found in Nova Scotia, western New Brunswick, Quebec's Eastern Townships and Lake Champlain.

The grass and redfin are known as the "little pickerel." In Canada they occur mainly in southeastern Quebec and Ontario. Grass pickerel seldom exceed 10 inches (25 cm) in length; the redfin pickerel may attain lengths of up to 14 inches (35.56 cm).

The large appetite of all pickerel and other pike help to keep down the numbers of other smaller species that could overpopulate some waters and cause stunting. Thoreau writes in *A Week on the Concord and Merrimack Rivers* about one that "had swallowed a brother pickerel half as large as itself, with the tail still visible in its mouth, while the head was already digested in its stomach."

THE MUDMINNOW FAMILY
Umbridae

Central mudminnow
(Umbra limi)

The central mudminnow is a small member of the Esociformes order. As well as being used for bait, it is suitable for aquariums.

This species, a member of the Umbridae family, occurs in the upper St. Lawrence, parts of southern Quebec, the Great Lakes, the Lake Nipissing district and eastern Manitoba. It averages 2 to 4 inches (5.08 to 10.15 cm) in length, and is full-bodied. It is brown with numerous irregular black vertical bars on the sides. It can be readily distinguished by the heavy black vertical stripe at the base of its rounded tail (not forked, as in true minnows).

The mudminnow is found in sluggish waters with a soft muddy bottom. It eludes its enemies by diving into the mud—an escape method aided by its dark coloration. It survives extremely harsh conditions. It is a spring spawner.

Hubbs and Lagler write in *Fishes of the Great Lakes Region* that anglers can change the mudminnow's dark colour—thought by some to render it unsuitable as bait—by keeping the fish in a light-coloured container in bright light. This hardy creature will long outlive other species in a minnow pail.

A similar species, the Olympic mudminnow *(Novumbra hubbsi)*, is found only in the Chehalis system of the Olympic Peninsula in Washington State. A third, the Alaska blackfish (*Dallia pectoralis*), occurs in North America only in Alaskan waters. A fourth species, *Umbra krameri*, occurs in Europe.

Smelt
ORDER OSMERIFORMES

Family Osmeridae of the Osmeriformes order has seven genera and thirteen species.

THE SMELT FAMILY
Osmeridae

Smelts are circumpolar fish restricted to the Northern Hemisphere. These slender, silvery, mostly small fish occur in temperate and cold coastal areas. Some spend their entire lives at sea, some are marine but enter fresh water to spawn, and some are strictly freshwater inhabitants. They occur in the Atlantic, Arctic and Pacific oceans and their drainages.

Four genera and species occur in Canadian fresh waters: the pond smelt (*Hypomesus olidus*), the rainbow smelt (*Osmerus mordax*), the eulachon (*Thaleichthys pacificus*) and the longfin smelt (*Spirinchus thaleichthys*).

The family is complex, and there is still uncertainty concerning the identity of some of its parts. Dr. Don McAllister's highly respected *A Revision of the Smelt Family, Osmeridae,* published in 1963 by the National Museum of Canada, has helped to clarify the status of some populations, however, and in this respect is the document still most frequently consulted.

Smelt are schooling fish. In spring, huge numbers move from their marine or freshwater habitat to small streams to spawn. The anadromous Pacific longfin smelt is an exception; it spawns during late fall and early winter. All smelt species spawn at night.

Both the pond smelt (*Hypomesus olidus*) and rainbow smelt (*Osmerus mordax*) are excellent food fish. Anglers have a high regard for rainbow smelts in many parts of their eastern Canadian range, especially the Great Lakes. Many are taken during the winter by dip-netting or seining through the ice. Scott and Crossman write that the "smelt is the only fish, other than bait fishes, that can legally be taken from Ontario waters at night by means other than angling."

The rich, oily Pacific eulachon has a long tradition—particularly among native peoples—as a food, as a source of cooking oil and for curative purposes. The longfin smelt, although it also occurs in great numbers along the British Columbia coast, has no value as a food or sports fish. Just as some people claim Arctic grayling smells like wild thyme or cucumber, some say smelts smell like cucumber. One writer, however, describes the smell as "putrid cucumber."

Sunfish, Bass, Perch & Drum
ORDER PERCIFORMES

The saltwater and freshwater Perciformes, or spiny-rayed fishes, make up the largest of all vertebrate orders. Its 18 suborders, 148 families and about 9,293 species occur in an incredible range of shapes and sizes.

Perciformes are widespread throughout the fresh and marine waters of the Northern and Southern Hemispheres, and are the dominant group in many tropical and subtropical waters. A few are deep-sea dwellers.

And what a diverse lot they are! They form a veritable aquatic zoo ranging in size from the 0.5 inch long (12.7 mm) Indian Ocean goby to the 1100 pound (499.96 kg) tuna. In between are such well-known creatures as swordfish, barracuda, marlin, freshwater sunfish, bass, yellow perch, walleye, sauger and the tiny darters—all related because of anatomical characteristics found in no other fish.

Most species in the Perciformes order, however, are known mainly to anglers and commercial fishers. This chapter describes only four freshwater families: sunfish (Centrarchidae), perch (Percidae), temperate bass (Moronidae), and drum or croaker (Sciaenidae).

THE SUNFISH FAMILY
Centrarchidae

Few fish in Canadian waters are subjected to more intensive angling than those of the Centrarchidae family. Although some twenty-nine species occur in North America—the only continent to which they are native—six hold greatest interest for anglers: smallmouth bass, largemouth bass, rock bass, pumpkinseed, bluegill and black crappie. Other sunfish—among them the white crappie, longear sunfish, green sunfish, redbreast sunfish and warmouth—are uncommon in Canada, although they have a wide United States range. COSEWIC considers the redbreast sunfish to be rare in the small area of New Brunswick which is its sole Canadian range.

Centrarchidae fish are commonly separated into three distinct families—bass, sunfish and crappies.

Sunfish occur in both cool and warm waters. That fine battler, the smallmouth bass, and several others are happy only in cool, clear lakes and streams. Others such as the largemouth bass inhabit warm and turbid waters.

All members of this family share much the same anatomical characteristics: the long continuous dorsal fin, the spiny-rayed front fin and the soft-rayed back fin (In the smallmouth and largemouth bass a prominent notch separates the two fins.).

This is a family of nest builders, but with a difference. The male assumes responsibility for excavating the nest and caring for the young once they hatch. Spawning and fertilization may be secluded operations, as among bass, or may be carried out in colonies. A female may be served by several males until spawning is over.

Sunfish frequently hybridize, mainly between congeneric species. Pumpkinseeds and bluegills may crossbreed, for example, and so may smallmouth bass and spotted bass. Largemouth bass are not known to hybridize in nature.

All sunfish are pugnacious, particularly males during spawning. Then their remarkably strong instinct to protect their families, either eggs or young fish, prompts them to attack just about anything that comes near their nests.

Anglers prize smallmouth and largemouth bass most highly of all the sunfish or centrarchids, although rock bass, bluegills and pumpkinseeds are fair game fish.

Freshwater bass have yet to establish themselves prominently in popular fishing literature, but references are growing more numerous, particularly in sporting journals. One of the earliest references was in the *Account of the natural history of eastern Canada,* published in the early 1800s by Charles Fothergill, an Upper Canada naturalist and compiler of almanacs. Another was Dr. James A. Henshall's 1881 *Book of the Black Bass,* in which he writes, "I consider him, inch for inch and pound for pound, the gamest fish that swims."

Important books have included *Freshwater Bass* by Ray Bergman and *Lucas on Bass Fishing,* by Jason Lucas. A great Canadian newspaperman, raconteur and fly-fisher, Gregory Clark, often wrote lovingly of the smallmouth. In the foreword to the first edition of *The Angler's Book of Canadian Fishes,* he writes that the battle with a smallmouth "is something that even the most callous angler shivers to." The species can also claim a long and impressive list of scientific studies.

Anglers and other students of natural history may ask why the smallmouth, largemouth and rock bass are classified as members of the sunfish family; a quirk in earlier classification and nomenclature is probably responsible. The white bass, striped bass and white perch are the only true bass in Canadian waters. All are members of the temperate bass family (Moronidae).

Several members of the sunfish or Centrarchidae family have

been introduced successfully in waters far beyond their native ranges. Smallmouth bass are now established in Europe and Africa; largemouth bass are now established in England, Scotland, France, the Low Countries, Germany and the basin of the Danube River. Adaptable creatures, indeed, they are splendid ambassadors of North America fishdom.

Largemouth bass
(Micropterus salmoides)

The largemouth bass can sometimes reach huge sizes. A 22 pound, 4 ounce (10.09 kg) fish was rod-caught in Georgia in 1932, and a 14 pound, 2 ounce (6.41 kg) fish was caught in Ontario in 1948. These weights are remarkable, considering that the largemouth—in Canadian waters at least—average only 2 to 3 pounds (1 to 1.4 kg).

Elassoma evergladei, one of six species known as pygmy sunfish and found only in the southeastern United States, is at the other end of the scale; it seldom reaches a length of 2 inches (5.08 cm). Even a 1.5 inch (3.81 cm) pygmy would be considered a trophy. Since it lives in the same environment as the largemouth, its only close acquaintance with its big cousin is probably when it becomes part of the largemouth's diet.

Like the smallmouth bass, the largemouth is winning a prominent place in fishing literature. In addition to the books devoted to it (notably Ray Bergman's *Freshwater Bass)*, hardly an issue of the many popular game fishing magazines fail to make mention of it.

How do largemouth rate as sports fish? That depends on the angler's environmental preferences. Largemouth bass most commonly inhabit shallow, weedy lakes and the warm, sometimes cloudy waters of languid rivers—hardly places suited to the elegant requirements of fly-fishers. Nevertheless, largemouth are worthy antagonists which fight strongly for their freedom. In the hands of a competent chef, they provide very acceptable meals.

153

The largemouth closely resembles the smallmouth, but there are recognizable differences such as a larger mouth and an upper jaw extending beyond the eyes. In addition, the membrane between the largemouth's continuous dorsal fin is more deeply notched, giving the impression of two separate fins. The lower first portion has ten strong spines and the rearward portion has a spine in its leading edge, followed by ten to fourteen soft rays.

The largemouth's body is deeper but less laterally compressed than the smallmouth's, and its ctenoid scales are larger. There are also noticeable differences in colouring, which varies depending on the environment. The largemouth's dorsal area and head range from dark green to olive, and the sides from green to yellow with a black midlateral stripe; this may be discontinuous or absent in adults. The sides are mottled with dark, narrow blotches mainly below the lateral line. Like smallmouth bass, largemouth have many fine brush-like teeth on both upper and lower jaws.

The largemouth bass occurs naturally in southern Quebec and Ontario, and throughout Atlantic coastal areas. It inhabits some lakes of the Columbia River system in British Columbia; some stocks introduced into Idaho waters in 1916 migrated north. In addition to widespread plantings in United States waters, introduced largemouth now live in England, Scotland, Germany, France, South Africa, the Philippines, Brazil, Hawaii and Hong Kong.

Largemouth bass spawn in the spring, usually in late May through June, when water temperature is 60 to 70° F (15.5 to 21.1° C). As with smallmouth bass (and other sunfish family members) the male builds the nest and cares for the young. The largemouth is an indifferent homemaker, however, for it may be content to deposit eggs and fertilize them wherever they settle. Each female lays from one to three thousand eggs per pound (4400 to 6600 per kg) of her weight. Eggs hatch in three to six days.

The largemouth is a faithful and courageous guardian of the eggs from spawning until the schooling fry become independent and free-swimming about a week later; in fact, parental protection may continue for as long as a month. By the first winter, the young are 3 to 5 inches (7.6 to 12.7 cm) long; by the end of the following year they reach 7 to 10 inches (17.8 to 25.4 cm). At three years, they are 12 inches (30.48 cm) long. The largemouth bass lives up to sixteen years.

Largemouth are round-the-clock feeders, but generally more active during the cooler hours of dawn and dusk. They respond to a wide variety of live bait and artificial lures presented by spin-fishing, trolling, still-fishing or fly-fishing. Experienced anglers claim the fish respond best to baits offered close to the water's surface rather than close to the bottom.

Smallmouth bass
(Micropterus dolomieu)

Smallmouth bass are often confused with largemouth bass because of their similar appearance. The easiest way to distinguish them is to remember that the smallmouth's upper jaw bone extends to about the centre of the eye, but the largemouth's upper jaw extends back beyond the eye.

The original Canadian range of smallmouth bass was the St. Lawrence River and the Great Lakes drainage systems. Plantings have greatly extended this range into parts of Nova Scotia, New Brunswick, Quebec, Ontario, Manitoba and Saskatchewan. Efforts have been made to establish the species in Alberta, but they may be unable to reproduce naturally there. They are present in British Columbia, where 1901 plantings established them in both mainland and Vancouver Island waters. Although respected in BC, they do not enjoy the popularity of native trout. Smallmouth have an extensive United States range, and have been successfully introduced to England, France, Germany, Russia and South Africa.

The smallmouth bass has a deep, compressed body and—in comparison with the largemouth—a moderately small mouth.

The jaws and roof of the mouth contain many small teeth. The two dorsal fins are joined by a broad, slightly dipped membrane, giving the appearance of a single structure (Largemouth bass have a broader and more deeply notched membrane, giving the appearance of two separate fins). The smallmouth's first dorsal has nine or ten needle-sharp spines. The second dorsal, higher and more fan-like, has twelve to fifteen soft rays. The broad caudal fin is moderately forked.

The smallmouth bass has a chameleon-like capability to change its colour quickly, particularly when it emerges from the subdued light of a bank overhang or large boulder. At first it may look almost black; after exposure to light or the sun's rays, it becomes dark green to dark brown on the upper parts and white on the belly. The sides have faint, wavy, olive-coloured blotches and pronounced tall, vertical, brownish green bars. The fry are jet black; the fingerlings have distinct vertical bars and an orange-tinged tail fin.

Smallmouth bass spawn in late spring, usually May or June (much later in some areas), when water temperature is 55 to 68° F (12.8 to 20°C). Males, which play the major role in parenthood, choose gravelly or sandy bottoms at depths of up to 20 feet (6.1 m) and scoop out saucer-shaped depressions from 2 to 6 feet (0.61 to 1.83 m) in diameter. These are usually on the sloping shores of rivers or lakes where there is protection from waves or strong currents. After completing each nest, the male awaits the arrival of a ripe female, and after a brief courtship of several advances and retreats, and rubbing and nipping of bodies, both fish circle the nest and settle in it to immediately release eggs and sperm. After spawning the female either leaves the nest area or the male drives her off. Both may soon spawn again, the female either mating again with the same male and adding more eggs to the nest, or choosing another male.

The number of eggs varies greatly, but the average is thought to be about seven thousand for each pound (15,400 per kg) of the female's weight. Mortality is often high, however, particularly

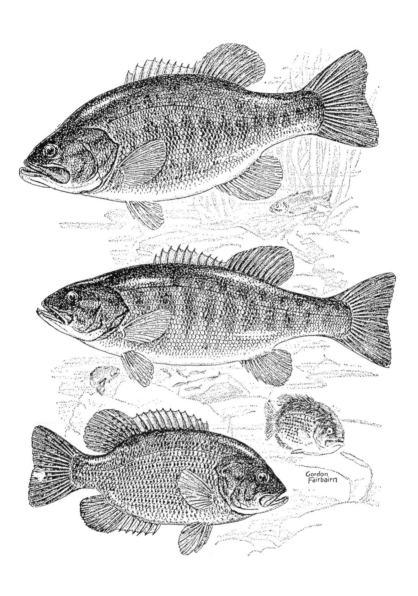

Top: LARGEMOUTH BASS
Centre: SMALLMOUTH BASS
Bottom: ROCK BASS

if the nests prove unsuitable or if there are severe variations in water temperature. (Scott and Crossman estimate that 40 percent of the nests are failures, but that "the larger the female and guarding male, the greater the hatching success.")

The smallmouth fry emerge from the eggs in four to ten days, but remain on the bottom for a week or so until they have absorbed the yolk sac which has nourished them. Now free-swimming, they make their way back to the surface where they mill about in compact schools. Pitch black except for the gold iris of their eyes, and about 0.5 inch (12 mm) in length, they are on their own; the male guardian, sensing its duties fulfilled, has by now abandoned them.

The fry grow fairly rapidly. By the end of August, they reach the fingerling stage and are from 3 to 4 inches (7.6 to 10.2 cm) long. By the end of the second fall, they are about 7 inches (17.8 cm) long, and by the third fall, about 9 to 10 inches (22.9 to 25.4 cm). Male smallmouth bass mature during their third to fifth year, and females during their fourth to sixth year. The maximum lifespan is estimated at fifteen years.

Smallmouth bass have a typical fish diet: plankton and immature insects at first, then crayfish, adult insects (with a special fondness for mayflies), leeches, frogs and small fish. Their enemies include walleye, yellow perch, catfish and rock bass.

Smallmouths favour rocky lakes and streams where the water is clean, cool and fairly deep. Unlike largemouths, they like moving water. They delight in basking in pools at the foot of riffles, or near boulders and other obstructions where the water is moving and well aerated. In lakes, smallmouths are more frequently found in fairly deep water along rocky shoreline.

Smallmouth bass respond to many types of live baits and artificial lures presented by still-fishing, casting or trolling. The average size in Canada is 2 pounds (0.91 kg); fish of 3 to 4 pounds (1.36 to 1.81 kg) are not uncommon. Although few over that weight are caught, in 1954 an exceptionally large specimen weighing 9 pounds, 13 ounces (4.45 kg) was taken from Birchbark Lake near Kinmount, Ontario. In the southern states, where some freshwater fish grow to larger sizes, an 11 pound, 15 ounce (about 5.41 kg) smallmouth bass, with a length of 27 inches (68.58 cm), was caught in 1955 in Dale Hollow Lake, Kentucky.

Rock bass
(Ambloplites rupestris)

Give a small child a can of worms, a willow pole, seven or eight feet of line fitted with a sinker and small straight-shank hook, find a place where the water is not too deep and the bottom is fairly rocky—and you just may make a small child's day.

Under such conditions and in such an environment, piscatorial monsters known as rock bass (some weighing as much as half a pound!) await a young angler's offering. If taken, they will battle so fiercely that the memory will likely last forever.

Rock bass are scrappers. No doubt when Nature planned the world of fish, rock bass (like the other sunfish) were included for the specific purpose of providing holiday fun for kids. Rock bass are known by a variety of names, for example *redeye bass* and *goggle-eye.*

This species is somewhat more sombre than most sunfish. It is olive brown on the back and sides—sometimes deep bronze to dull gold—and silver, grey or white on the belly. There are about four shadowy, wide, vertical bars above the lateral line, and the scales below the lateral line have a dark brownish spot; this combination gives the fish a striped appearance. The tip of the gill covers has a bluish black blotch—a distinguishing characteristic—and the eyes are bright red to orange. The rock bass is somewhat oblong; the back is quite elevated and the large head is narrow, rounded and deep.

Rock bass have a limited Canadian range extending through southern Quebec, southern Ontario and southern Manitoba, and in a small area of southeastern Saskatchewan. They spawn from late May to early July in shallow, circular excavations made in sandy or gravelly areas. They prefer sites near weed beds or other protection such as rocky outcroppings, submerged tree trunks or bank overhangs. Male rock bass—like many other sunfish family males—prepare the redd and stand guard until the eggs hatch and the young are free-swimming. Females, which may spawn in more than one nest, lay from three to eleven thousand eggs.

Rock bass average 6 to 10 inches (15.2 to 25.4 cm), although Scott and Crossman write that one fish of 13.4 inches (about 34.04 cm) and about 3 pounds, 10 ounces (1.64 kg) was caught in 1974 in York River, Ontario. The maximum age of this species is thought to be ten to twelve years.

Rock bass respond to a variety of natural baits and artificial lures, and are especially attracted to live minnows, a glob of worms or grubs, and small crayfish. Dr. Robert Campbell, himself an ardent angler, told me that he has "even taken them on a bare hook or one with bits of red flannel as bait." Rock bass seize a bait with much enthusiasm, but their vigour wanes and they are relatively passive when lifted from the water.

Rock bass taken from cool, clear waters are generally scrappier, and when cooked are better flavoured than those taken from warm, murky areas. These schooling fish are often found in the company of smallmouth bass and other sunfish. One of their drawbacks is that they tend to overpopulate; in small lakes, especially, control measures are frequently necessary.

Bluegill
(Lepomis macrochirus)

No one could have been more lavish in praise of the beauty of the sunfish than William Bartram, the eighteenth-century naturalist who related his wilderness excursions in his now famous *Travels Through North and South Carolina, Georgia, East and West Florida*. William, son of John Bartram, who established near Philadelphia the United States' first botanical garden, was a peripatetic wanderer who spent a lifetime studying natural history. He writes of the "yellow bream," undoubtedly the fish we refer to today as the bluegill:

> Gliding to and fro, and figuring in the still clear waters, with his orient attendant and associates: the yellow bream or sunfish. It is nearly of the shape of the trout, of a pale, gold (or burnished brass) color, darker on the back and upper sides; scales everywhere variably powdered with red, russet, silver, blue, and green specks, so laid on the scales as to appear like real dust of opaque bodies, each apparent particle being so projected by light and shade, and the various attitudes of the fish, as to deceive the sight; for in reality nothing can be of a more plain and polished surface than the scales and whole body of the fish; the fins are of an orange colour; and, like all the species of the bream, the ultimate angle of the branchiostegal terminates by a little spatula, the extreme end of which represents a crescent of the finest ultramarine blue, encircled with silver and velvet black, like the eye in the feathers of a peacock's train; he is a fish of prodigious strength and activity in the water; a warrior in a gilded coat of mail.

Did Bartram overindulge in superlatives—was the fish as beautiful as he claimed? The colour of fish is strongly influenced by the clarity and purity of their water home, and Bartram's travel took him along rivers that—in those days—were clean and sweet. Nature was not then assaulted by acid rain, industrial pollution and other environmental poisons now produced by humans. Next time you see a bluegill, make your own assessment. My own? Bluegills are indeed clothed in a "gilded coat of mail."

The bluegill's many hues are matched by its many colloquial names: *bluegill sunfish, northern bluegill sunfish, blue sunfish, common bluegill, blue perch, bream* (pronounced "brim" in the southern states), *copper-nosed bream, roach, sun perch* and *dollardee.*

The bluegill is the largest member of the sunfish family, apart from the basses. Its body is deep and compressed, and the sides generally have six to eight vertical bars. Its two dorsal fins appear to be one; the first is moderately high and has ten (sometimes eleven) sharp spines, the second has ten to twelve soft rays with a black blotch on the posterior. The pectoral fins are long and pointed. The large eyes are slightly above and forward of the centre of the head. The scales are ctenoid. As to colour, Bartram has said it all.

Bluegills spawn from late spring to midsummer, depending on water temperature. The males carry out communal nest building in shallow water where the bottom is sandy or gravelly. Scott and Crossman write that they may excavate as many as thirty nests within 160 square feet (14.86 m²). The females arrive and pair off with the males; soon they begin spawning and fertilization. Several females may spawn in the same nest. Each female releases from seven thousand to more than thirty thousand eggs, depending on her size. Studies have shown that some large females may carry as many as sixty thousand eggs. Hatching takes only three to five days, and the survival rate is generally high.

The males are vigorously territorial and defensive throughout nest building, spawning and hatching, and often until the fry become free-swimming. They aggressively chase off any predator, especially another sunfish.

Bluegills prefer warm, quiet lakes or streams with shallow water, an abundance of weed beds and—ideally—cool deep holes. There they can retire to feed when water temperatures rise above tolerance levels. In winter, when thick ice lowers oxygen production, winterkill often brings high mortality.

Bluegills feed mainly on insects such as mayflies and damselflies, but small crustaceans and vegetation are also part of their diet. Males may reach sexual maturity between their second and third year, females between their third and fourth year. Longevity is estimated at up to eight or ten years. Mature bluegills may attain lengths of about a foot (30.48 cm), but they average 6 to

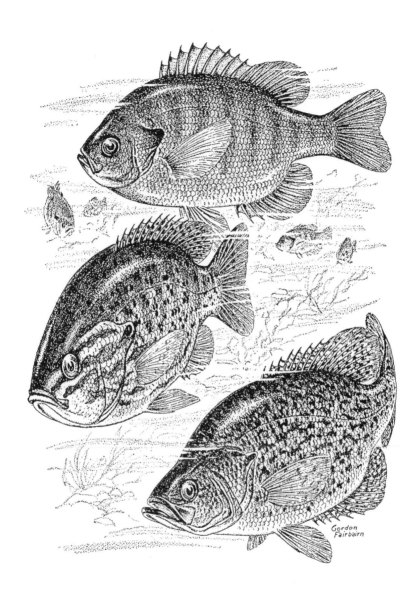

Top: BLUEGILL
Centre: PUMPKINSEED
Bottom: BLACK CRAPPIE

8 inches (15.24 to 20.32 cm). Howard T. Walden II writes in *Familiar Fishes of America* of one hardy bluegill that grew to 15 inches (38.1 cm) and 4 pounds, 12 ounces (2.15 kg). It was caught in Ketona Lake, Alabama, in 1950.

Bluegills are among the most popular of panfish. They take most natural baits such as little minnows, grubs and worms, and also respond to small artificial lures. They do vigorous battle when hooked on a dry or wet artificial fly.

Canada's largest bluegill populations occur in the upper St. Lawrence region of Quebec, throughout most of southern Ontario (particularly in the Rideau Lakes systems) and in the Quetico-Rainy River section of the Nelson River-Hudson Bay drainages.

Pumpkinseed
(Lepomis gibbosus)

Why this species is called pumpkinseed is anyone's guess (perhaps because it has the shape of a pumpkin seed?). But it's a pleasant name, and appropriate for the most colourful of the freshwater sunfish family—even more colourful than the bluegill. Young pumpkinseeds are often captured for aquariums, but are generally short-term residents because of their rapid growth.

Arrayed in all their finery, and observed as they move about in schools in the shallow, clear, quiet waters of lakes and streams, pumpkinseeds display Nature's mastery of colour arrangement. To mention only the prominent tones would do the species an injustice, so I draw on the sensitive observations of Scott and Crossman:

> Dorsal surface of head, body and upper sides golden brown to olive, lower sides golden with irregular, wavy, interconnecting blue-green lines, ventral surface bronze to red-orange; sides of body and head flecked with spots of olive, orange or red and with blue, emerald, or green reflections. Sides with several vague, vertical bars; sides of the head with

prominent, wavy, blue-green stripes, pupil of eye black, a narrow, iridescent, golden ring around this and larger area brown dorsally, blue-green ventrally; opercular flap with wide, black centre, a narrow border of white, yellow, orange, or blue with small halfmoon spots of bright red (sometimes orange, pink, or yellow) at tip; leading edge of dorsal spines black, membranes of second dorsal, caudal, anal, and pelvic fins black but no pronounced or distinct large black spots, small vague orange to olive spots on membrane of second dorsal and caudal fins, leading edge of pelvic whitish, trailing edge of second dorsal, caudal, and anal with narrow, iridescent yellow or blue-green edge; pectoral fins amber and clear.

What nature did to make the pumpkinseed one of the Beau Brummels of freshwater fishdom, however, was not carried through to its structural appearance. Its body, rather bumpy in shape, is deep and laterally compressed. Its two dorsal fins appear as one, the first with ten (sometimes eleven) spines, the second with ten to thirteen rays. The pectoral fins are long and pointed. The small scales are ctenoid, as is characteristic of sunfish. The small mouth does not extend back beyond the eye. The pumpkinseed can be distinguished from other sunfish by the brilliant scarlet spot on the ear flap.

Pumpkinseeds are now well established far beyond their native ranges because of transplantation. Originally restricted to eastern North America, the species is now found in England, France, the Low Countries, Germany and the basin of the Danube River. They are present in the Maritime provinces, southern Quebec, Ontario and southeastern Manitoba. Migrants from stocks planted in the Columbia River have moved into southeastern British Columbia. They also have been stocked in some waters of Vancouver Island, where they threaten some native species such as sticklebacks.

Spawning takes place mainly during late spring and early summer. Since a male and female may spawn in the same nest more than once, the total number of emerging fry may be as many as eight thousand. The male stands guard through the incubation period of about three days, and for a week or so after the fry have hatched, and vigorously chases off intruders.

Pumpkinseeds feed mainly on insects, molluscs, crustaceans and other small fish. The size and weight of this species varies, but in Ontario waters (the area of their greatest abundance) their maximum length is approximately 10 inches (25.4 cm) and their maximum weight 17 ounces (0.48 kg). Pumpkinseeds live six to ten years.

Like bluegills, pumpkinseeds respond readily to natural baits including worms and grubs, and small artificial lures. They give a good account of themselves when taken on dry or wet flies. Pumpkinseeds hybridize with other sunfish.

Longear sunfish
(Lepomis megalotis)

Green sunfish
(Lepomis cyanellus)

Redbreast sunfish
(Lepomis auritus)

Small populations of these three sunfish occur in limited areas of eastern Canada; they are abundant in United States waters. Because of their relative scarcity, they are not well known to anglers in Canada, although they continue to be of much interest to scientists. All three species are colourful creatures.

The longear sunfish in Canada, found mainly in Quebec and Ontario, seldom reaches 4 inches (10.16 cm). It is beautifully garbed, and small individuals are frequently added to aquarium collections.

The green sunfish, seldom exceeding 8 inches (20.32 cm), is more elongate in shape than other sunfish, and much duller in coloration. In Canada it occurs only in a few small Ontario lakes.

Its small size gives it angling value only for children, although it responds readily to worms and similar baits. This species hybridizes with other sunfish.

The redbreast sunfish, known to some as the *yellowbelly*, occurs in Canada only in a small area of New Brunswick. In 1988 COSEWIC rated this species as vulnerable.

Black crappie
(Pomoxis nigromaculatus)

White crappie
(Pomoxis annularis)

The natural range of the black crappie in Canada is Quebec's St. Lawrence River and its tributaries, Southern Ontario including all of the Great Lakes, and southeastern Manitoba. It is also present in lakes and streams of the lower Fraser River Valley in British Columbia, but how it became established so far from its native range is not well known. Small populations of the white crappie occur in Canada only in western Lake Ontario and in lakes Erie, St. Clair and Huron.

These two crappies are so nearly identical in shape and colour that it is sometimes difficult for the untrained eye to distinguish between them. Both are deep-bodied—the black crappie a bit more so—and laterally compressed. Both have prominent depressions in the forehead, very large dorsal and anal fins of about the same size, and a large mouth with protruding jaws. Their general colouring is dark green to olive to bronze on the head and dorsal surface (often with an overcast of silver or blue), brassy to light green on the sides, and silvery on the belly. The upper and middle sides of the black crappie have irregularly placed dark blotches; those of the white crappie have seven or eight vertical bands. Colouring and markings, depending on the clarity or turbidity of the water, may vary in intensity. They may vary, as well, during the spawning season.

The spine and ray counts differ, however. The first dorsal fin of the black crappie carries eight (rarely seven) spines and the second dorsal fourteen to sixteen rays, whereas the first dorsal of the white crappie carries six or seven spines and the second sixteen to eighteen rays. The dorsal, anal and caudal fins of both species are covered with dark green speckles.

The biology of the two crappies is identical in most ways. They spawn in late spring and early summer in nests excavated by the males in sand, gravel or mud, generally in weedy areas. The females lay a few eggs at a time during the morning hours, and may eject them in more than one nest. Depending on their size, they are capable of spawning from about twenty-seven thousand to more than sixty-eight thousand eggs. Black crappie eggs incubate for three to five days, and white crappie eggs for two to four days. Both black and white crappies mature in their second to fourth year, and both are thought to live about ten years at most.

Crappies are schooling fish, and like all members of the family, respond readily to natural baits such as worms, grubs and small minnows. They are rather good fun when hooked on either wet or dry flies. They are also highly edible—but bony.

THE PERCH FAMILY
Percidae

In Izaak Walton's time as in ours, perch rated highly as quarry—one that not only helped to satisfy angling expectations, but that when cooked to a turn and accompanied by appropriate condiments, provided a delectable dish.

Early Greeks and Romans knew these ubiquitous creatures, resident throughout a vast European and North American range. Aristotle (384–322 BC) writes about them in his monumental study of the fish of Greece. Some 1800 years later in 1495, in the first important book written especially for anglers, *The Treatyse*

Of Fysshynge wyth an Angle, the legendary Dame Juliana Berners writes that "the perche is a daynteous fysshe & passynge holsom with a free biting."

Although it can't be said with certainty that a perch was one of the fish referred to in the Biblical miracle of loaves and fishes, interestingly, a Sea of Galilee fish classified as *Tilapia galilea** is often called a perch. This species is commonly known in the Holy Land as "St. Peter's fish," a name given in the belief that some of its markings resemble St. Peter's fingerprints! According to St. Matthew's gospel (17:27), when Jesus was in Capernaum, he instructed his disciple Peter to pay the taxes due the temple. "Go down to the shore," he said, "and throw in a line, and open the mouth of the first fish you catch. You will find a coin to cover the taxes for both of us. Take it and pay them." Could this have been the perch-like *Tilapia galilea*?

Yellow perch
(Perca flavescens)

Why the yellow perch has traditionally stood fins and tail above so many other fish in fame and popularity is easy to understand. One can readily imagine small boys and girls of Greek and Roman times setting forth—much as children do today—in search of these challengers. Since then, generation upon generation of anglers first felt the call of the Gentle Art as a result of their childhood introduction to this species. Of all the panfish, yellow perch, in both Canada and the United States, are most associated with youth. One of their attractions is that they are commonly found in schools and in readily accessible places. They prefer clear, quiet streams and lakes with weed beds and bridge and

---

* *Tilapia galilea:* This species, while perch-like, is not of the Percidae family. Nelson in *Fishes of the World* writes that it belongs to the family Cichidae—the second largest family in the Perciformes order.

dock pilings; other sunfish such as bluegills, pumpkinseeds and rock bass often share their habitat.

A typical yellow perch is oblong and laterally compressed. The back is dark to olive green, the sides yellow or green and the belly pearly white. The sides generally display six to eight broad, dark vertical bars. The pectoral fins are light-coloured, and the pelvic fins are pale or bright orange. The two separated dorsal fins are high and rounded, the first containing thirteen to fifteen needle-sharp spines, the second containing one or two spines and twelve to fifteen soft rays. The scales are ctenoid. The mouth, which extends to the middle of the eye, contains many small sharp teeth but no canine teeth. This lack of canines provides a sure method of distinguishing perch from young walleye and sauger.

Perca flavescens is one of the prettiest of all freshwater fishes. The noted English author and angler, Stephen Downes, bluntly asserts that "its shape and colouring are so distinctive that anyone who cannot make a reasonable likeness of it had better take up photography."

The original North American range of yellow perch is uncertain, but is thought to have been from eastern Canada south to Missouri. Extensive transplanting has made them the most widely distributed of all Percidae except for the walleye, *Stizostedion vitreum*. Today they occur in every Canadian province except Newfoundland, and are found as far north as Great Slave Lake, NWT; they also inhabit some brackish waters of the Gulf of St. Lawrence and the Atlantic coast. Yellow perch introduced into Washington spread into British Columbia, and now inhabit the Pend Oreille, Columbia, Kootenay and Okanagan watersheds.

Yellow perch usually spawn from mid-April to May and early June, when the water temperature is 44 to 55°F (6.7 to 12.8°C). The adult males, followed later by the females, migrate shoreward to clean, shallow areas, sometimes with sand or gravel bottoms but more often with weeds, submerged logs, tree branches and other objects.

From dawn to dusk each female randomly extrudes tubular,

gelatinous ribbons 2 to 7 feet (0.61 to 2.13 m) long and 2 to 4 inches (5.08 to 10.16 cm) in diameter, containing two thousand to ninety thousand eggs (the average is about twenty-three thousand). The males immediately fertilize these. As the bands sink they normally attach to submerged objects or find anchorage on the bottom. Waves or storms wash some free-floating bands ashore, where they perish. Predator fish readily consume newly spawned eggs of other species, but perch eggs are protected by what has been described as an "antipredator mechanism," which makes them inedible.

Once spawning is over, the parent fish abandon the eggs. The young, when they hatch about ten days later, receive no parental protection; they are transparent and less than 0.25 inch (6 mm) in length. For the first five days they derive nourishment from their yolk sac. Once they absorb this, they begin moving about in dense schools, feeding heavily on zooplankton and insect larvae. During these early stages they are at great risk; enormous numbers of the little fingerlings are eaten by walleye, sauger, northern pike, muskellunge, bass, sunfish, lake trout and even large perch. Predator birds such as herons, mergansers, loons and kingfishers also take their toll.

Young perch grow rapidly during their first months, but development then slows. By the end of the year, they may only attain a length of 2 to 4 inches (5.08 to 10.16 cm). The size of mature perch varies, however, and some fish grow to more than 12 inches (30.48 cm) and more than 4 pounds (1.81 kg). The average size of perch caught by anglers and commercial fishers ranges from 8 to 12 inches (20.32 to 30.48 cm). Perch are relatively shallow-water fish, but in large rivers and lakes they may be found as deep as 30 feet (9.14 m) or more. Large individuals are frequently caught in deep waters of the St. Lawrence, where they are known as *channel perch*.

The diet of yellow perch ranges from aquatic insect larvae and other invertebrates to the young and eggs of other fish. They feed mainly during morning and evening throughout the year.

Yellow perch, desirable though they are, can be a threat in some waters if they are allowed to become the dominant residents. This often happens when anglers, using them as bait fish, dump unused live stocks into all-trout lakes or streams. Having a high reproductive capacity as well as an insatiable liking for trout eggs and fry, perch can threaten the very existence of other species. In waters where perch populations become abnormally high, stunting often occurs, and many fish become infested with parasites.

Although yellow perch are not heart-throbbers as game fish, they do provide year-round sport for anglers of all ages. Voracious feeders, they can be readily taken by still-fishing, using hooks baited with worms, minnows, grubs, crawfish and the like. They also respond to artificial wet and dry flies and various small spinning lures. For best results, the lure should be kept as close to the bottom as possible and retrieved slowly. Perch strike hard, but tend to approach most natural baits (worms and grubs, for example) cautiously, nibbling before seizing them. They are a favourite winter food fish of intrepid souls who enjoy angling for them through holes cut in the ice.

What perch lack as rod-bending opponents is more than compensated by their superb eating qualities. Their flesh is white, firm and sweet—and good medicine too. Konrad von Gesner, the fifteenth-century Swiss biologist, writes that the "perch is so wholesome that physicians allow him to be eaten by wounded men, or by men in fevers, or by women in child-bed." Admittedly, preparing perch for the skillet is not the most pleasant way to spend one's time. The spines of the first dorsal fin are sharp, and the ctenoid scales on the body are prickly and hard to remove.

Walleye
(Stizostedion vitreum)

Most fly-fishers would scoff at the suggestion that any species claims greater prominence than do salmon, trout and charr. Yet the walleye is not only one of North America's most popular sports fish, it is also one of the most commercially valuable of all freshwater species.

Fly-fishers (who consider themselves the purists of the angling fraternity) do have a point, at least in nomenclature. How can one equate the walleye with such splendid appellations as "Atlantic salmon," "rainbow trout," "brook trout," "Arctic charr" or "Dolly Varden"?

The name walleye has long provoked heated debate. Many die-hard anglers, as well as chefs at summer resorts, flatly refuse to call this species anything but pickerel. It is a gross misnomer; pickerel are small members of the pike family (Esocidae) and bear no resemblance to the walleye. Walleyes have a number of other unpolished aliases, among them *yellow pike, pike-perch, walleye pike, walleye perch* and *walleye pickerel*. The French common name is *doré,* meaning the gilded one, and somehow that seems appropriate.

The walleye comes by its name honestly, however, since the word refers to an unusually large, white or opaque eye. The walleye's big eyes look almost blind because of the *tapetum lucidum*, a membrane which covers the retina and protects it from bright light.

The walleye is a cylindrical fish with a long head (a little like a pike's), large mouth, forked tail and ctenoid scales. It has two well-separated dorsal fins. The first dorsal fin has twelve to sixteen strong spines; at the base of each of the back two or three spines there is a large black blotch. The second dorsal has one spine and eighteen to twenty rays. The mouth contains many sharp teeth; the canines are most conspicuous. The strong, sharp opercle bones on the gill covers can give a nasty cut, and should be avoided when handling this fish.

The walleye's coloration is influenced by habitat, and varies considerably. In clear waters, a typical walleye is dark green on the back, yellow on the sides and white—often with a yellow-green tinge—on the belly. In some areas, the back may be olive or dark brown. Yellow to golden flecks (sometimes black or brown) sprinkle the upper part of the body and the head. Six to seven vertical bars are usually present across the back and along the sides. The lower lobe of the tail carries a prominent white tip. This tip, absent on the walleye's somewhat look-alike cousin the sauger, shows clearly when a hooked fish is drawn close to the boat. Walleyes in turbid waters are less heavily patterned.

Walleyes live only in large lakes and rivers. Native and extensively introduced populations occupy an enormous range throughout Canada and the United States. In Canada they are most abundant in Lake Erie and the Prairies, where they support important commercial fisheries. Walleyes occur in all provinces except the Maritimes and insular Newfoundland. They inhabit St. Lawrence River tributaries, the east coast of James Bay, the Peace River drainage of northeastern British Columbia and areas of the Rocky Mountain foothills. They occur in Great Slave and Great Bear lakes, and in the Mackenzie River right to the estuary. Walleye are major sports fish in virtually all midwestern states, and transplanted stocks now thrive in areas including the Columbia River drainage; they may have dispersed from here into southeastern British Columbia. In many areas stocks have been seriously declining, however, because of environmental deterioration and overexploitation by commercial fishers and anglers.

Walleyes spawn in lakes and their tributary rivers from early spring to late summer, depending on water temperature and location. In southern areas this occurs from early April through June. Just before or after the ice breaks up, males move to shallows with a bottom cover of rocks, gravel or rubble, and a strong flow of water. Often they choose spots below falls or rapids, or in shoals with frequent wave action. Some walleyes migrate up tributary streams to spawn, and there are reports of journeys of over 100 miles (160.93 km).

As Scott and Crossman describe, "Spawning takes place at night in groups of one large female and one or two smaller males, or two females and up to six males. Males are not territorial, and no nest is built. Prior to spawning there is much pursuit, pushing, circular swimming, and fin erection. Finally, the spawning group rushes upwards into shallow water, stops, the females roll on their sides, and eggs and sperm are released. Apparently most individual females deposit most of their eggs in one night of spawning."

The eggs may number from twenty-five thousand to as many as seven hundred thousand. Promptly abandoned after spawning, they fall into bottom crevices, and if water temperature and oxygenation conditions are favourable, hatch in twelve to eighteen days. Mortality is severe; only 5 to 20 percent hatch successfully.

The fry remain near the gravel beds for about fifteen days, nourished by zooplankton and their yolk sac. During their second week they disperse and move closer to the surface, where they feed eagerly and grow rapidly. Within a few months they grow to several inches, and their diet includes invertebrates and other fish—especially yellow perch, which walleyes of all ages seem to prefer. Scott and Crossman write, however, that "some populations, even as adults, feed almost exclusively on emerging larvae of aquatic insects and adult mayflies or chironomids* for part of the year."

In southern Canadian waters, male walleyes mature at two to four years and females at three to six years. Both sexes average about 3 pounds (1.36 kg) at maturity, but walleyes of up to 20 pounds (9.07 kg) are frequently recorded. If they survive predators such as northern pike and muskellunge, the onslaught of commercial and sports fisheries, and increasingly serious environmental destruction by acid rain and other pollutants, walleyes may live from ten to twelve years in southern waters to a possible twenty years in northern waters. In some areas hybridization occurs between walleyes and saugers.

---

* Chironomids: midges, delicate gnat-like flies. The larvae of some of the two thousand known species can live at great depths, such as the bottom of Lake Superior.

Because of their sensitivity to light, walleyes are most commonly found in turbid lakes and rivers. There they tend to feed throughout the day. Those inhabiting clear waters generally avoid daytime light, however, by remaining near the bottom or in spots shaded by fallen trees, bank overhangs, boulders or weed beds. These fish move late in the day into shallow areas and feed mainly from dusk to dawn. Favourite haunts are sand bars and quieter water at the foot of falls or rapids.

Daytime fishing for walleyes can be productive, though. The usual procedure is to use live bait—preferably small perch or an artificial lure resembling a small fish—trolled slowly as close as possible to the bottom. Walleyes are year-round feeders and can also be caught readily through holes cut in ice. They are a schooling species; when one is caught, others are generally close by. Walleyes are not grabbers. They take bait gently, and it is wise to wait a second or two before setting the hook. They struggle hard to regain their freedom and are worthy antagonists.

Properly prepared, their flesh can be delicious.

Blue walleye
(Stizostedion vitreum glaucum)

This extinct smaller walleye, once abundant in lakes Erie and Ontario, was highly valued as a commercial and sports fish. Precise reasons for its extinction twenty-odd years ago are not known; according to "Rare, Endangered and Extinct Fishes in Canada" in *Syllogeus 54,* causes "probably include pollution, oxygen depletion, exploitation by commercial and sports fishermen, and introduction of non-native species."

The report's authors (Drs. Don E. McAllister, Brad J. Parker and Paul M. McKee) in summation make a simple but sensitive plea: "Save other fishes before it is too late."

Sauger
(Stizostedion canadense)

Saugers are similar to walleyes in most ways, though uniformly smaller. A trained eye can quickly tell the difference, however, notably in coloration (variable depending on habitat), the absence of a black blotch on the rear membrane of the first dorsal fin, and the absence of the white tip on the lower lobe of the caudal fin.

Saugers—often found with walleye, yellow perch, northern pike, goldeye and whitefish—are fair to middling as sports fish, but as food they equal the highly rated walleye. They have commercial importance in Ontario and Manitoba.

The sauger shares the walleye's body conformation. It has a round and elongate body, forked caudal fin, spines on the first dorsal fin, and large, sharp canine teeth on the jaws and roof of the mouth. Eyes are large and misty, and like the walleye's, sensitive to bright light; a membrane covering the retina offers protection. The back and sides are generally olive grey, often with a brassy or golden tinge, and the belly is white. Three or four dark saddles mark the sides, and the paired fins are orange with black spots. The sauger, like the walleye, has sharp opercle bones on the gill covers. It has ctenoid scales.

Saugers in Canada occur in large, shallow, warm lakes and rivers from southern Quebec to central Alberta; there they inhabit only rivers.

The sauger's life history appears almost identical to the walleye's. Spawning takes place at night during the spring, shortly before or after the ice breaks up and immediately after the spawning of the walleyes. Saugers often spawn on the same gravel beds, sand bars and rock reefs as walleyes. Once released and fertilized, eggs drop to the bottom where they lodge in crevices and places with good water circulation and protection from predators. Females shed seven to twenty thousand eggs for each pound (15,400 to 44,000 kg) of their weight. Once spawning is over, the eggs are abandoned.

Depending on water temperature, the young hatch after twenty-six to twenty-eight days. For the first week or so they swim in compact schools, deriving their nourishment from their yolk sac. When they have absorbed the sac, they disperse and begin feeding on foods such as zooplankton and the larvae of chironomid midges. As they grow, they prefer mayflies and other insects, and eventually become large enough to consume crustaceans and small fish. They provide food in turn for northern pike, walleyes and other saugers.

Female saugers reach maturity between four and six years, and males between two and four years. Longevity in southern waters is five to six years; in colder northern waters it may be as long as fourteen years. The weight of this species varies with locality, but the average is about 2 pounds (0.91 kg). Larger saugers are common, however, and fish of 3 to 5 pounds (1.36 to 2.27 kg) have been taken from reservoirs and tail waters of some Missouri dams. An 8.75 pound (3.97 kg) sauger was taken from Lake Sakakawea, North Dakota, in 1971.

Saugers respond to most lures and techniques used to catch walleyes, including live bait slowly retrieved along the bottom, worm-spinner combinations, and jigging with live or dead minnows. Since saugers live in turbid waters which prevent strong light penetration, they are often active throughout the day. Nevertheless, the best fishing times for saugers, as for walleyes, are usually dusk and early morning.

The flesh of this species is firm, white and exceedingly tasty.

THE DARTER SUBFAMILY—Etheostomatinae

Darters, the smallest members of the perch family, occur only in North America. Of more than one hundred and forty-two species, only twelve occur in Canada. Darters belong to the perch subfamily Etheostomatinae, which consists of three genera: *Etheostoma*, *Percina*, and *Ammocrypta*.

These creatures are among the most beautiful and interesting

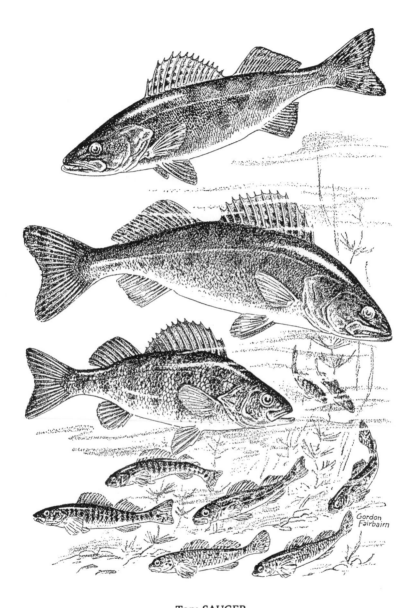

Top: SAUGER
Centre: WALLEYE and YELLOW PERCH
Bottom: LOG PERCH, BLACKSIDE DARTER, IOWA DARTER and
JOHNNY DARTER

of all freshwater aquatic life. The diversity of their habitats also makes them, as Kuehne and Barbour write in their remarkable *The American Darters*, "subtle indicators of water quality, much as the miners' canaries once served to verify pure air."

The diminutive darters are mostly similar in shape to their larger Percidae cousins, the walleyes and saugers. A major difference is that darters either lack an air bladder or have a deficient one. This reduces or eliminates their buoyancy, making them bottom-dwellers; they are rarely seen suspended in the water. One species, the blackside darter (*Percina maculata*), has a partially developed bladder that enables it to swim in midwater and even leap out of the water to capture flying insects. The largest darter in Canadian waters is the log perch (*Percina caprodes*), which can reach 5 inches (12.7 cm).

The serious angler who is interested in aquatic life has undoubtedly seen these miniature creatures on occasion and has been fascinated at their remarkable ability to move with lightning speed. To try to catch one by hand is an interesting, but seldom successful, experience; the moment it seems within your grasp it darts away in an almost imperceptible movement. Then it comes quickly to rest on its extended pectoral fins.

Darters are so beautifully coloured and patterned (especially at spawning) that they are often referred to as the hummingbirds, or wood warblers, of the freshwater fish world. The rainbow darter, for example, is so splendidly attired that hobbyists frequently add it to their aquariums. But there are exceptions, as is customary in nature; some species such as the johnny darter are so sombre that they blend almost perfectly into the sand.

The habitat of darters varies from rivers, streams, creeks and reservoirs to lakes, ponds and swamps. Their most common habitat is shallow gravel or sand riffles with an abundance of microcrustaceans and insect larvae. Darters are spring to early summer spawners. Their upstream or downstream migrations from deeper waters to shallower spawning grounds are seasonal events.

Detailed accounts of darters in Canada are contained in *Freshwater Fishes of Canada*, by Scott and Crossman, and accounts of all North American species (with remarkable colour photographs) in *The American Darters*.

THE TEMPERATE BASS FAMILY
Moronidae

Until 1966 the striped bass, white bass and white perch (genus *Morone*) were classified as part of the Serranidae family, a large and poorly defined group of about three hundred and seventy sea bass found throughout the world in tropical and temperate waters. In 1966, these three species were brought into the Percicthyidae or temperate bass family to help clarify the systematic relationship of the Serranidae family. Johnson (1984), however, placed the Morone and Dicentrarchus in their own family.

The Moronidae family worldwide consists of two genera and six species.

Striped bass
(Morone saxatilis)

As game fish striped bass are considered by some anglers to be the equal of Atlantic salmon or barracuda. There is no doubt that these schooling, mainly anadromous creatures have succeeded in developing a race of anglers frantically devoted to their pursuit.

Angling for striped bass is no sport for the timid soul. These are fish of unbelievable power. Whether you cast into the surf from the beach, perilous lichen-covered rocks, jetties or the shore of a freshwater lake or stream, be prepared for a mammoth task. If you do connect, you will need muscle and imagination to outwit a cunning and explosive warrior.

Striped bass inhabit coastal waters and tidal streams throughout most of eastern North America, from the St. Lawrence River to northern Florida, Louisiana and the Gulf of Mexico. Pacific Ocean stocks descend from fry transplanted in 1879 and 1882 from New Jersey's Navesink River to San Francisco Bay. Although now most abundant in the Bay area, some migrate as far north as Oregon, and they are occasionally reported on the west coast of Vancouver Island.

They occur naturally in the upper St. Lawrence River, and in coastal waters and rivers of all the Maritime provinces except Newfoundland. Stocks in these areas have declined in recent years, however, and their status is closely monitored.

This species is olive green to bluish or black above, paling to silver on the sides and white below. The upper sides carry six to nine uninterrupted horizontal blackish stripes, the highest stripe being the most distinct. Its body is long and moderately compressed laterally; it has a long head and projecting lower jaw. The eyes are noticeably small. The first dorsal fin, with seven to twelve (generally nine) stiff spines, is high and quite separate from the second dorsal, which has one sharp spine and eight to fourteen (generally twelve) soft rays. The tail fin is forked.

Striped bass spawn from late May to July in strong currents of fresh water. The semibuoyant eggs often drift many miles, some even into tidal waters, before hatching. The eggs hatch in forty-eight to seventy-four hours, depending on water temperature. Records show that a 4.5 pound (2.04 kg) female can produce as many as two hundred and sixty-five thousand eggs in one season; thus a very large fish can spawn several million eggs each year.

Striped bass move in big schools, except for large fish, which tend to travel alone or with a few others of their own size. In Canadian waters they appear to remain close to their natal rivers. Some United States populations are long-distance seasonal migrants, however, swimming north in summer and south in winter. They remain mainly inshore, although they may go farther seaward to cross bays.

Stripers are voracious feeders and consume large quantities of herring, menhaden (a kind of herring), flounders, alewives, eels and smelt, as well as invertebrates such as worms, squid and crabs. Their feeding times vary; they can be taken from dawn to dusk, but their most active periods are generally at night.

Along the coast these fish frequent sandy beaches and bays with relatively shallow water and submerged boulders. They also dwell in estuaries. In open water, where the surf is strong, they favour the troughs behind bars and rocks. Many anglers seek striped bass among rafts of floating weeds; a breaking sea is usually more productive than smooth water.

Although striped bass fishing is not as popular in Atlantic Canada as salmon fishing, the sport is gaining increasing attention, especially among fly-fishers. Commercially, these fish are caught in hoop and trap nets, generally along with other species such as salmon and cod. Striped bass are highly rated for their eating qualities.

The average weight of striped bass is 5 to 10 pounds (2.27 to 4.53 kg) but some reach far greater weights; a 78 pound, 8 ounce (35.6 kg) individual was caught in New Jersey in 1982. A bass weighing more than 55 pounds (24.94 kg) was rod-caught in 1979 below the reversing falls of the St. John River in New Brunswick. Several striped bass, said to be the largest ever caught commercially, were taken from North Carolina waters in 1891. Their average weight was 125 pounds (56.7 kg).

White bass
(Morone chrysops)

White bass, it was once thought, arose from populations of anadromous striped bass (*Morone saxatilis*) that eons ago became landlocked during migrations to freshwater spawning areas. Anatomical and morphological differences make this unlikely, despite similarities in appearance between the two species. The white bass is also a consistently much smaller species which, in Canadian waters, seldom exceeds 1.5 pounds (0.68 kg).

The white bass has a compressed, deep body, a somewhat

elevated back and a rather conical head. Its two dorsal fins—the first with nine spines, the second with one spine and twelve to fourteen rays—are separate. Many small, sharp teeth line the jaws and base of the tongue. The white bass is dark green or grey on the back, silvery on the sides and white beneath. Several narrow dusky stripes, about five above the lateral line, mark the back. The eyes have a yellowish tint.

White bass, which occur widely throughout the United States, in Canada are confined mainly to the St. Lawrence River, Lake Nipissing and all Great Lakes except Superior. Their area of greatest abundance in Canada is Lake Erie, where they support a small but valuable commercial fishery.

White bass spawn in shallow water from late April to June, choosing rocky reefs or gravelly bottoms over which to shed their tiny, heavy, adhesive eggs. The parent fish do not protect their eggs or young. Eggs hatch within a few days. Females are remarkably fecund; during a season each may lay one-half to one million eggs. When spawning is over, adult fish go to deeper water; there they swim in compact schools, often close to the surface.

White perch
(Morone americana)

White perch, despite their common name, are not part of the Percidae family; they don't even look like perch. They belong to the temperate bass family, (Moronidae) as do the striped bass and white bass.

This species, neither well known nor popular in Canada as a sports fish, is native to fresh and brackish waters from the upper St. Lawrence River to the Gulf of St. Lawrence. Freshwater populations occur in the Maritime provinces, Quebec and lakes Ontario and Erie. White perch first entered the Great Lakes from the United States, it is believed, by way of the Erie Barge Canal and the Oswego River. The body of the white perch is deep, laterally compressed and heavily covered with ctenoid scales. The large, triangular head has a projecting lower jaw. Freshwater populations are normally olive to dark greyish green on the back, silvery or silvery green on the sides, and silvery white on the belly. Those inhabiting salt or brackish water are usually lighter in colour. The pelvic and anal fins sometimes have a rosy tint.

White perch are spring spawners. They lay their eggs in shallow water, where they attach to whatever object they fall on. A small female may lay about twenty-two thousand eggs, a large female as many as two hundred and forty thousand. Hatching, depending on water temperature, occurs within five days. The young congregate in small schools, living at first on nymphs, insect larvae and water fleas. As they grow older, they feed on small fish. They reach maturity during their second year. The average lifespan is believed to be five to seven years, but an authentic record shows that one fish reached seventeen years.

White perch bite freely on almost any bait, but they are often wary, especially when close to the surface; wet and dry flies are then productive. During the day, when they are in deeper water, they respond to still-fishing with baits such as worms, minnows, and hellgrammites (larvae of the Dobson fly). Spinner-fly combinations are also effective. The average weight of this species is about 1 pound (0.45 kg), although in United States waters 3-pounders (1.36 kg) are occasionally reported. The flesh of the white perch is white and flaky, and of excellent flavour.

THE DRUM OR CROAKER FAMILY
Sciaenidae

This family numbers about seventy genera and about two hundred and seventy species of bottom-dwelling fish found in tropical and temperate coastal waters of the Pacific, Atlantic and Indian oceans. Thirty-three species inhabit North American waters but only one, the freshwater drum (*Aplodinotus grunniens*), is a freshwater fish.

Members of the Sciaenidae family range from a few inches—the tiny jackknife fish (*Equetus lanceolatus*) of Caribbean waters, for example—to the 6-foot (1.83 m), 225 pound (102 kg), totuva (*Cynoscion macdonaldi*) of Mexican and Panamanian waters.

Most members of this family have specialized muscles which, especially during the spawning season, can be made to vibrate against the swim bladder, creating grunting or drumming sounds. These sounds can sometimes be heard from the water if the fish are swimming not too deeply and are moving ahead in schools. Also characteristic of most sciaenids are one or several barbels on the chin; the large, ivory-like "ear bones" or otoliths: and the heavily dentured lower jaws with strong, crushing teeth in the pharyngeal arches.

Sciaenids feed mainly on invertebrates such as crustaceans and molluscs, although larger specimens include fish in their diet. They are not greatly esteemed as food, but some are taken by anglers or commercial fishers.

Freshwater drum
(Aplodinotus grunniens)

The most imaginative of this species' common names is *sheepshead,* said to derive from a comment in Alexander Wilson's 1815 book, *The Fishes of New York,* the first American book on ichthyology: "The form of the mouth and a certain smuttiness of the face . . . have a distinct resemblance to the physiognomy of a sheep."

Freshwater drums inhabit large lakes and rivers in Canada and the United States. Their Canadian range includes the upper St. Lawrence and Ottawa rivers, and they are well established in all Great Lakes except Superior. They occur as far north as the Nelson River in Manitoba, in the Hudson Bay drainages of Manitoba and in southwestern Saskatchewan. The major Canadian fishery for this species is in Lake Erie.

The freshwater drum is laterally compressed, and its back arches near the shoulder. The first dorsal fin is short, with eight or nine sharp spines. The second dorsal, with twenty-five to thirty-three soft rays, extends almost onto the rounded caudal fin. The two dorsal fins are connected by a narrow membrane, but separated by a deep notch. The mouth is overhung by the snout, and prominent crushing teeth line the pharynx or upper digestive tract. These teeth enable the fish to break up the hard shells of the invertebrates they feed on. Large ctenoid scales are present on most parts of the body, including the head.

The large, ivory-like "ear bones" or otoliths inside the ear, are often called *lucky stones*; according to Cooper in *Fishes of Pennsylvania*, some found in Mississippi Valley middens have been carbon-dated to 3600 to 3700 BC. Indians often used otoliths and pharyngeal teeth for ceremonial adornments and to ward off sickness.

Adult freshwater drums vary from 2 to 5 pounds (0.91 to 2.27 kg). Drums taken from Canadian waters have reached the uncommon size of 24 pounds (10.89 kg). The largest drum on record weighed 54 pounds 8 ounces (24.72 kg), and was rod-caught in 1972 in Nickajack Lake, Tennessee. Drums, though not significant to the sports fishery, are usually caught by casting, trolling or still-fishing. They respond to artificial lures and natural bait such as crayfish, worms and pieces of other fish. Drums are bottom-dwellers and often swim in schools. When hooked they put up a spirited fight.

Catfish, Bullhead, Stonecat & Madtom
ORDER SILURIFORMES

The Siluriformes include 34 families and more than 2405 species—some of them marine—distributed worldwide. About 1200, including the infamous Amazon piranhas (family Characidae of Order Characiformes), are native to South America. The 45 or so North American species are of the freshwater family Ictaluridae. The seven species found in Canada are the channel catfish, brown bullhead, yellow bullhead, black bullhead, and the tiny stonecat, brindled madtom and tadpole madtom.

All Siluriformes are scaleless, except for several freshwater families of South American armoured catfish, whose bodies have bony plates. Nearly all have barbels or "whiskers" around their mouths. The barbels are extremely sensitive. By extending them forward and waving them, the fish can intercept the smell and taste of food. Sensory cells on their bodies perform the same function.

CATFISH

Catfish range in size from the European *Siluris glanis*, which reaches more than 727.5 pounds (329.99 kg), to the North American least madtom (*Noturus hildebrandi*), usually weighing a few grams and seldom exceeding 1 inch (2.54 cm) in length. North American blue catfish (*Ictalurus furcatus*) have reached weights of 120 pounds (54.43 kg), and the channel catfish (*Ictalurus punctatus*) reaches up to 58 pounds (26.31 kg). The average weight of bullheads is 2 to 3 pounds (0.91 to 1.36 kg).

Catfish around the world show remarkable variations in form and behaviour. Some "walk" on land; some make barking or grunting sounds; some produce electrical currents; some "climb." Others are blind and toothless. There are also parasitic catfish, which enter the gill covers of their large armoured relatives, make cuts in the gill filaments and drink the blood that oozes out.

The "upside-down" catfish swim on their backs and feed on algae growing on the underside of floating vegetation. Naturally, their bellies are dark and their backs light. Most catfish, however, have stiff, sharp spines at the front of their dorsal fins that are capable of inflicting painful wounds. The little madtoms and stonecats have a gland at the base of the pectoral spine containing a venom that can cause serious infection.

As noted in Nelson's *Fishes of the World*, one catfish species (*Plotosus lineatus*) of the eeltail catfish family—found in both marine and freshwater tropical habitats—can inflict wounds potentially fatal to humans. Nelson also lists an aggressive Indian species (*Heteropneustes fossilis*) with a painful, potentially dangerous sting. This species, he writes, has "an aggressive behavior with records of attacks on humans."

All but two North American ictalurids inhabit lakes, rivers, streams and ponds with plentiful weeds and other aquatic vegetation. The exceptions are the big catfish and the little stonecat; these generally inhabit clean, cool, free-flowing waters.

It's no exaggeration to say that catfish will eat almost anything.

Their stomach contents have included not only natural foods—minnows, frogs, worms, crayfish, clams, aquatic insects and algae—but also unlikely tidbits such as chewing gum, old cheese and offal. Some anglers swear by "stink bait" (concoctions of blood pudding, cheese balls or pig liver, among other ingredients).

Anglers usually try to get their bait as close to the bottom as possible, whether they are fishing from a boat, a bridge or the shore. A bobber keeps the bait free-moving and acts as an indicator when the fish nudges or swallows the hook. Catfish have not only a highly developed sense of smell but extreme sensitivity to sound. Unnecessary noises when boating or walking along a bank can drive them away.

Catfishing is less popular in Canada than the United States, but it does attract many anglers. Enthusiasts claim that the larger species resist capture with as much determination as other fish of their size.

Channel catfish
(Ictalurus punctatus)

Channel catfish, the largest of the Ictaluridae family in Canadian waters, are eagerly sought by anglers. Native Indians have traditionally used the spines of this and other catfish to make artifacts. Scott and Crossman write about the discovery of such an artifact on the shores of Lake Huron, carbon-dated to 1000 BC.

The channel catfish is slender with a long, wide head and small eyes. The channel catfish and blue catfish have a deeply forked tail as a distinguishing characteristic; other catfish have either a square or fan-shaped tail. Eight sensory barbels are present on the head, one near each nostril, one at each corner of the mouth and four under the chin. A sharp spine is located at the front of the dorsal fin and in front of each pectoral fin. The smooth, leathery skin is scaleless. Colour varies widely depending on environment, but a typical specimen is dark on the back and grey on the belly. Some are irregularly spotted.

Channel catfish occur throughout an extensive area including the St. Lawrence River and its tributaries, southern Quebec, the Ottawa River, all Great Lakes except Superior, and southeastern Manitoba. They inhabit many Ontario lakes and rivers and their drainage systems. They are thought to have been present at one time in Saskatchewan and Alberta. Nelson and Paetz write in *Fishes of Alberta* that channel catfish bones a few thousand years old have been found in the South Saskatchewan River; the fish may have been present in Alberta until about two hundred years ago.

Channel catfish are late spring and summer spawners. They deposit their eggs in gelatinous clusters in nests made under logs or rocks, and sometimes in submerged muskrat runs. Depending on size and age, females lay three thousand to twenty thousand or more eggs. These hatch in five to ten days. Males guard the nests during the incubation period and remain with the fry until they can fend for themselves. For a few weeks the young, protected by one or both parents, move in schools, feeding mostly on the larvae of insects such as midges, mayflies, black flies and caddis flies. Eventually the schools break up, and the young fish become independent.

Mature catfish prefer cleaner, cooler and deeper waters than do bullheads, and often seek areas with strong current. Unlike other ictalurids, which feed mainly at night, channel catfish also feed during the day. They retire to shallower, more protected waters at night.

Channel catfish will respond to slowly retrieved artificial lures such as spoons, spinners and plugs. Anglers also catch them on jig lines with hooks baited with minnows, frogs, worms, pieces of meat and "stink bait." Most productive areas are the deep runs and riffles of streams and waterfalls.

Flathead catfish
(Pylodictis olivaris)

Flathead catfish have only recently been recorded in Canadian waters, in the Point Pelée area of Lake Erie, where they are being watched with interest. They have a large range in the United States, from Pennsylvania south throughout the Mississippi Valley, and west to Mexico.

Flathead catfish are primarily inhabitants of large, warm, sluggish rivers and lakes. Adults average 2 to 5 pounds (0.91 to 2.27 kg), although fish of 20 to 40 pounds (9.07 to 18.14 kg) are not uncommon in the US. Occasionally commercial fishers take large flatheads of 60 to 100 pounds (27.21 to 45.36 kg).

The flathead is comparable in biology to other members of the Ictaluridae family. Two major structural differences are its long, flat head—which inspired its name—and its square tail.

Angling for flatheads is the same as for other catfish. They are well regarded as food fish.

BULLHEADS

Bullheads compare with perch, sunfish and rock bass in the special pleasure they give children. They are fun fish, ready to take any bait offered, capable of putting up rod-bending scraps, and certainly tasty when seasoned, pan-fried and served with trimmings. As Dr. Robert Campbell points out, however, it may be unwise to eat bullheads taken from polluted waters; like other bottom-feeders, they are bioaccumulators of pollutants.

Bullheads in Canada occur primarily in all eastern provinces except Newfoundland, but there are introduced populations in the prairie provinces and British Columbia. They occur widely in the United States. Bullheads thrive in lakes and streams with tepid, slow-moving water and muddy, weedy bottoms.

Yellow bullhead
(Ameiurus natalis)

Yellow bullheads compare with brown bullheads as sports fish, and are frequently mistaken for them. They are commonly dark on the head, slate black to yellow-lime on the back, bright yellow on the sides, and yellow to white under the head and on the belly. Their chin barbels are white to yellowish. Unlike black and brown bullheads, they have no mottling on the body. The head and mouth are large. The body is short with a fan-like tail. The leathery, scaleless skin is thinner than that of other bullheads.

Yellow bullheads usually inhabit lakes and streams with thick vegetation. They spawn during late May and June in nests made beneath bank overhangs, under stumps and in other protected areas. Females deposit about three hundred to six thousand eggs depending on their size. In *Familiar Freshwater Fishes of America*, Walden writes: "During the five to ten day incubation one or both parents may inhale an egg cluster, move it around like a mouthwash and expel it again. This practice is assumed to clean and aerate the eggs."

Yellow bullheads reach maturity during their second or third year and live to about seven years. Adults can reach 18.3 inches (46.48 cm) and sometimes attain a weight of 3 pounds (1.36 kg).

The Canadian range of the yellow bullhead is restricted to the Ontario section of the St. Lawrence River and its tributaries, and to all Great Lakes except Superior; it is well known in the Rideau Lakes district. Fishing for yellow bullhead is most productive at night; they respond to baits including meat and offal.

Yellow bullheads are among the tastiest of all panfish. Some anglers claim that they should be iced as soon as possible after catching to prevent quick loss in texture. At its best the flesh is of excellent quality.

Brown bullhead
(Ameiurus nebulosis)

Brown bullheads are the largest of the bullhead clan, yet their average weight is under a pound (0.45 kg). Individuals of 2 to 4 pounds (0.91 to 1.81 kg) are occasionally caught.

The brown bullhead's head is large compared to its rounded, pot-bellied body; this is an ictalurid characteristic. It is generally olive to brown on the back with dark mottlings on the sides, and cream to white underneath. Its tail is square or slightly notched. A barbel is located near each nostril and at each corner of the mouth, and there are four barbels under the chin. A sharp spine is found at the front of the dorsal fin and in front of each pectoral fin. The skin is leathery, smooth and completely without scales.

Brown bullheads occur in Canada from Nova Scotia westward to Saskatchewan. They are common in the St. Lawrence River and in all Great Lakes and their tributaries, except Lake Superior. Introduced stocks are present in British Columbia's Fraser River system and in a few lakes of southeastern Vancouver Island.

Brown bullheads inhabit warm, sluggish and often stagnant waters. They spawn during April and May in nests made by fanning out saucer-shaped depressions in the mud or sand. The eggs—two thousand to ten thousand depending on the size of the female—are cream-coloured and hatch in about a week. The young fish are jet black, and can be seen swimming in large schools near the surface. The male parent protects them from predators until they are about 2 inches (5.08 cm) long and able to fend for themselves. During their baby stages they resemble, and often are mistaken for, tadpoles.

Brown bullheads have a typical catfish diet of insect larvae, worms, minnows, crustaceans, offal and other things that smell and taste enticing—to a bullhead.

Brown bullheads are commonly caught by still-fishing methods, mostly at night. They will respond to almost anything an angler attaches to a hook. One "killer" which I proved successful after a venerable French-Canadian angler recommended it, is blood pudding, available in some butcher shops. When a piece of the coagulated blood begins to melt, and the smell and taste permeate the water, the bullheads go into a frenzy. The angler will tire of fishing long before the fish will tire of eating. Bullheads usually greedily swallow the bait immediately upon taking it, which makes removal of the hook difficult. In handling bullheads,

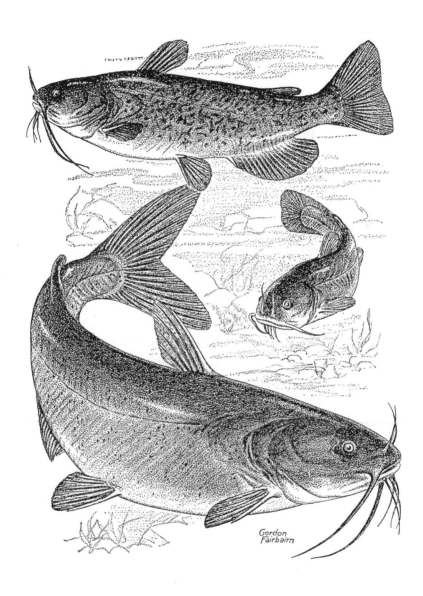

Top: BROWN BULLHEAD
Centre: STONECAT
Bottom: CHANNEL CATFISH

take care to avoid the sharp spines; they can cause painful wounds.

Brown bullheads are also known as *bullpout, horned pout, mudcat, barbottle, squaretail* and (for some reason) *minister.*

Black bullhead
(Ameiurus melas)

This species is relatively rare in Canada, though it has a wide range in the midwestern United States. Its natural range in this country is Lake Erie and its tributary waters. Small introduced populations occur in southern Manitoba, Saskatchewan and British Columbia.

Black bullheads are typically dark or yellowish green on the back, yellow or white on the sides, and paler yellow or white on the belly. Their chin barbels are dark and spotted. They seldom exceed 6 to 7 inches (15.24 to 17.78 cm). Black bullheads are similar in biology and habitat to other ictalurids. Scott and Crossman write that they seem to be more tolerant of pollutants than other bullheads, however, and capable of surviving in water at a higher temperature.

This species is considered a delicacy and reared artificially in some states for market. In their natural habitat they provide good sport. Angling methods are the same as for other bullheads.

STONECATS & MADTOMS

Stonecat
(Noturus flavus)

Madtom
(Noturus gyrinus and Noturus miurus)

Most people, apart from fishery workers and those especially interested in aquatic life, never see these creatures.

Madtoms are tiny, averaging only 1 to 3 inches (2.54 to 7.62 cm) in length; stonecats sometimes grow to 8 inches (20.32 cm). One characteristic distinguishes both from other Canadian freshwater fish: a poison gland in the spines of the pectoral fins can cause a painful wound. The sting compares in unpleasantness to a bee-sting.

Madtoms and stonecats are indigenous to Canada only in the upper St. Lawrence River, Great Lakes except for Superior and northern Ontario. Their spotty occurrence in the Prairies is thought to result from transplanting. They have a vast range in the United States, particularly throughout the Mississippi drainage.

Canadian waters are home to one species of stonecat (*Noturus flavus*) and two species of madtoms, the tadpole madtom (*Noturus gyrinus*) and the brindled madtom (*Noturus miurus*).

Madtoms and stonecats prefer shallow parts of lakes and streams, often where there is a current. All in this group are secretive, hiding during the day under rocks and stones, and in other protective places. Spawning patterns of madtoms and stonecats are much the same as among other catfish. They likewise feed on immature insects and other tiny vertebrates, and algae. Stonecats are not much bigger than common shiners, but their flesh is said to be tasty. Smaller madtoms are sometimes sold as aquarium fish, and anglers often use them as bait.

Incidentally, the "mad" part of the madtom apparently refers to the creature's strange swimming behaviour. Another explanation is that a madtom stung an angler called Tom with poison from its pectoral fin spine. Tom got mad. In reality, then, he was the "madtom!" There are reports (COSEWIC's *Rare and Endangered Fishes and Marine Mammals of Canada*) that one relative of the brindled madtom is apparently even madder; it is called the "furious madtom."

Tomcod & Burbot
ORDER GADIFORMES

his order includes pelagic, deepwater dwellers found in a vast range from Arctic to Antarctic. Some are among the world's most valuable commercial fish. Twelve families include about four hundred and eighty-two species. Among the best known Northern Hemisphere species are cod, haddock, pollock, cusk and hake.

Three members of the Gadidae family spend some time in fresh water, however. One primarily marine member, the Atlantic tomcod, commonly enters fresh water to spawn. A second member, the burbot, is strictly a freshwater resident. A related marine species, the Pacific tomcod (*Microgadus proximus*), occurs sporadically in coastal waters of the Pacific from California to the Bering Sea.

Atlantic tomcod
(*Microgadus tomcod*)

Atlantic tomcod, sometimes called *tommy cod* and *frostfish*, occur along the Atlantic seaboard from northern Labrador to

Virginia. Although tomcod are a primarily marine species, many enter brackish and fresh water to spawn. There are also land-locked freshwater populations in at least two areas: Lake St. John, Quebec, and Deer Lake, Newfoundland.

Atlantic tomcod closely resemble young Atlantic cod (*Gadus morhua*); they are elongate in shape, with the front of the body rounded and the rear compressed. They differ from *Gadus morhua* in the long, tapering filaments of their pelvic or ventral fins, and in the rounded tail fin (the tail fin of the Atlantic cod is slightly concave). Another distinguishing feature is the barbel-like appearance of the pelvic fin and the slender barbel on the underside of the lower jaw.

The tomcod's colour varies, but is generally olive or yellow-green on the back and sides, and grey or white on the belly. A white lateral line, arching slightly over the pectoral fin, clearly marks both sides of the body. Tomcod seldom exceed 13 inches (33.02 cm), however, though the saltwater species sometimes grow to prodigious sizes. A venerable granddaddy of the Gadidae family, captured on a longline off the Massachusetts coast in 1895, weighed more than 211 pounds (95.71 kg) and was 6 feet (1.83 m) in length!

Tomcod spawn in midwinter, normally under ice in shallow brackish or fresh water, although some spawn in saltwater shallows. The females lay from six thousand to sixty thousand small, adhesive, spherical eggs. As they sink they become attached to sand, gravel or other detritus. They hatch in three to four weeks.

Anglers and commercial fishers take great numbers of tomcod during their spawning migrations in late fall and winter, especially when fairly thick ice has formed in the rivers. Water pollution has seriously curtailed the fishery in recent years, although it is still popular recreationally, especially in the lower St. Lawrence. (Pollution in the same areas now also threatens the once abundant beluga or white whale.)

Huts have long been used on frozen rivers, as Dr. Vadim Vladykov described so colourfully:

Winter fishing for Tomcod already has a history: it goes back to the days of the colonists, and Bougainville spoke of it in 1757. Today *cabins* are installed on both shores of the St. Lawrence River, from Cap-de-la-Madeleine to Neuville, and from St. Angèle to Lotbinière. The best known localities are Batiscan and Ste. Anne de la Pérade. At this last place, there were some 400 cabins during the winter of 1954. These wooden cabins, measuring 7 feet by 9 feet, can house 4 fishermen and be used for several seasons. Moreover, larger cabins can be found, where 18 persons can fish. All these cabins are painted in gay and vivid colours, lighted with electricity and heated with a wood stove.

As soon as the ice is from 4 to 5 inches thick, which is normally formed towards the 20th of December, the first cabins appear in the estuary of St. Anne de la Pérade. As the season progresses and winter's rigors thicken the ice up to 2 feet, it can then support a veritable village of fishing cabins, and many automobiles. In each cabin a rectangular hole is cut in the ice, some 6 feet long and 16 inches wide, which is kept covered with a wooden board outside the hours of fishing to prevent freezing. In these comfortably heated cabins, each fisherman uses 2 lines. Each line, provided in the middle with a match stick, has two hooks baited with a small piece of pork liver. A pound of pork liver gives some 400 baits, $1/4$ of an inch thick. Some prefer to use larger size baits. A jigging movement of the match indicates that there is a bite. With a single jerk the fisherman brings up the Tomcod, and then throws it out through the window. The fish freeze instantly, thus conserving their flavour.

Tomcod can bite any time of the day, but the best fishing is done at night. A person can catch up to 500 or 600 Tomcod, between 7 o'clock at night and 7 o'clock in the morning. A 60 pound potato sack can hold 400 or 500 Tomcod. In winter, Tomcod is delicious and satisfies the most demanding tastes. The average rate for a cabin is $2.00 a day per person; on weekends the price is somewhat higher. The fishing season normally lasts from Christmas to the beginning of February. This winter sport attracts not only fishermen from different parts of Quebec, but also from Ontario and the United States. In spite of their small size, Tomcod bite freely and thus give the satisfaction of great numbers caught.

The best fishing period coincides with the full moon, which adds an enchanting allure to this unique winter sport. The cold of the night air contrasts pleasingly with the warmth of the cabin and the cordiality of the neighbours. All the fishermen, even the unlucky ones, are amply recompensed by the infectious gaiety and pleasure of hearing joyous French-Canadian songs floating out and mingling with the aroma of burning wood in the invigorating winter air.

Close to half a century has passed since Dr. Vladykov wrote about the tomcod, but the little fish are still there. When winter arrives and the ice is thick, the huts go up again, and the songs—so dear to the hearts of fishermen—fill the air. But one thing has changed—no longer is it possible to rent a cabin, or even a seat in one, for two dollars a night!

Burbot
(Lota lota)

In the world of freshwater fishes the burbot—alias *ling, eelpout, loche, freshwater cod, maria* (in Saskatchewan, Manitoba and Ontario) *methy* (in Northern Canada), *lush* (in Alaska), and *lawyer* (Great Lakes)—could never win a piscatorial beauty contest on its appearance. It's a cod, all right, and though its familial respectability is beyond question, it simply isn't a creature of elegance. And to make its acquaintance is an experience not soon to be forgotten.

The burbot has a large, flat, pointed head, almost a quarter the length of the body, which is severely compressed at the rear. It has small, beady eyes, a projecting mouth, a barbel on the tip of the chin and a small barbel near each nostril. Its first dorsal fin is small, but the second—like the anal fin—continues almost to the rounded tail. All fins are soft-rayed. Colour varies depending on habitat; the fish may be light brown, dark brown, dark olive or even yellow. All are heavily mottled on the body and fins, however. A heavy covering of mucus hides fine scales. Least enchanting about this species are its extreme sliminess and occasionally its foul smell. Burbot are cold-water dwellers. They are exceedingly voracious and live mainly on other fish, occasionally fish of almost their own size. One report tells of a 15-inch (38.1 cm) burbot whose stomach contained a 12-inch (30.48 cm) walleye—as good an example of gorging as one might find. Their diet also includes aquatic insects, molluscs, crustaceans, plankton and fish eggs.

Spawning times of the burbot vary according to geography. It may begin in late November and continue through to March or April, but it invariably ends before the breakup of the ice. Females lay eggs at night in shallows of lakes or tributary streams, and are left unguarded. They hatch in three to four weeks, and the young soon move into deeper waters. The mating act of burbot is of special interest. Males and females, as McPhail and Lindsey describe it, "come together and form a globular mass of squirming bodies." These communal ecstasies may result in the ejection and fertilization of a million or more eggs.

Why is the burbot a freshwater fish in a totally marine order of 482 species worldwide, except for the anadromous or freshwater tomcod? This raises an interesting question. Why does this member of Order Gadiformes alone dwell in a freshwater habitat? It is a yet-unsolved evolutionary puzzle.

By all accounts, however, Nature did anglers no great favour in consigning the burbot to fresh waters. Few species, other than the piscivorous bowfin which it resembles, have drawn more disdain than this creature. Some consider the flesh insipid. Yet some claim that burbot, especially from very cold waters, are firm and well flavoured, and make excellent eating. It's all a matter of taste. The burbot does rate well for its superior liver oil, however, especially for its content of vitamins A and D. It also makes very acceptable food for dogs.

The burbot occurs throughout a wide Eurasian and North American range. In Canada it is present in all provinces except Newfoundland, Nova Scotia and Prince Edward Island. Its habitat also includes the drainage systems of Hudson Bay, and the Mackenzie and Yukon rivers.

Sturgeon & Paddlefish
ORDER ACIPENSERIFORMES

Sturgeon and their distant, lesser-known relatives, the paddlefish, are among the largest and most ancient of bony fish. Recognizable fossils of both species date to the Cretaceous period that ended around sixty-four million years ago—about when dinosaurs, which had dominated the earth for a hundred and fifty million years, became extinct.

Sturgeon and paddlefish inhabit the temperate fresh waters of the Northern Hemisphere, although some sturgeon spend part of their lives at sea and return to fresh water to spawn. Paddlefish dwell only in fresh water.

Order Acipenseriformes consists of two families, with twenty-four species in the sturgeon family (Acipenseridae) and two species in the paddlefish family (Polyodontidae). Seven of the sturgeon species occur in North America, five in Canadian waters. One of the two species of paddlefish occurs only in the United States, the other only in China.

THE STURGEON FAMILY
Acipenseridae

Sturgeon have two distinguishing characteristics: their long almost scaleless body, supported by a largely cartilaginous skeleton; and the unique, prominent, shield-like plates which partially cover the thick, tough skin of their back and sides. Conspicuous, too, are the long shark-like tail—the upper lobe curves far beyond the lower, and has rhombic ganoid scales —and the long, conical snout. In front of the toothless mouth are four barbels which serve as sensory organs for locating food.

Sturgeon—in fresh, brackish or saltwater environments—are bottom-feeders. They live primarily on insect larvae, molluscs, worms, small crustaceans and a variety of aquatic vegetation. This they scoop up from the mud with their long, underslung, protrusible lips and ingest with their suctorial mouth. If this seems a slim diet for such large fish, remember that the blue whale—the largest of the cetaceans—lives almost exclusively on small, shrimp-like crustaceans known as *krill*.

Sturgeon are slow-growing, take many years to reach sexual maturity (up to twenty years in some species), and live very long lives. A sturgeon's age, according to Dr. Peter B. Moyle, "is determined by taking cross sections of fin rays or spines and counting the number of rings visible, on the assumption that a new ring is laid down every year."

The five species of sturgeon occurring in Canadian waters are lake sturgeon (*Acipenser fulvescens*), a freshwater form found over a wide range from Quebec to Alberta, and northward to the Hudson and James Bay areas; Atlantic sturgeon (*Acipenser oxyrhynchus*), an anadromous form found in the St. Lawrence River and in some eastern seaboard areas; white sturgeon (*Acipenser transmontanus*), a Pacific species present in both anadromous and strictly freshwater forms in British Columbia; green sturgeon (*Acipenser medirostris*), found infrequently on the east and west coasts of Vancouver Island and rarely in the Fraser and Skeena rivers; and shortnose sturgeon (*Acipenser breviros-trum*), an Atlantic anadromous species which in Canada occurs only in the St. John River, New Brunswick.

The white sturgeon is thought to be the largest North American freshwater fish. It sometimes grows to enormous sizes; one weighing 1800 pounds (816.48 kg) was caught in the Fraser River. Others, such as the shortnose sturgeon, grow only to about 33 inches (83.82 cm) with weights of up to about 10 pounds (4.54 kg). The lake sturgeon is probably the second largest North American freshwater fish. A fish taken in 1922 from Lake Superior holds the record; it was nearly 8 feet (2.44 m) long and weighed 310 pounds (140.62 kg). The 2860 pound (1297.3 kg) beluga sturgeon (*Huso huso*) netted in Russia's Volga River, also in 1922, may hold the unbeaten world record.

Sturgeon have played an interesting part in human affairs for many years. In medieval times they were an important source of food, and even in those days gourmets and other venturesome cooks found ways to change or improve on things. They discovered, for example, that they could dress the flesh so that in texture and flavour it resembled chicken, pork or—if preferred—lamb! Later, when Europeans discovered Russian caviar, the roe gained immediate popularity, particularly in royal circles. Caviar producers have never looked back. Possibly the world's choicest caviar comes from the roe of the Russian beluga sturgeon (*Huso huso*)—a fish of the Volga and Caspian seas that reaches weights of more than 2000 pounds (907.2 kg).

In England, where sturgeon are known as "royal fish," a royal decree of Edward II still stands as (updated) law: "The King shall have the wreck of the sea throughout the land, whale and the great sturgeon . . . except in certain places privileged by the King." This inspired the English writer George Herbert to write whimsically:

The sturgeon belongs to the King,
And if in some desolate chasm
You feloniously catch one or two on a string
You must see that His Majesty has 'em.

Stephen Downes writes in *The New Compleat Angler* of the 1933 experience of Alexander Allen. While fishing in the Towy River in Wales, Mr. Allen accidentally hooked a 338 pound (153.32 kg) sturgeon; he could subdue the monster only by smashing its head with a boulder. Then the trouble began. By terminating the sturgeon's life, Mr. Allen had broken the ancient law. Discussions with representatives of the Crown followed and Mr. Allen, although not sequestered for his "crime," was obliged to relinquish his catch—for which he received the princely sum of fifty shillings!

The lake sturgeon is the most commercially valuable of the five species inhabiting Canadian waters. But these have been controversial fish. Up until the mid-1860s their market value was so low that many caught were killed and thrown back into the water. Because of their large size, they destroyed nets used to catch smaller species such as lake trout and whitefish; this deepened contempt for them. Some were used as fertilizer or animal food. Scott and Crossman write in *Freshwater Fishes of Canada* that sturgeon were "even stacked like cord wood on the wood dock at Amherstburg, Ont., and used to fire the boilers of steamboats plying the Detroit River." Later it was found that the lake sturgeon's skin would tan into a good quality leather, and that the boiled carcass produced a liquid suitable as a paint base. Then it emerged that the swim bladder contained isinglass, a clear, pure gelatin necessary for clarifying beer and wine, and for the setting of jams and jellies. That wasn't all. The isinglass also proved effective for waterproofing fabrics and cementing pottery. Happily, however, technology came to the rescue when researchers developed an isinglass substitute from Irish moss and seaweeds, making the swim bladders commercially unnecessary.

Few anglers fish for sturgeon. They are difficult to locate and do not respond well to baited hooks or other lures. Those who seek them generally use handlines, spinning gear or, at times, spears. Commercial fishers frequently find them trapped in gill-nets. Now and again sturgeon reportedly jump clear of the water and land in an angler's boat—a type of aquatic acrobatics not to be encouraged!

The flesh of most sturgeon is of acceptable table quality when fresh or smoked, but it calls for considerable skill in preparation. There is also a market demand for the roe of some species, which is processed as caviar.

The status of sturgeon in Canadian waters is closely monitored by COSEWIC. In some areas stocks are relatively secure, but in other areas declines continue.

As evolution continues many forms of life disappear and new forms emerge—the passenger pigeon is now extinct, for example, but a new form of stickleback has emerged in a small Vancouver Island lake. Humans have demonstrated their ability to hasten the demise every day of enormous numbers of living creatures. Well within our reach is the termination of at least two species of sturgeon—the shortnose sturgeon (*Acipenser brevirostrum*) and the green sturgeon (*Acipenser medirostris*)—living relics of ancestors that roamed the Earth's waters millions of years ago.

Need we let this happen?

Lake sturgeon
(Acipenser fulvescens)

"Sturgeons," observed the late Dr. Vadim Vladykov in his treatise on *Acipenser fluvescens*, "are the Leviathans and Methuselahs of fresh-water Fish."

Perhaps Dr. Vladykov indulged himself a little in making such a comparison, for although Acipenseriformes evolved long before *Homo sapiens* appeared, none of the sturgeon species has ever managed to attain Methuselah's alleged 969 years.

The longevity record for the North American lake sturgeon appears to be a fish weighing 208 pounds (94.35 kg) and estimated to be 154 years old. It was caught in 1953 in Lake of the Woods, Ontario. Scott and Crossman write that it must have been born in 1801, four years before the Battle of Trafalgar! As for Leviathan, Vladykov was closer to the mark. A fish caught in Lake Superior in 1922 was 7 feet, 11 inches (2.42 m) long and weighed 310 pounds (140.62 kg)!

Lake sturgeon in Canada are less abundant than in earlier years. They occur in many Quebec lakes and rivers including the St. Lawrence, all Great Lakes and most of their drainages, waters

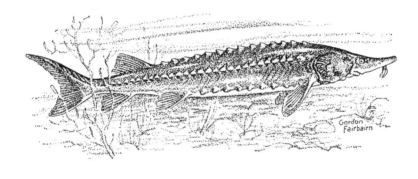

LAKE STURGEON

draining into Hudson Bay and James Bay, and some lakes and rivers in Manitoba, Saskatchewan and Alberta. Their presence in the Northwest Territories and Labrador has not been confirmed. Although this is a freshwater species, during the autumn rainy season some populations descend to brackish waters. These are temporary migrations; shortly afterwards they return to fresh water.

The lake sturgeon's colour changes with size. Juveniles are buff or reddish, commonly with dark grey or black blotches on the snout, back and sides. Adult lake sturgeon are olive brown to grey on the back and sides, and white on the ventral surface of the head and body.

Lake sturgeon, which reach sexual maturity only in their twelfth to twentieth year, spawn every two or three years. In the spring and early summer, preceded by the males, they leave the lakes and migrate up streams to areas with a fast flow of water and bottoms covered with stones, gravel or other detritus. These areas are sometimes at the foot of falls where the tumbling water may be 2 to 20 feet (0.61 to 6.10 m) deep. Sturgeon sometimes remain in lakes to spawn, choosing rocky, shallow sites with strong wave action. They make no nests but release their sticky eggs—dark-coloured and up to $1/8$ inch (0.32 cm) in diameter— randomly over a period of several days. Eggs may number in the hundreds of thousands, depending on the size of the female. They hatch in about a week.

"Many observations," write Scott and Crossman, "of sturgeon rolling near the bottom and then leaping completely out of the water to fall back with a considerable splash and noise have been recorded during the spawning or the prespawning season."

Lake sturgeon are still a commercially valuable species, especially in their eastern range. Anglers also seek them, wherever laws permit, perhaps more for their sporting value than for their edibility. Their flesh is inclined to be rich and oily, but is pleasant when smoked. The eggs make excellent caviar.

Atlantic sturgeon
(Acipenser oxyrhynchus)

Atlantic sturgeon, also known as sea sturgeon, occur on the Atlantic coast from Labrador to Florida. They spend part of their lives at sea, frequently migrating long distances back and forth before returning to fresh water to spawn. Vladykov records that an individual tagged in 1945 at Kamouraska, Quebec, was recaptured eight years later on the south coast of Newfoundland. Three other fish tagged and freed in 1947—one near Isle aux Coudres, the others near Kamouraska—were retaken a year later near Halifax, Nova Scotia, after travelling about 870 miles (1400 km)!

This species is the second largest member of the Acipenseridae family occurring in North American waters. Only the sometimes anadromous white sturgeon of the Pacific is larger. The largest Atlantic sturgeon on record was taken in 1924 off the estuary of the St. John River, New Brunswick. The female was 14 feet (4.27 m) long and weighed 811 pounds (367.87 kg).

The Atlantic sturgeon has a typical appearance for its family. It differs in coloration, however. The blue-black of its head and dorsal surface fade on the sides. The undersides of the body and head are white.

Although much remains to be learned of the species' life history, it is known that sexually mature fish in their Canadian range move from the sea into rivers in late spring. They are thought to spawn when the water temperature reaches about 56° F (13.33° C). In Quebec waters, according to Vladykov, spawning extends from early May to early July. Females randomly scatter the eggs, light to dark brown and $1/12$ to $1/10$ inch (0.21 to 0.25 cm) in diameter. Typically viscid, they adhere to vegetation and bottom detritus. Vladykov writes that one specimen of 352 pounds (159.67 kg) had 3,755,764 eggs in her 91 pound (41.28 kg) ovaries!

Atlantic sturgeon are of little importance as game fish. They put up a fierce struggle when taken on light tackle, however, calling for great skill in capturing them. This species, no longer plentiful in its native waters, is not significant in its commercial fishery; those caught are usually marketed in smoked form. Limited quantities of roe are processed into caviar, which is considered to be of high quality.

White sturgeon
(Acipenser transmontanus)

Scotland's Loch Ness has its Nessie, British Columbia's Lake Okanagan has its Ogopogo, and somewhere in brackish West

Coast waters there must be an equally elusive white sturgeon whose size would bring similar worldwide fame. If it exists, it would have to outweigh the 1387 pound (629.14 kg) fish captured in the Fraser River in 1897 near New Westminster—thus far the undisputed champion. A record specimen taken at Astoria, at the mouth of the Columbia River in Oregon, in 1892 weighed 1900 pounds (861.84 kg). The really big *Acipenser transmontanus*, however, is out there somewhere. When discovered—and hopefully allowed to live!—it, too, will become legend.

White sturgeon are the largest North American freshwater fish. Their classification as freshwater fish may seem somewhat contradictory, for they spend most of their lives in river estuaries and sometimes make extensive saltwater journeys. But they are mostly anadromous; when mature they migrate, sometimes far inland, to spawn. Some populations, on the other hand, spend their lives in fresh water.

White sturgeon occur only on the North American side of the Pacific Ocean. Their range extends from Mexico to the Gulf of Alaska. In Canadian waters they inhabit only two river systems. One is the Fraser River and its numerous tributaries such as Harrison River, Lower Pitt River, Williams Lake, Stuart Lake, Takla Lake and Stellako River. The other system includes the Columbia River above Revelstoke, Kootenay Lake, Kootenay River and possibly Okanagan Lake.

A typical white sturgeon is characterized by a body and snout that are more rounded than in other sturgeon. Their caudal fin is heterocercal; its upper lobe is longer and more pointed than the lower lobe. In other significant respects it has a typical sturgeon appearance. Why it is called white is open to question, however, for its predominant colouring is grey. Moyles suggests that the name may refer to its pale flesh compared to that of another Pacific species, the green sturgeon. The body colour of young white sturgeon is a lighter grey.

Age of sexual maturity varies and is different in each sex. Fraser River males are thought to spawn first at eleven to twenty-two years, females at twenty-six to thirty-four years. When ready to spawn, sturgeon migrate upstream and spawn during May and June (mid-March to early June in southern waters). Little is known of their spawning habits. It is believed that parent fish release eggs and sperm randomly on gravel or rocky bottoms in deep rapids or at the foot of falls. The number of eggs may range from about a million to as many as three or four million, depending on the size of the female. The eggs are believed to hatch in about two weeks. It is also believed that adult fish return to the estuaries soon after spawning. White sturgeon are commercially valuable; the flesh is flavoursome and the eggs can become above-average caviar.

White sturgeon—being large, strong and tenacious—perform vigorously when caught on sports fishing gear. COSEWIC classifies the species as vulnerable.

Green sturgeon
(Acipenser medirostris)

In the sturgeon world, this species is reminiscent of the tale of the beauty and the beast. While it has most of the ancient, fascinating anatomical characteristics of other members of the family, it is a dead loser (from a human point of view) when it comes to the edibility of its flesh or its eggs. To be specific, its flesh—once thought to be poisonous (it isn't)—is dark, exudes what most people find a disagreeable odour and has an objectionable flavour. But *Acipenser medirostris* is not aware of this and goes on its way, abandoned and disdained by most commercial fishermen and anglers.

Green sturgeon, which are less common than white sturgeon, are found in Pacific coastal regions of both Asia and North America. In North America their range extends from Mexico to the Bering Sea. In Canadian waters they occur off Kyuquot Sound on the west coast of Vancouver Island, and in the Fraser and Skeena rivers.

Very little is known about this species. It is believed to migrate from estuarine waters in fall and winter, and to spawn in the spring. Average size is thought to be 50 to 100 pounds (22.68 to 45.36 kg), although there are references to weights of up to 350 pounds (158.76 kg). It is commonly called green sturgeon because of the olive green colour of its body.

Green sturgeon have limited commercial or sporting value. COSEWIC classifies this species as vulnerable.

Shortnose sturgeon
(Acipenser brevirostrum)

The shortnose sturgeon, native to Canada only in New Brunswick's St. John River and its estuary, occurs in eastern coastal waters as far south as the St. Johns River, Florida. This smallest of all North American sturgeon seldom exceeds 36 inches (91.44 cm) at maturity. The smallest on record, at 7.3 inches (18.54 cm), was found in North Carolina waters in 1963. The largest on record, weighing 52 pounds (23.59 kg), was taken from the Bay of Fundy in 1975.

This species is dark brown to almost black on the head, back and sides, and light brown, yellow or white on the sides and belly. Little is known of the early freshwater lives of the young, which are seldom seen. Their growth is slow, as with all members of the Acipenseridae family, and their lifespan can be long. One female examined in the St. John River estuary was sixty-seven years old.

Shortnose sturgeon have a limited role in the commercial and sport fishery, and most are taken when anglers and commercial fishers are seeking other species.

Because it occurs in Canada only in the St. John River and its tributaries, (it is also uncommon in United States waters) COSEWIC is closely monitoring its status. At the moment it is rated as vulnerable.

PADDLEFISH
Polyodontidae

These distant relatives of sturgeon merit mention because of their uniqueness. Also, though now extinct in Canadian waters, they are still present in the United States, principally in the Mississippi River system.

They belong to Order Acipenseriformes, but are of the family Polyodontidae. There are only two living species, the North American *Polyodon spathula,* and *Psephurus gladius,* an inhabitant of the Yangtze River in China.

Paddlefish are of special interest because of their snout, which is broad, flat, long and flexible. This handy attribute makes it easy for them to take in plankton (their main source of food) as they lazily move about open-mouthed. Their gill arches filter this food.

Paddlefish live on the muddy bottoms of lakes and rivers. They spawn in the spring over gravel beds with a flow of water. Growth of the young is believed to be rapid, and at maturity they weigh up to 40 pounds (18.14 kg); fish of 90 pounds (40.82 kg) are sometimes captured. Paddlefish do not respond to any bait offered by anglers. They are caught only by netting or spearing—illegal procedures in some states. Their flesh is of good quality, but the paddlefish is more highly prized for its roe.

Eel

ORDER ANGUILLIFORMES

This order of fish, with its origins in the Cretaceous period some sixty to one hundred and thirty-six million years ago, consists of fifteen families and about seven hundred and thirty-eight species worldwide. With the exception of the Anguillidae family of fifteen species, all are marine and inhabit sub-tropical and tropical seas and oceans.

The Anguillidae family is represented in North Atlantic waters by two freshwater species, the American eel and the European eel. Until recently these were accepted as one species, but it is now believed that the American eel and the European eel are distinct. Both are catadromous; in other words, although born in salt water, they migrate to fresh water where they live out most of their lives and then return to salt water to spawn.

The marine families include such well-known species as conger eels, moray eels and the burrow-living garden eels. Some species are found at great depths. One—the snubnose parasitic eel—is often found at nearly 6000 feet (1828.8 m) and is known at times to live at depths of more than 8000 feet (2438.4 m).

Eels are not to be confused with saltwater and freshwater lampreys which, although also snake-like in appearance, belong to a different order, Petromyzontiformes. Lampreys are sometimes wrongly called "lamprey eels."

Eels have fascinated mankind for more than two thousand years. Strange and wonderful is the mystique that has been built around them, and especially around the catadromous Anguillidae family in North America.

Perhaps the first to write about the catadromous eels was Aristotle (384–322 BC). He helped to promote the theory that because no sexual organs were apparent, eels reproduced by means of "spontaneous generation." How this was accomplished inspired the imagination of other classical authors. Among the theories advanced were that eels developed from horsehairs (of stallions!) that found their way into streams or from worms that inhabited mud, or that they were offspring of intercourse between eels and snakes (but which of the two gave birth was not recorded!) There was, as well, a belief (as Izaak Walton described it—a belief he wisely attributed to "others") that spontaneous generation occurred "as pearls are made of glutinous dew-drops, which are condensed by the sun's heat—so eels are born of a particular dew, falling in the month of May or June on the banks of some particular ponds or rivers (adapted by nature for that end) which in a few days are, by the sun's heat, turned into eels."

There were even more theories. Defenders of each, as in witchcraft, tried to outdo each other. There was one belief that eels had a particular fondness for dead human flesh!

The different theories held sway in various degrees of belief and disbelief until 1774 when a Professor Mondini of the University of Bologna identified, through microscopic study, the ovaries of females, and a scientist by the name of Syrski, who was director of the Museum of Trieste, by the same means identified testes of males.

This was followed by the exciting discovery in the Strait of Messina, between Italy and Sicily, of hitherto unknown tiny, leaf-shaped, transparent fish. One can but speculate on the discussions which then took place within the scientific community. Eventually scientists agreed that the creatures were in a state of metamorphosis and that they were, indeed, immature eels. They were given the name *Leptocephalus brevirostris*.

For a time it was thought that eels lived and bred in Italian waters. This was proved wrong when Johannes Schmitt, a Danish biologist and oceanographer, found the same creatures in the North Atlantic between Iceland and Scotland. The highly imaginative Schmitt, determined to solve the puzzle of the eels, gained the support of the Danish government and took a calculated gamble. He pursued his investigations, first by way of the Faeroe Islands, the Azores and Newfoundland, and finally to the Antilles and beyond to the northern edge of the Sargasso Sea—a vast area of highly saline, stagnant water southwest of Bermuda where an unending mat of vegetation gently sways over the abysses two to three miles (3.22 to 4.83 km) in depth. There, after eighteen years of determined and amazingly dedicated search, and that at depths of about 350 feet (106.68 m), he brought up great quantities of newly hatched larvae of eels in his plankton nets.

A discovery of major importance had been made, but it created questions that were even more perplexing—questions that even to this day have not been full answered.

What strange compulsions or involuntary influences cause these creatures, known as *leptocephali*—when barely one inch (2.54 cm) in length, flat, transparent and looking like little willow leaves—to undertake their incredible mass migration, 2000 to 3000 miles (3218.6 to 4827.9 km) north, to freshwater rivers and lakes in North America and Europe, where they live out most of their lives?

Although they are different species (the most significant distinction being that the American eel has 103 to 111 vertebrae and the European eel has 110 to 119 vertebrae), why does one species migrate to waters on the North American side of the Atlantic, and the other species to waters on the European side? And why, when mature fish, do they migrate back to the Sargasso Sea to spawn, never to be seen again?

The astonishing thing about the migration north is that, despite the fact that the European-bound leptocephali have three times farther to travel than do the North American-bound lepto-cephali, both migrants, under the influence of the ocean's currents, arrive at their freshwater destinations with the same growth attainment of 3 to 4 inches (7.6 to 10 cm), at the same larval stage, and at the correct period for the metamorphosis that will adapt them to freshwater life!

As Brian Curtis writes in *The Life Story of Fish*, "it is a beautiful arrangement of variables into an equation in timing, in which the speed of the Gulf Stream, the distance from the Sargasso Sea, and the length of time required to reach the stage of metamorphosis, have all been perfectly correlated."

At this early stage of their lives the young eels bear little resemblance to the appearance they will later assume. In fact, while they have now developed the outline shape of adults, they are still quite flat and transparent. Fins have also developed. Little black eyes and the dark outline of their mouths are more noticeable. Their mouth also contains many teeth.

Just before entry into fresh water, which is generally a mass movement during May and June, there occurs a gradual loss of their transparency as a grey pigmentation spreads over their bodies and they become more cylindrical in form. Now they are known as *elvers*. But then another interesting thing happens: for some reason not all of the young go upstream. Many choose to remain permanently in the brackish waters of the tidal marshes, harbours and the like, and in some coastal areas where there is a thick growth of eelgrass.

And this, too, is interesting: although it is still difficult to distinguish males from females, it is believed that of the young eels that do migrate upstream, by far the greatest number are females.

What drives the elvers often many miles inland (in Canada as far inland as the Great Lakes and in Europe as far east as the Baltic Sea!) is a mystery, but the migratory urge is so compelling, so insistent, that dams, waterfalls, weirs and other obstacles offer only temporary barriers. In their determination to leave main rivers and lakes to reach landlocked lakes and ponds they will journey (mostly on warm, dark nights) over fields wet from rain or dew, through marshes and underground channels, and even across roads on stormy nights.

Dr. Vladykov wrote that in certain rivers in Europe "ribbons of elvers, formed by millions of individuals, several miles long, about 91 cm (3 feet) wide and some 45 cm (18 inches) in depth were observed. These runs can last many days." Somewhat the same phenomenon occurs in North American waters.

The young elvers grow slowly and during this time they are eaten in great quantities by game fish. When they become larger the situation is reversed and they become exceedingly voracious. They have a highly developed sense of smell and will eat all kinds of animal food, particularly fish and their eggs, snails, and crustaceans, but not, as a rule, decaying or dead matter.

Eels are highly sensitive to light intensity and so are most active during hours of darkness; very dark, warm nights mark the peak of their activity. During daylight hours they generally remain hidden in mudholes, as they do throughout the winter months when they become torpid and inactive. Because nearly three-quarters of their intake of oxygen is through the skin, eels are able to live out of the water for long periods. Carbon dioxide is excreted through the skin when the animal is out of water, but in water it is excreted through the gills.

Eels remain in fresh water for many years—some for as long as ten years—and grow to lengths of up to 4 feet (121.92 cm) and occasionally to weights of more than 7 pounds (3.17 kg).

Their coloration is variable and is strongly influenced by light changes. Yellow eels have completed their northern migration and are now residents of estuarial or freshwater areas; silver eels have completed their estuarial or freshwater stay and have now reached the time to return to the spawning grounds. Their outward migration takes place in the fall, mostly at night, and in great numbers.

The eels' departure from the waters of North America and Europe and their return to the Sargasso Sea is shrouded in mystery, for once they have left they are rarely seen again. But whether all spawn in the Sargasso Sea is now open to question. Dr. J.G. Eales in *The Eel Fisheries of Eastern Canada* suggests that this may not be so. This puzzling aspect of their life history has yet to be resolved. In any case, it is estimated that each female will randomly spawn between ten and twenty million eggs. These, once released and fertilized by males, gradually float to the surface where, soon afterwards, they hatch.

Exhausted after their long sea journey and the intensity of their spawning, the parent fish die, their cycle of life completed. According to Dr. Eales, the entire North American population could be sustained by the spawning of adults from only a few freshwater populations.

Such, then, is a fragment of the story of freshwater eels—as strange a story as any to be found in the whole realm of nature.

American eel
(Anguilla rostrata)

This species resembles all eels in having a long, snake-like body. Caudal, dorsal and anal fins run continuously along the dorsal surface and around the tail to the rear of the anus on the belly. It has no pelvic fins. On each side of the paired pectoral fins is a small gill opening, and the nostril lies forward of the snout. The American eel has a pointed jaw, the lower part projecting beyond the snout. Its mouth contains many small, needle-like teeth. The tiny scales on its head and body are not apparent to the human touch because of their size and because of the thick layer of mucus covering them. This, as Vladykov observed, inspired the common expression "slippery as an eel."

Freshwater American eels occur in Canada in rivers and lakes and their drainages, from the tip of Labrador south throughout Newfoundland, the Maritime provinces, Quebec and much of eastern and southern Ontario. Some are said to have entered the Great Lakes by way of the Welland Canal.

Eels in the yellow and silver stages are fished commercially, especially in the St. Lawrence River. Smaller fisheries operate in the Maritimes.

This species can hardly be considered a sports fish, but when taken on light tackle they provide a good deal of squirming action. Many people consider eels a gourmet food, especially when smoked or pickled. Most of the Canadian catch is shipped to foreign markets.

Gar

ORDER SEMIONOTIFORMES

These elongate, armour-plated creatures, once widely distributed throughout the world, are living fossils of an order that began during the Cretaceous period. They now occur only in eastern Canada, central and eastern United States, and Central America.

They have survived throughout the millennia, changing little in appearance or characteristics. In this they resemble other primitive species such as sturgeon, lampreys, paddlefish and bowfins.

The order has seven living species, two of which occur in Canadian waters—the longnose gar (*Lepisosteus osseus*) and the spotted gar (*Lepisosteus oculatus*). COSEWIC rates the spotted gar in Canada as vulnerable.

Gars are pike-like in appearance but can be distinguished by their long, pointed snouts and their large, hard, diamond-shaped ganoid scales. In earlier times First Nations peoples used gar scales as arrowheads. Farmers often used whole gar skins to cover their wooden ploughshares in the days before steel ploughs.

Gars have a single dorsal fin at the far end of the body, just ahead of the rounded tail fin. Markings vary in different species, but all have roundish dark spots on the tail and some also have spots on the fins.

Like other fish with vascularized air bladders (which serve as extra lungs), they can thrust their long snouts out of the water, expel the stale air in their bladder and gulp in a fresh supply. This supplementary air supply permits them to live in stagnant water with a low oxygen content and to live out of water for fairly long periods.

To come upon gars in the silence of a canoe's passage through still waters is to enjoy the thrill of seeing the ancient past entering the present. There, sometimes just inches below the surface, you can observe them floating motionless or cruising slowly, waiting for some unsuspecting food fish to come within range. They make their attack on a quarry in a sudden, swift thrust of their long, lean bodies and wide open beak-like mouths. The victim has little chance of escape.

Gars have little appeal to anglers in Canada. Ordinary fishing methods are futile, of course, for it is almost impossible for a hook to penetrate the hard bones of the mouth. In any case, the mass of razor-sharp teeth can quickly cut through the stoutest line. In some parts of the United States, where they can threaten the young of sports fish, anglers help to reduce their numbers by catching them in wire snares.

In Canada gars are rarely (if ever) used for food, mostly because of the difficulty of removing the hard, heavily scaled outer skin. They are said to be tasty, however, when fried, roasted or baked with a stuffing. Smoked gar is popular in some parts of the United States. The eggs of these fish are poisonous.

Although gars have no significant sporting or commercial value, they have an important part in our aquatic fauna and are fascinating to those interested in fish behaviour.

Longnose gar
(Lepisosteus osseus)

Spotted gar
(Lepisosteus oculatus)

Longnose gars are spring spawners. They deposit their small, dark eggs in shallow water, generally over aquatic vegetation; the eggs hatch in about eight days and the young almost immediately take up an independent and frequently solitary life.

Growth is rapid for the first few months; at the end of the first season they may reach 8 inches (20.32 cm). At maturity they can reach 3 feet (91.44 cm). The range of the longnose gar in Canada includes the lower St. Lawrence River and all Great Lakes except Superior. It occurs also in Quebec's Eastern Townships and numerous Ontario waters as far west as Lake Temiskaming.

This species is dark green on the back, light green on the upper sides, silvery on the lower sides and white on the belly. The anal, dorsal and tail fins are yellowish with pronounced green or black spots. The young, often beautifully coloured, are readily identified by a broad, dark wavy band running along the lateral line.

The now rare spotted gar—the only other representative of the Lepisosteidae family in Canadian waters—is slightly different in colour from the longnose gar; it is olive green on the back, grey-green on the sides and grey on the belly. It also has a shorter beak. It is predacious, as is the longnose gar, and eats large quantities of other fish. At maturity it reaches about 2 feet (61 cm). Its range in this country is limited to the Great Lakes basin.

Lamprey & Hagfish
ORDERS PETROMYZONTIFORMES AND MYXINIFORMES

A friend of mine, a distinguished fisheries scientist, said of fish that "to know them is to love them." But it wasn't all true love, for he drew the line at the anadromous and freshwater lampreys and saltwater hagfish. To most people, he admitted, these are not lovable creatures.

Lampreys and hagfish are the closest living relatives of the first backboned animals to evolve on earth—the small and heavily armoured fish known as *ostracoderms* in the class Agnatha.

Lampreys, then not much larger than a minnow, evolved during the Ordovician period between 450 and 500 million years ago—more than 250 million years before the Jurassic period and the rise of the dinosaurs. Complete skeletons of their relatives found in ancient rocks show that, at that time, their heads and bodies had a protective covering of large, bony plates. This—despite the small size of the fish—must have made them formidable looking indeed. They were jawless and fed on minute sedimentary organisms which they ingested through their underslung, suctorial mouths. The other Agnathan was the jawless saltwater hagfish, of which only one possible fossilized remain has been found. The line of succession is not clear, however. Most paleoichthyologists now believe that the hagfish is the most primitive of all living vertebrates, which would put lampreys in second place.

With the passing of the millennia other Agnathans evolved and became extinct. Then emerged the Chondrichtheys (jawed, cartilage fish such as sharks and rays), and later the Teleostomi. The Teleostomi, which introduced the "age of fishes," embraces most of the species we know today.

Lampreys, members of the Petromyzontidae family, occur throughout the Northern Hemisphere and in parts of the Southern Hemisphere.

The ocean-dwelling hagfish, members of the Myxinidae family, occur in temperate zones.

Nelson recognizes forty-one extant species of lampreys, eleven of which occur in Canadian waters. Seven of these are parasitic, most notably the anadromous sea lamprey (*Petromyzon marinus*), which once nearly destroyed the Great Lakes commercial fishery. Even today it requires intensive and costly control measures. Two of the eleven species were discovered as recently as 1992—one in Greece and the other on Vancouver Island.

Of the forty-three species of hagfish, two occur in Canadian waters—one Atlantic (*Myxine glutinosa*) and the other Pacific (*Eptatretus stouti*).

All lampreys die after spawning.

Lampreys
(Class Cephalaspidomorphi, Order Petromyzontiformes)

Lampreys are a far cry from being game fish, but if you chance to hook into a large one, it will certainly be a rod-bouncing experience. Some people consider them gourmet food. An unconfirmed story claims that King John died from indulging in too many lampreys at one sitting. There is no record of the recipe or method of preparation, which may be just as well.

Lampreys are scaleless and eel-like in appearance. They have one or more separate dorsal fins but lack the paired fins that characterize most other fish. They also have three eyes. Two on the back sides of the head are used for vision. The third, a pineal eye, is located behind the single nostril on top of the head; it has a retina and is capable of perceiving light. There are seven external gill openings on each side of the head.

The parasitic lampreys, including the anadromous sea lamprey, which reaches lengths of around 34 inches (86.36 cm) are: the Pacific lamprey (*Lampetra tridentata*), around 27 inches (68.58 cm); the river lamprey (*Lampetra ayresi*), around 12 inches (30.48 cm); the chestnut lamprey (*Ichthyomyzon castaneus*), around 15 inches (38.1 cm); the silver lamprey (*Ichthyomyzon unicuspis*), around 13 inches (33.02 cm); and the newly discovered Vancouver lamprey (*Lampetra macrostoma*), around 12 inches (30.48 cm).

The American brook lamprey (*Lampetra appendix*), western brook lamprey (*Lampetra richardsoni*) and northern brook lamprey (*Ichthyomyzon fossor*) are nonparasitic. Beamish describes the lampreys resident in two lakes on Vancouver Island, however, as posing "a definite threat to freshwater fish."

The dominant anatomical feature of the parasitic species is their underslung suctorial mouth, which is heavily ringed with strong, rasping teeth. The tongue is also covered with sharp, horny "teeth" and operates like a piston. When they attach themselves to the bodies of larger fish such as lake trout, they rasp a hole and draw out blood and other body juices. Lampreys are assisted in this procedure by an anticoagulant saliva that keeps the victim's blood flowing, and by juices that help to soften the flesh and aid digestion. They may remain attached to a fish until it dies, which could take several days. Fish that manage to shake free of a lamprey's grasp generally carry ugly, circular scars.

The most predacious of all lampreys is the Atlantic sea lamprey.

The populations now common in the Great Lakes probably adapted to fresh water in Lake Ontario. In postglacial times, this lake was a brackish gulf that freshened as the St. Lawrence River rapids gradually rose and cut off the salt water. Geologically speaking, this happened in recent times. Their migration beyond Lake Ontario was blocked by the force and height of Niagara Falls, but when the original Welland Canal was completed in 1829, a new migration route opened. Not until 1921, nearly a century later, did scientists become aware of the lampreys' presence in Lake Erie. The lampreys quickly moved on to Lake Huron and Lake Michigan. Their presence in Lake Superior was undiscovered until 1945.

Hagfish
(Class Myxini, Order Myxiniformes)

Hagfish are also known as *slime eels*. They commonly reach about 25 inches (63.5 cm); they dwell mainly in deep water and on soft, muddy bottoms, such as substrates of the continental shelf.

Hags, as they are often called, have a highly developed sense of smell which enables them to find their prey, generally dead or dying fish. They have repulsive table manners. They enter the victim's body through its mouth, gills or anus, and consume the intestines first and then the flesh. This continues until nothing is left but skin and bones.

Hagfish sometimes have communal scavenging habits; Hart recorded that "as many as four hagfish have been found in a single dogfish skin." This species often destroys valuable food fish, such as salmon and steelhead trout, captured by deep-sea anglers and in trammel nets of commercial fishers.

Hagfish excel in their ability, when disturbed, to discharge huge amounts of viscous, toxic slime from glands located on both sides of their body. This slime adheres to anything it touches. Being soft-bodied, they can use their suctorial mouth as an anchor to literally tie themselves in an overhand knot to pull flesh from their victims.

Hagfish are considered inedible. Any human who develops an affection for these creatures should immediately consult a psychiatrist—on the other hand, perhaps we should reserve a little affection for these evolutionary relics.

Bowfin
CLASS ACTINOPTERYGII, ORDER AMIIFORMES

T he bowfin, *Amia calva,* is the only existing member of the order Amiiformes. It occurs in Canada in only a small part of the upper St. Lawrence River and Great Lakes, but is present in many eastern United States waters south to the Gulf of Mexico.

This is one of the ancient creatures. In *Fishes of the World,* Nelson writes that "fossil amiids are known from marine and freshwater deposits from North America, Brazil, Europe, Asia, and Saudi Arabia (on the African continental plate); the oldest fossils are of Jurassic age."

This species, the last of a family of several members, is still secure throughout its present range. It can tolerate warm, stagnant water—conditions under which most other species cannot survive.

Anglers frequently catch the bowfin, which puts up a spirited fight, but it is not highly regarded as food.

Bowfin
(Amia calva)

The bowfin is roundish, with a long, spineless dorsal fin which extends over much of the back and almost to the fan-shaped tail fin. It has a very large, broad, naked head. Anterior nostrils are short, barbel-like tubes. The large mouth contains numerous sharp teeth.

Its colour is most frequently described as dark green or brownish green on the back and lighter on the sides and belly; the sides carry lighter-hued, irregular chain-like markings. The male, which is generally much smaller than the female, has a yellow-bordered black spot on the base of the tail. The scales are known as *polygono cycloid,* and are large, soft and fleshy. The average weight of this species is 2 to 3 pounds (0.91 to 1.36 kg).

Bowfins spawn in the spring.

Goldeye & Mooneye
CLASS ACTINOPTERYGII, ORDER OSTEOGLOSSIFORMES

This order of freshwater bony fish consists of six families and about two hundred and seventeen species. All but two species inhabit tropical fresh waters of northern Australia, Africa and Southeast Asia.

The goldeye and mooneye are the two living representatives of the order in North America, and the only members of the freshwater family Hiodontidae.

Both species superficially resemble shad, freshwater herring and whitefish. They are easily distinguishable because they lack an adipose fin, have teeth on the jaws and tongue, and have a dorsal fin located far toward the rear. They are blunt-nosed, deep-bodied and laterally thin. Their large scales are cycloid.

Goldeye
(Hiodon alosoides)

Goldeye occur in Canada in the western fringe of Ontario, Manitoba, Saskatchewan, Alberta, the Northwest Territories and northeastern British Columbia. Scott and Crossman write that an isolated population is present in Ontario and Quebec south of James Bay. At one time their area of greatest abundance was Lake Winnipeg. Catches primarily from that lake, smoke-cured, were once featured as Winnipeg Goldeye in the menus of transcontinental trains. The limited numbers of goldeye still smoke-cured command a high market price.

Goldeye occur in turbid lakes, rivers and other waters. They spawn in the spring. In their book *Fishes of Alberta,* Nelson and Paetz refer to the long migrations sometimes made by this species and write that B.A. Munson "observed downstream movement in one individual of up to about 2000 km in fifteen days"—approximately 1243 miles!

Goldeye are dark blue to blue-green on the back and upper sides, silvery on the lower sides and white on the belly. The large eye is high on the forward part of the head and the iris is a bright golden colour—the reason for its name. When smoked-cured or brined, the fish become bright red or orange.

Goldeye have limited appeal to anglers, although Nelson and Paetz write that they are not given the credit they deserve as good game fish. "When taken on light tackle," they contend, "this fish can provide sport comparable to some species of trout of equivalent size. They will take both wet and dry flies, but most of the goldeye taken by anglers are caught on baits and small spinning lures."

The maximum size of goldeye is about 20 inches (50.8 cm) and their weight averages from 2 to 3 pounds (0.91 to 1.36 kg).

Mooneye
(Hiodon tergisus)

Mooneye have a limited eastern and midwestern Canadian range including Quebec's Nottaway, Ottawa, St. Lawrence and Richelieu rivers; Lake Champlain; part of the lower Great Lakes west to Lake Superior; Lake of the Woods; southern Manitoba; southeastern Saskatchewan north to the North Saskatchewan River; and Alberta north to the Red Deer River.

This species is somewhat similar in appearance to the goldeye; unlike the goldeye it has little potential as a food or sports fish. Smoked and sold as "smoked shiner," is is sometimes used as a substitute for smoked goldeye. It reaches lengths of nearly 18 inches (45.72 cm) and weights of close to 3 pounds (about 1.36 kg).

Shad, Herring & Alewife
ORDER CLUPEIFORMES

This order of primarily marine fish consists of five families and three hundred and fifty-seven species. One of the most widely dispersed orders, it has representatives in most parts of the world except the cold waters of the Arctic and Antarctic. Dr. Alex Peden caught one Pacific herring, however, at the mouth of the Mackenzie River.

The most commercially valuable clupeiform fish are those in the herring family, Clupeidae, which numbers about a hundred and eighty-one species worldwide. Twenty-five species of herring, sardines, shads, alewife and menhaden occur in Canadian and United States salt and fresh waters. In the closely related family Engraulidae, with a hundred and thirty-nine species, there are thirteen species of saltwater anchovies in North American waters.

Four species—each a landlocked form of an anadromous species—occur in Canadian fresh waters: the American shad, blueback herring, alewife and gizzard shad. The food fishery for these species is limited; their economic worth depends primarily upon their value as pet and cattle food, and fertilizers. They are important food for game fish, however, and in some instances provide good sport for anglers.

The saltwater members of this family, on the other hand, are considered the world's most valuable commercial species (in tons landed). This is especially true of the Atlantic and Pacific herring fisheries. Western Atlantic and Eastern European stocks have been seriously overfished, however, and like northern cod are facing extinction. The Pacific herring retain their relatively secure status.

Clupeidae fish range from about 6 to 12 inches (15.24 to 30.48 cm); they are slender and noticeably laterally compressed. The mouth is small to moderate, and a transparent tissue is visible around the eyes. They may be toothed or toothless; all have cycloid scales. An unusual feature in some is that the midline of the belly is compressed to a sharp-edged ridge from which project sharp and somewhat saw-toothed scales. There is no lateral line.

In fresh water they live on plankton, amphipods, small fish and fish eggs. They in turn provide food for larger fish such as lake trout, pike, bass and introduced salmon such as coho. All are spring spawners.

American shad
(Alosa sapidissima)

This species is the largest of the Clupeidae fish occurring in Canadian fresh waters. Its Atlantic range extends from Newfoundland to Florida. It spawns in freshwater streams throughout its coastal range and as far inland as the St. Lawrence and Ottawa rivers. Its Pacific coastal range extends from California—where it was introduced in the early 1870s—north along the British Columbia coast to Alaska and west to the Kamchatka Peninsula. Unlike its Atlantic relative, it spawns mainly in salt water, but spawning runs do occur in the Fraser River and (less abundantly) in Rivers Inlet.

This species is more popular as a game fish in the United States than in Canada. There is a commercial market for it, and in limited quantities its roe is processed as caviar.

Blueback herring
(Alosa aestivalis)

This species is similar in appearance to the alewife (*Alosa pseudoharengus*); it is often difficult to distinguish between them. It occurs in Atlantic coastal waters from Cape Breton Island south to Northern Florida.

The blueback herring spawns in freshwater rivers and streams, generally just above the head of the tide, and in brackish waters. Most of the catch is used to manufacture pet food, although some enters the consumer market in fresh and smoked forms. The flesh is tasty but contains many bones.

Alewife
(Alosa pseudoharengus)

The alewife is a tiny anadromous species of about 6 inches (15.24 cm) inhabiting coastal waters from Newfoundland to North Carolina in great abundance. It occurs inland in Quebec drainages of the St. Lawrence River, and in lakes Ontario, Erie, St. Clair and Huron as well as many smaller inland lakes.

This is one of the most controversial of all species because of its periodic mass dieoffs in the Toronto-Hamilton region of Lake Ontario. For reasons not yet fully understood, during the spring and early summer, enormous numbers of dead or dying bodies drift to shore. The task of cleaning up is always a difficult one.

Although alewife have a limited market appeal in fresh or frozen form, most are processed for pet food.

Gizzard shad
(Dorosoma cepedianum)

Gizzard shad occur in Atlantic coastal waters from New York State south to the Gulf of Mexico and eastern Mexico. Freshwater stocks occur in the St. Lawrence River and Lake Ontario (now rarely), and in lakes Erie, St. Clair and Huron. They are most abundant in Lake Erie.

The gizzard shad is a larger species, averaging about 10 inches (25.4 cm). Its flesh is soft, bony and not particularly appetizing; most fish caught are processed for animal food and fertilizer. It is important food fish for game and predacious species.

Carp, Goldfish, Squawfish, Dace, Shiner & Chub
ORDER CYPRINIFORMES

This order of freshwater fish is the second largest of all vertebrate orders, exceeded in number of species only by the highly diversified saltwater and freshwater Perciformes (sunfish, perch and related species). Cypriniids represent just under 10 percent of all the living fish species known to science.

It is an extraordinary conglomeration, consisting worldwide of about 2662 species. Their greatest diversity is in southeast Asia. The two North American families (Cyprinidae and Catostomidae) are believed to have originated in Asia, from where they dispersed and reached North America, perhaps by way of the Bering Sea.

CARPS AND MINNOWS
Cyprinidae

The Cyprinidae family in Canada consists of minnows, dace, shiners, chubs, squawfish, peamouth, tench, chiselmouth, fallfish, carp and goldfish. The Catostomidae family consists of suckers, redhorses, bigmouth buffalo and quillback.

Most cyprinids, however, are of interest mainly to scientists. The species referred to here are those best known to or most widely used by anglers. Anyone seriously interested in gaining more knowledge of the status or life histories of all freshwater cyprinids should refer to the superbly written and comprehensive accounts in *Freshwater Fishes of Canada* by Scott and Crossman and *Freshwater Fishes of Northwestern Canada and Alaska* by McPhail and Lindsey.

Other "minnow-like" fish referred in this book, but belonging to different orders, are trout-perch (Order Percopsiformes); banded killifish, mummichog, and blackstripe topminnow (Order Cyprinodontiformes). The central mudminnow (Order Esociformes) also has minnow-like characteristics.

Satisfying though it would be to be able to identify all of the species, most anglers and other observers will be content to be able to tell a true minnow from the fry and fingerlings of other fish, particularly game fish. But the problem of identification, even to taxonomists, is often difficult and in some instances it is possible only by minute examination of the pharyngeal teeth in the throat—a job that could challenge the dissecting ability of a dentist.

The following guide will help in distinguishing true minnows from the young of other fish.

- **Trout, charr, grayling, salmon, whitefish, cisco and smelt:** The fry and fingerlings of these fish all have an adipose fin, a fleshy appendage on the back near the tail. The adipose fin is lacking in true minnows.
- **Catfish:** Catfish lack scales and are also characterized by the presence of barbels or "whiskers" on the head and under the chin. They possess an adipose fin.
- **Northern pike, muskellunge and pickerel:** The young of these fish are characterized by the position of

the dorsal fin, which is far back on the body near the tail. The head and jaws are long and the mouth has many sharp teeth.

- **Yellow perch, walleye, and sauger:** All members of this family have two large dorsal fins, the first spiny-rayed. The mouth contains many sharp teeth.
- **Darter:** The smallest members of the perch family are also generally found in areas where minnows are present. They can be distinguished by the presence of two dorsal fins—the first spiny-rayed. The spines are weak, however, and not readily recognized in small specimens. Their pectoral fins are highly developed. Darters move in sudden, fast spurts, and spend most of their time on the bottom.
- **Sunfish (which includes smallmouth bass, largemouth bass, pumpkinseed, bluegill and crappie):** The young of these fish have spiny-rayed dorsal fins and are deep-bodied. True minnows are usually more elongate and slender.
- **Stickleback:** These fish have two to ten isolated dorsal spines in front of the soft-rayed dorsal fin. They are commonly found with true minnows.
- **Sucker:** Suckers can be identified by their protruding snout and fleshy lips that have wrinkle-like folds. the mouth of most species of true minnows is usually terminal.

In at least two respects cyprinids are fairly sophisticated: they have an acute sense of hearing and a well developed sense of smell. Peter B. Moyle in *Inland Fishes of California* writes that the olfactory sense of minnows is important in helping them to avoid predators. If one of their number is attacked by a predator and its skin broken, a special chemical present in the skin is released into the water and acts as a fear stimulant. "When they detect it in the water," he writes, "the minnows immediately go into a protective behavior pattern, usually fleeing or hiding."

There is no uniformity in the behaviour and spawning patterns of minnows or their choice of habitats. For example, while most species spawn over an extended season, some have a relatively short spawning season. Some make elaborate nests and guard their young; some place them under protective covering such as stones. Some lay their eggs in gravel, mud or sand, while others lay their eggs in vegetation. Some are more abundant in big lakes, others in clear, cool streams; some in fast-running water, others in warm, weedy lakes or in boggy ponds. Some live almost entirely on algae and diatoms, some on aquatic insects, larvae and plants. Some eat other small fish, snails and crustaceans, and some will eat all of these foods and anything else that happens along.

Perhaps the most interesting period in the lives of minnows is the time of their spawning, and many are the accounts of their curious behavior. Romeo Mansueti, writing in *Nature* magazine half a century ago, spoke of a series of observations made by Dr. Jacob Reighard. "He described a peculiar ceremonial behavior as a 'deferred combat' between two male creek chubs that were fighting for possession of a nest," Dr. Mansueti wrote. "He observed that, in starting a nest, the male picks up pebbles from one area and carries them short distances against the current before depositing them, finally forming a mound of washed stones with a cavity downstream. The laborious building of the nest and the careful guarding of the eggs are the exclusive tasks of the male. The odd behavior occurs when a strange male approaches the side of the nest where he is joined by the guarding male, whereupon the two fish as a pair swim upstream with great deliberation for a distance of 15 to 20 feet [4.57 to 6.1 m]. In their course they move slowly and swing their tails from side to side in unison, as they keep in step with one another. Dr. Reighard wrote that 'at the end of their course they settle down to the bottom and bring their heads together and finally separate, the owner to return to his nest, his companion to some nearby shelter'. This curious behavior also has been observed in other minnows."

Frank Sawyer, when head keeper of the Officers' Fishing Association water at Netheravon, England, wrote with particular sensitivity about minnows in his delightful book *Keeper of the Stream*:

> I like to watch minnows in March and early April. To me they are very interesting when they congregate. It appears like a rally or an assembly of the tribe, for an initial party may start with a few dozen yet, at the end of an hour or two may swell to ten thousand or more . . . Somehow, I think there must be a superior among these minnows—a commander, like a queen in a swarm of bees, or the leader of a colony of migrating ants. Perhaps in this case it is a king; it is hard to say. What is certain, is that the gathering of the clan is always started by a limited number, who travel about collecting, gradually, what becomes an army . . . I have seen the initial band pause by a big stone until 20 or 30 others of all sizes have come out from beneath it. The same thing has been repeated, by the ever-increasing horde, time and again, up and down the stream, until the assembling has been complete, and the numbers swell from scores to perhaps many thousands. The time of the year has come for them to move. The urge to feed is prevailing, and they know sufficient food is not to be obtained in the side streams for such a mighty throng. With what appear to be one general impulse they all move from spring stream to river. And after they have gone you can search the banks and delve in the mud where, but a few days previously, there were minnows concealed everywhere, now not a single one is to be found. They have gone to places where, in the higher temperature water of the main river, their food is daily becoming more plentiful, and where the gathering for spawning will take place.

The largest concentrations of cyprinids in North America are found in the Mississippi drainage. Every Canadian province, as well as the Northwest Territories and Yukon, has some type of minnow, but most species in Canada occur in British Columbia, Manitoba, Ontario, Quebec and the Maritimes. The minnow with the largest distribution is the lake chub, which is found in every province except Newfoundland as well as in the Northwest Territories, Yukon and Alaska. Some species, however, are found only marginally in Canada. For example, the speckled dace is confined to the Kettle River in extreme south-central British Columbia, and the redside dace is confined to streams tributary to western Lake Ontario.

Many minnows are widely used as bait fish, but their importance depends on their availability and on their keeping qualities. In some areas the use of goldfish, carp and other minnows is forbidden. Most minnows make excellent bait, but not all are able to live long in the confinement of a pail or other container. An exception is the spottail shiner, which is used extensively in northern Ontario. It can be carried for long periods, but only if the water is constantly well-oxygenated and kept at a relatively low temperature. The northern redbelly dace also has a high degree of hardiness.

Anglers using minnows as bait should use only species found in the same lakes or rivers in which they are fishing, and under no circumstances should forage fish such as small perch or suckers be used, or left, in all-trout waters. In some lakes and streams populations of trout have been decimated by forage fish and restoration measures are not always biologically or economically feasible.

Minnows are a vitally important link in the chain of aquatic life. They, in turn, are food for larger fish, as well as for such birds as loons, kingfishers, terns and herons. And what would anglers of all ages do if these little creatures were not available for use as bait for the capture of game fish?

Carp
(Cyprinus carpio)

The carp is an Oriental species that was introduced into waters of Europe and England about five hundred years ago, where it successfully established itself as both a food and a sports fish. It became highly regarded by anglers and, as Izaak Walton writes, "the carp is accounted the water-fox for his cunning."

Stocks introduced into Ontario and New Brunswick in 1880 came from rearing ponds in the United States, where it arrived about 1831. Propagation failed in New Brunswick but the carp later became well established in Quebec, Ontario, Manitoba, Saskatchewan and British Columbia.

The carp is laterally compressed and heavily scaled. While its colour varies greatly, it is typically olive green or brown on the back and sides, and yellowish on the lower sides and belly. Its lower fins are reddish. The head is short, the snout somewhat rounded with an overshot upper jaw; the mouth is toothless and somewhat sucker-like. Two pairs of barbels, one pair more prominent than the other, are present at the mouth.

Carp are schooling fish and inhabit both lakes and rivers, often in waters more favourable to plant life than to other fish life. They spawn in shallow, weedy water in June and July. At that time they often splash and jump noisily near the surface.

The fecundity of the carp is astonishing—a large female can discharge more than two million eggs at one spawning. The eggs are strongly adhesive; once ejected and fertilized they cling to plants, roots and other submerged objects. The young hatch three to twelve days later, depending on water temperature. Neither eggs nor young fish receive parental care. The young fish grow rapidly and reach about 9 inches (22.86 cm) in their first year.

This is a durable species. In our waters the carp has a lifespan of about twenty years. Some caught commercially have weighed up to 50 pounds (22.68 kg).

Juvenile carp make good bait fish, but their use is forbidden in some areas where trout are the main species. Anglers catch carp by still-fishing, using worms or dough balls as bait. They sometimes respond to artificial lures.

In China, parents often hang paper models of carp when a child is born to give it the strength and vigour of this fish.

Goldfish
(Carassius auratus)

Goldfish were brought to North America in the late 1800s from their native Asia, it is believed. In Canada, goldfish occur only in Ontario, with limited numbers in Alberta and British Columbia; they were either deliberately planted or accidentally released by anglers using them as bait fish. Goldfish are widespread throughout the United States.

Goldfish have exerted impressive influence in Oriental art, and in enhancing the ponds of gardens, parklands and even domestic aquariums. They are also important to science, Scott and Crossman write, and "are widely used as laboratory animals . . . in physiological work developing techniques in measuring sensitivity to, and rate of uptake of various dissolved gasses such as carbon dioxide and oxygen, sensitivity to temperature, measuring swimming speeds, and toxicity to industrial wastes. The goldfish is the aquatic counterpart of the guinea pig and rabbit."

Goldfish closely resemble carp. They have similar large scales, but lack the barbels under the chin which characterize carp. In the wild, their colour is generally olive green on the dorsal surface and dull yellowish on the sides, belly, tail and fins. Goldfish bred for aquariums or ponds are generally brilliantly attired in black, yellow, red, gold or yellow markings.

Spring spawners, they seek out weedy shallows where they lay their adhesive eggs on the vegetation. The eggs hatch in three to seven days under favourable conditions. Their diet consists largely of larvae, aquatic insects, worms, small molluscs and vegetation. Mature goldfish, which reach 5 to 10 inches (12.7 to 25.4 cm), hybridize readily with carp. Although juvenile goldfish, especially the more colourful ones, make good bait fish, they should never be used for that purpose except in their own habitat.

Northern squawfish
(Ptychocheilus oregonensis)

This large minnow occurs in coastal drainages from British Columbia to Oregon. It is common in the Nass, Skeena and Fraser river drainages, and also occurs in the Peace River in both British Columbia and Alberta. It is primarily a lake-dweller.

The squawfish is a predatory species, reaching a length of about 18 inches (45.72 cm) in Canadian waters and up to 36 inches (91.44 cm) in some United States waters. It has a long, somewhat compressed body. It has a long, pointed head and a large, toothless mouth. Its cycloid scales are small. The squawfish is usually greenish on the back shading to silvery on the sides. During the spring spawning season, its fins are tinged with red or orange.

Anglers generally consider the squawfish undesirable because it consumes young salmon and trout, although its diet also includes small fish, aquatic and terrestrial insects, plankton and crustaceans. It does not rate highly either as a sports fish or food fish, but it does readily take a lure.

Finescale dace
(Phoxinus neogaeus)

The finescale dace's discontinuous Canadian range includes New Brunswick, southern Quebec, most of Ontario, a small section of southeastern Manitoba and Hudson Bay. It is absent from the rest of Manitoba, occurs again in southwestern Saskatchewan, and occurs spottily in Alberta and a few areas of northeastern British Columbia. It is also found in the Mackenzie River drainages.

The finescale dace inhabits cool, sluggish streams and lakes. It is dark brownish olive on the back and silvery on the sides. A dark band, topped by a silvery yellowish band, runs laterally from the gill cover to the tail. At spawning—thought to take place during June and July—the sides and belly of the male turn yellow or red.

The mature finescale dace reaches about 3 inches (7.62 cm). This species hybridizes with northern redbelly dace. Anglers familiar with the finescale dace rate it as a hardy fish, and because of this and its small size, it makes excellent bait. In Quebec and northern Ontario, according to Scott and Crossman, it is often sold under the name *chub.*

Blacknose dace
(Rhinichthys atratulus)

This stream-dwelling minnow rates highly as a bait fish, and provides important food for trout and larger game fish. In Canada its range stretches from Nova Scotia westward through southern Ontario to the Lake of the Woods and the southern half of Manitoba.

The overall colouring of the blacknose dace is olive green to dark brown, and the sides carry many specialized darkened scales. It spawns in the spring, and is believed to have a lifespan of up to four years. Its average length at maturity is about 2.5 inches (6.35 cm).

Anglers familiar with the blacknose dace and finescale dace rate them as hardy fish; because of this and their small size, they make excellent bait. In Quebec and northern Ontario, according to Scott and Crossman, both dace are often sold under the name "chub."

Nelson and Paetz note that three other species of *Rhinichthys* occur in the Columbia River drainage of British Columbia: leopard dace, *Rhinichthys falcatus,* speckled dace, *Rhinichthys osculus,* and umatilla dace, *Rhinichthys umatilla.* They suggest that *Rhinichthys umatilla,* however, may be a variant of the speckled dace.

Golden shiner
(Notemigonus crysoleucas)

The golden shiner is native to eastern North America, and occurs in Canada from Prince Edward Island westward to Saskatchewan. Anglers consider it one of the best bait fish.

This species inhabits warm, weedy lakes and quiet streams and generally swims in large schools. It is laterally compressed, with a small pointed head and small mouth. It is dark brown or olive green on the back, and brassy on the sides and belly. Spawning over a long period during the summer, it scatters its eggs randomly over vegetation. Its diet consists of plant life, insects, plankton, crustaceans and sometimes smaller fish. The golden shiner in Nova Scotia is said to tolerate salt water for a short time. It reaches a length of up to 10.5 inches (26.67 cm).

The golden shiner is also known as *butterfish, bream, roach* and *eastern golden shiner.*

Lake chub
(Couesius plumbeus)

Lake chub inhabit lakes, rivers and streams throughout their vast range throughout all provinces (except Newfoundland), the Yukon and Northwest Territories, except the Arctic islands. They also occur in Alaska and some midwestern states.

They spawn in spring and early summer, and move to streams together in large numbers (as do rainbow smelt); there they lay and fertilize their eggs randomly over rocky bottoms. Parent fish provide no care to either eggs or young. In waters tributary to Lake Ontario and Lake Huron, lake chub are sometimes mistaken for—and eaten as—smelt. Anglers in some areas use lake chub as bait fish.

This species has a rounded body, and is dark brown or greenish on the back and silvery on the sides. The scales are often noticeably dark, and young fish have a particularly distinct lateral line. At spawning time, males develop reddish dashes, especially at the inner base of the pectoral fin. Lake chub feed mainly on aquatic insects and plankton, but larger ones eat smaller fish. In turn they are eaten by larger fish such as lake trout, northern pike and walleye, and birds including kingfishers and mergansers.

Lake chub are also commonly known as *northern chub, creek chub* and *chub minnow.*

Common shiner
(Luxilus cornutus)

The common shiner, primarily a stream-dweller, inhabits many waters from Nova Scotia to Saskatchewan. Deep-bodied and laterally compressed, it is characterized by its scales; on the forward part of the body they are much higher that they are wide. The back is olive green, the sides are silvery and the belly is white. A purple or grey-blue stripe is pronounced along the back. At spawning time the male becomes rather gaily coloured in overall salmon pink; outer areas of the dorsal and lower fin and tail become bright red to orange.

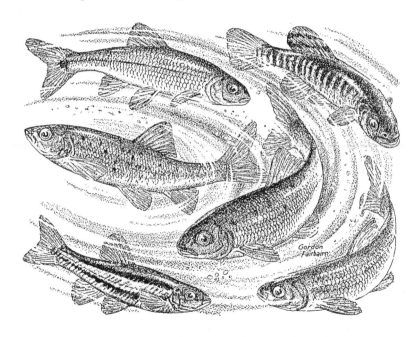

Top left: SPOTTAIL SHINER, Top right: BANDED KILLIFISH
Centre left: LAKE CHUB, Centre right: COMMON SHINER
Bottom left: NORTHERN REDBELLY DACE, Bottom right: EMERALD SHINER

The common shiner spawns from May to August in nests of pebbles or gravel excavated by the male, or in nests already made by other minnows. The male guards the eggs and is often pugnacious when threatened by intruders. The food of this species consists mainly of insects, algae, and to a lesser extent, crustaceans and other small fish. At maturity it averages 4 inches (10.16 cm), but it often reaches a length of up to 8 inches (20.32 cm).

The common shiner is a popular bait fish and sometimes gives good sport on a fly-rod. It is edible but bony.

Among its common names are *redfin shiner, silver shiner, hornyhead, rough-head,* and *creek shiner.*

Emerald shiner
(Nortopis atherinoides)

The emerald shiner is important not only as food for larger fish, but as one of the best live baits.

In Canada the emerald shiner occurs in the upper St. Lawrence River, Lake Champlain, all Great Lakes and many of their tributary lakes and streams, the prairie provinces and the northeastern corner of British Columbia. It also occurs in waters tributary to the lower Mackenzie and Liard rivers.

This is a slender, streamlined minnow of 2 to 3 inches (5.08 to 7.62 cm) whose translucency gives it the impression of fragility. It is emerald green on the back and sides, silver on the lower flanks and white on the belly. It is found mainly in larger lakes and rivers, where it moves in schools, and spawns in the spring in shallow water. It lives mainly on plankton and insects.

Spottail shiner
(Notropis hudsonius)

The spottail shiner occurs from Quebec westward to all of the Great Lakes and throughout Ontario. It has a far northerly limit in Manitoba, Saskatchewan and Alberta, and occurs throughout much of the Mackenzie River system as far downstream as Fort Good Hope. Mcphail and Lindsey write that the spottail shiner is the most northerly species of the large North American genus *Notropis.*

A slender, deep-bodied fish, the spottail shiner is green to olive on the back, silvery on the sides and white on the belly. Overall it has yellow or golden hues. It has a blunt nose, small mouth and large scales. An identifying characteristic of this minnow is the pronounced black spot on the base of the tail fin of small fish. As they grow larger this spot becomes obscured by silvery guanine and large scales, according to Scott and Crossman, but reappears after death. (A similar black spot occurs, less conspicuously, on the pugnose shiner and creek chub).

The spottail shiner inhabits large lakes and rivers in its eastern range, but thrives in small, shallow lakes in its western range. It spawns in May and June, the eggs receiving no parental care. Its diet consists mainly of insects, plankton, aquatic vegetation and small, free-swimming crustaceans. At maturity it averages 3 inches (7.62 cm), although some Manitoba spottail shiners are reported to reach 6 inches (15.24 cm). The spottail shiner is an important food for larger fish, and an excellent live bait for anglers.

Other common names are *spottail minnow, shiner, spawneater,* and *sucking carp.*

Northern redbelly dace
(Phoxinus eos)

The northern redbelly dace occurs from Nova Scotia westward to the Peace River district in northern British Columbia. One of the smallest and most beautiful minnows, it is highly regarded by anglers because of its hardiness as a bait fish.

This dace, which averages 2 to 3 inches (5.08 to 7.62 cm), is dark brownish on the back. Dark lateral lines are sometimes joined by an oblique line just before the tail. Its sides and belly are silvery, white or yellow, but turn bright red in the breeding male. This species has very fine scales. It has large eyes and a small mouth.

Northern redbelly dace are found in boggy parts of lakes and streams, usually in shallow water with an abundance of algae, diatoms and aquatic insects.

Creek chub
(Semotilus atromaculatus)

The creek chub's widespread occurrence in eastern North America and its abundance make it one of the minnows best known to anglers. It is also one of the most extensively studied by scientists.

This species is stout-bodied, olive brown on the back, silvery on the sides—which have a noticeable violet or purple iridescence—and creamy white on the belly. A black spot is prominent at the base of the forward part of the dorsal fin. The head is blunt and the mouth is large. Four to eight large, thorn-like tubercles occur on the head of the male during the spawning season.

The creek chub is found in cool, clear streams, where it often competes with trout for food. Although it consumes trout eggs and fry, its principal diet consists of insects, aquatic vegetation and crayfish. This large minnow sometimes reaches 12 inches (30.48 cm). It is quite edible—if you can make your way through the tiny bones!

Among its common names are *creek chub, horned dace, common chub, brook chub, northern creek chub, silvery chub and mud chub.*

Redside shiner
(Richardsonius balteatus)

The redside shiner inhabits Pacific coast drainage systems from the Nass River in the north to the Columbia River and some Oregon rivers in the south. It is also found east of the Continental

Divide, from British Columbia's Peace River system downstream to around Fort Vermilion in Alberta.

This is a controversial species, for its introduction into some lakes to provide food for rainbow trout has proved detrimental to the native game species. Although rainbows feed heavily on the shiners, the shiner population often increases enough to compete with young trout for both space and food. Shiners are also known to eat small trout. The problem has been sufficiently serious to lead to poisoning of some waters.

The redside shiner is deep-bodied and laterally compressed. It grows to a maximum of about 7 inches (17.78 cm). Perhaps its most distinguishing characteristics are its long anal fin base and the far backward position of its dorsal fin. Its colour is steely blue, olive or dark brown on the back and silvery on the lower sides and belly. A dark lateral band extends from the snout to the base of the tail, and a light streak above the eye fades out below the dorsal fin. At spawning time both sexes are strikingly coloured with metallic gold on the head, fins and sides, alternating with vivid crimson. The redside shiner spawns from late May to early August. It is a good bait fish.

Among its other common names are *red-sided bream, silver-sided minnow, silver shiner* and *Columbia River minnow.*

SUCKERS
Catostomidae

The Catostomidae family is made up of thirteen genera and sixty-eight species. All—except two species in China and north-eastern Siberia—inhabit freshwater rivers and lakes throughout North and Central America as far south as Guatemala.

Seventeen species occur in Canada. Catostomidae are present in every province and territory, and their northern range also extends throughout Alaska.

In their *Freshwater Fishes of Northwestern Canada and Alaska,*

McPhail and Lindsey write that a relic form of the sucker family living in China's Yangtze drainage, and fossil remains found in both Asia and North America, "leave the question open as to which continent was the original home of the group." Perhaps one day the answer will be found. Its significance to anglers will be minimal, but no doubt it will be of immense importance to scientists, particularly those specializing in evolution, taxonomy and morphology.

Canada's seventeen sucker species range from about 5 inches (12.7 cm) to 20 inches (50.8 cm); the average size is 10 to 12 inches (25.4 to 30.48 cm). Most have roundish bodies. All but one have protrusible sucking mouths with fleshy lips. The exception is the bigmouth buffalo (*Ictiobus cyprinellus*), which in some midwest United States waters reportedly reaches more than 3 feet (0.91 m) and weighs up to 80 pounds (36.29 kg).

Suckers spawn from spring to early summer, depending on geography and water temperature. Their choice of nursery areas ranges from stream shallows with gravel bottoms and a fast flow of water to quiet pools and sandy lake shores. Suckers build no nests and give neither eggs nor young parental care. A juvenile sucker has a mouth in terminal position and feeds mainly on plankton, but as the fish grows older a remarkable transformation takes place: its mouth eventually moves under the snout. This change, along with the development of sucking mouths, enables suckers to draw up ooze from the bottom and sift out food such as small crustaceans and insect larvae through their gill rakers. Suckers also have pharyngeal teeth which enable them to crush the shells of small molluscs and crustaceans. Some species are able to overturn stones and feed on the insect and other animal life they expose.

Suckers are not significant as game fish, but in some areas, especially in the spring when they are in shallow lake water or are on their way to their spawning grounds, white suckers provide good sport. News that "suckers are running" acts as a clarion call to hundreds of young and old who head for the streams to capture these creatures on hook and line, with dip nets and even with bare hands. At that time they are at their edible best—if you can put up with the mass of small bones in the flesh—and their great numbers moving through the shallows can provide exhilarating, wholesome outdoor fun. The "sucker run" is as exciting as the "smelt run" in Ontario and the "roll" of the capelin in Newfoundland.

But others hold suckers in contempt and consider them a nuisance our waters would be well rid of. Nevertheless, suckers have their value. Some serve as useful bait fish at minnow size (never in all-trout waters!), and they also provide important food for larger game fish. They have commercial value, too; considerable quantities are marketed each year under the name "mullet." In the far north they are important as dog food.

Most species of suckers in Canadian waters have limited distribution, and many are considered by COSEWIC as rare or endangered.

These sucker species inhabit Canadian waters:

- bigmouth buffalo (*Ictiobus cyprinellus*)
- lake chubsucker (*Erimyzon sucetta*)
- spotted sucker (*Minytrema melanops*)
- northern hog sucker (*Hypentelium nigricans*)
- bridgelip sucker (*Catostomus columbianus*)
- mountain sucker (*Catostomus platyrhynchus*)
- largescale sucker (*Catostomus macrocheilus*)
- copper redhorse (*Moxostoma hubbsi*)
- river redhorse (*Moxostoma carinatum*)
- black redhorse (*Moxostoma duquesnei*)
- greater redhorse (*Moxostoma valenciennesi*)
- shorthead redhorse (*Moxostoma macrolepidotum*)
- golden redhorse (*Moxostoma erythrurum*)

Several species are plentiful enough in Canada to have significance as sports fish:

The quillback (*Carpiodes cyprinus*) occurs from the St. Lawrence River to western, central and southern Ontario. The Mississippi River in Ontario is noted for its "sucker run." Size ranges from 10 to 15 inches (25.4 to 38.1 cm).

The longnose sucker (*Catostomus catostomus*) occurs in every province but Newfoundland and Nova Scotia. It also occurs in the Northwest Territories, the Yukon, Alaska and the arctic drainages of Siberia. Caught commercially in the Great Lakes, it is marketed as "mullet." It forms part of the diet of northern people and is also used as dog food. Size ranges from 12 to 14 inches (30.48 to 35.56 cm).

The white sucker (*Catostomus commersoni*) is widely distributed from Nova Scotia west to British Columbia, and in the central and western Northwest Territories. It is taken commercially and has some appeal as a game fish. It is valued as live bait at minnow size. Mature fish are 12 to 20 inches (30.48 to 50.8 cm).

The silver redhorse (*Moxostoma anisurum*) occurs in a narrow, mostly southern range from the St. Lawrence River west to Alberta. It is caught commercially in some areas. Size ranges from 12 to 15 inches (30.48 to 38.1 cm). Scott and Crossman write that a redhorse 24 inches (60.96 cm) long was reportedly taken from Sparrow Lake, Ontario, after giving an angler a two-hour battle!

Fish described as redhorses belong to the genus *Moxostoma* and are the largest of the Catostomidae family. Much has yet to be recorded regarding their life histories.

It is mainly in Canada that suckers are rated low as sports fish. In the United States a number of species, such as the white sucker and northern redhorse, provide good sport, especially during the spring; there they are often called "pig heads" (a reference to their down-turned snouts and suctorial or sucking mouths). Some species are highly regarded for their good flavour despite their multitude of small bones.

Trout-Perch
ORDER PERCOPSIFORMES

This order of North American freshwater fish includes six genera and nine species grouped in three families. Only the family Percopsidae, with one species—the trout-perch—occurs in Canada.

Trout-perch
(Percopsis omiscomaycus)

The trout-perch, also known as *silver chub*, occurs over a wide Canadian range: the St. Lawrence River watershed, Lake Champlain, numerous lakes including the Great Lakes, James and Hudson bays, the Northwest Territories, and some parts of the Yukon and Alaska. It is present in all western provinces.

This unusual species combines the head and scale characteristics of perch and the adipose fin of salmonids—hence its name. Its colour is silvery with the three rows of dark spots running along the back and sides. Its lower sides show a blue or purple iridescence which gives it a transparent appearance when fresh from the water.

Trout-perch inhabit deep lakes and slow streams, and live mainly on aquatic insects and small crustaceans. Spawning takes place in the spring, generally along the shores of lakes and in small streams. Some individuals mature and spawn at one year. This species, which is sometimes used for bait, is an important food source for larger fish such as walleye and lake trout. In southern waters trout-perch may grow to up to 8 inches (20.32 cm), but in more northerly waters their maximum size is about 4 inches (10.16 cm).

Killifish, Mummichog & Topminnow
ORDER CYPRINODONTIFORMES

Members of this order are found on every continent except Australia. Nelson recognizes eighty-eight genera and about eight hundred and seven species, of which three in the Fundulidae family inhabit Canadian waters.

TOPMINNOWS AND KILLIFISHES
Fundulidae

Banded killifish
(Fundulus diaphanus)

The banded killifish occurs in Canada in lakes and rivers from the Maritime provinces to southwestern Ontario. It is minnow-like in appearance, but can be distinguished from true minnows by its dorsal fin, large anal fin and upturned mouth. Its tail is square; in minnows the tail is noticeably forked.

The banded killifish is olive green on the back and silvery on the sides, which also carrying eighteen to twenty vertical bars. It lives mainly on aquatic insects and vegetation, and is a midsummer spawner. In the Maritimes the banded killifish is used as live bait.

Livingstone writes in *The Fresh Water Fishes of Nova Scotia* that "anglers keep *Fundulus* alive by packing it in dry leaves in an old tin can. It will live in this way, completely without water for several days . . ."

This species averages about 3 inches (7.62 cm) in length.

Mummichog
(Fundulus heteroclitus)

The mummichog lives in brackish water of sheltered inshore areas and tidal creeks on the Atlantic seaboard. It has a stout, rounded body, blunt nose and round tail fin. Popularly known as *mummy* and *chub,* it averages about 3 inches (7.62 cm) in length, is extremely hardy and can survive for long periods without oxygen. It is a good bait fish.

Blackstripe topminnow
(Fundulus notatus)

The blackstripe topminnow occurs only in a few streams in southern Ontario, where it feeds on food from the surface film. It is rated by COSEWIC as rare.

Sculpins
ORDER SCORPAENIFORMES

This order of scorpionfish, sculpins and gurnards consists of 25 families, 266 genera and 1271 species. They inhabit salt and fresh water in tropical and northern areas through much of the world. All are bottom-dwelling creatures as adults.

Sculpins are generally characterized by their broad, flat head and heavy body which tapers to a slender caudal peduncle and large tail fin. The pectoral fins are large and wing-like; there are two large unconnected dorsal fins, the first spiny-rayed, the second soft-rayed and running almost to the tail fin. The anal fin is without spines. All sculpins have a bony support beneath the eye. They may have scales—usually in the form of prickles—or they may be scaleless. Among the largest sculpins are the saltwater cabezons (*Scorpaenichthys marmoratus*), which occur from California to Alaska. They can weigh up to 30 pounds (13.61 kg).

Scorpaeniforms are among the spiniest of all fish. Many in

marine environments are grotesquely beautiful, but some have stout spines containing venom that can cause excruciating pain or even death.

There are 300 species in the family Cottidae. Among them are the freshwater sculpins, which are widely distributed throughout the Northern Hemisphere. Tiny creatures, they range in size from about 2 inches (5.08 cm) to 7 inches (17.78 cm), and are of interest mainly to scientists and serious students of nature. They play an important role, however, as food for larger fish. Some, despite their small size, are significant predators of the eggs and young of game fish. Freshwater sculpins tend to hide under stones and similar protection; they dart out when food appears, but are seldom seen unless disturbed. Most are spring spawners.

Eight species of freshwater sculpins occur in Canada. The slimy sculpin (*Cottus cognatus*) has the widest range; it is found in all provinces and territories except Nova Scotia and the island of Newfoundland. COSEWIC rates the shorthead sculpin (*Cottus confusus*), found only in the Columbia River in southeastern British Columbia, and the deepwater sculpin (*Myoxocephalus thompsoni*) of the Great Lakes, as threatened. The fourhorn sculpin (*Myoxocephalus quadricornis*) of Victoria Island, Western Arctic, is rated as vulnerable.

Many freshwater scorpaeniforms are too small for human consumption. In salt water the well-known Pacific ling cod, which provide good sport for anglers, and the deep-dwelling sablefish of Family Anoplopomatidae (smoked and marketed as Alaska black cod) are highly rated food fish. The marine rockfish (Scorpaenidae) are equally important commercial fish.

Grunion & Silverside
ORDER ATHERINIFORMES

This is a complex order consisting of eight families, forty-seven genera and two hundred and eighty-five species occurring around the world in marine, tropical and temperate seas. A few species occur in fresh water. The brook silverside (*Labidesthes sicculus*) is the only member of family Atherinidae in Canadian waters.

But this order of fishes cannot readily be bypassed. One species in the Atherinidae family in every sense is about as remarkable a creature as one could find. It is the little grunion (*Leuresthes tenuis*), a 6 inch (15.24 cm) smelt-like fish occurring only near the sandy beaches of Southern California. Schultz describes it as "practically the only kind of fish known along North American shores that comes out of the sea to mate and lay its eggs in the sand of beaches."

During their March to July spawning season, great numbers of these little creatures congregate at night in the surf and wait for the second highest wave of the highest tide. Then, en masse, they move with that wave to the beaches where each female, tail down, wriggles out a hole in the sand. The eggs are released and immediately fertilized by the males. Then, on the following highest wave, the parent fish are carried out to sea. The whole process takes less than a minute.

About two weeks later the next series of high tides occurs. When the highest wave comes in it uncovers the eggs, which *immediately* hatch, and the young are carried out to their home in the sea as that wave recedes.

Surely these little creatures are among the wonders of the world.

Brook silverside
(Labidesthes sicculus)

The brook silverside occurs in the upper St. Lawrence and Ottawa rivers, in lakes Erie, Ontario and St. Clair, and in Georgian Bay. It is a slender fish, translucent pale green in colour, with a prominent lateral band on the side—hence the name silverside. It seldom exceeds 3 inches (7.62 cm). It can also be identified by its two dorsal fins; the first dorsal is tiny and contains four spines. It has a long anal fin.

The brook silverside, a spring spawner, lives close to the surface and is also known as *skipjack* because of its ability at times to skip into the air. When large numbers of schooling fish do this, the surface water fairly boils with activity.

Brook silverside feed mainly on aquatic and terrestrial insects as well as plankton, and are important forage fish for larger species.

Sticklebacks

ORDER GASTEROSTEIFORMES

Sticklebacks belong to an order that includes seahorses, sand eels, pipefish, snipe fish and tube-snouts—all spiny-rayed fish inhabiting marine, brackish and fresh water almost worldwide. Most forms have a high salinity tolerance and many are anadromous.

Sticklebacks belong to the family Gasterosteidae, made up of five genera and seven species; at least five are found in Canadian waters. Their name relates to the short, stout spines on the first dorsal fin, the spine at the front of the anal fin and the spine on each pelvic fin. The number of spines on the first dorsal fin is the common way of identifying each species. Sticklebacks are scaleless, but most species have bony plates along the sides. They are tiny creatures. The largest in Canadian waters is up to 4 inches (10.16 cm), but normally they are under 2 inches (5.08 cm).

This family continues to challenge scientists, and many studies have been made of their mating behaviour and nest-building activities. Of particular importance are the ongoing studies being made of the differences between the anadromous and freshwater forms.

Under study by Dr. J.D. McPhail and his associates at the University of British Columbia, along with Dr. Alex Peden of the Royal British Columbia Museum, Victoria, are the 1.5-inch (3.81-cm) threespine sticklebacks (*Gasterosteus aculeatus*)—a species found throughout the Northern Hemisphere—which taxonomically appear to be evolving into two distinct forms in Enos Lake, Vancouver Island. Scientists are describing it as a "biological wonder," but as COSEWIC's Dr. Robert Campbell says, "it is sad to note that this important event has been over-shadowed by urban development, which could lead to the extinction of the species pair."

Four lakes on northern Texada Island, British Columbia, are also known to have newly evolved species, but these have yet to be named. A species that evolved on nearby Lasqueti Island is now believed to be extinct—the result of the illegal introduction of predacious catfish.

"There is also," writes Izaak Walton, "a little fish called Sticklebag; a Fishe without scales, but hath his body fenc'd with several prickles. I know not where he dwells in winter, or what he is good for in summer, but only to make sport for boyes and women-Anglers, and to feed other Fishe that be Fishe of prey, as Trouts in particular, who will bite at him as a Penk, and better, if your hook be tightly baited with him, for he may be so baited as his tail turning like the sail of a windmill and make him turn more quick that any Penk or Minnow can."

It is surprising that the Old Master, a sensitive observer of stream life, by his own admission knew so little about these interesting creatures, for the "sticklebags" are quite unlike most other fish found in fresh water. We can only hope that he did get to know more of their odd habits and that he spent many pleasant hours, as so many fish-watchers have done since his time, enjoying their behaviour in the quiet streams and small ponds in which they commonly make their homes.

Sticklebacks are tiny, with the exception of the giant stickle-back, and seldom exceed 3 inches (7.62 cm). What they lack in size they more than make up in courage. They are pugnacious creatures that, especially during the mating season, show little fear of fish considerably larger than themselves. Their pugnacity has physical capabilities to back it up, too. All members of the family carry strong spines, not only on the back, but sometimes on the belly as well. Dr. Lionel Johnson reminds us that one species—the three-spined stickleback (*Gasterosteus aculeatus*)—"has a pair of spines on the pelvic fin which, like the dorsal spines, can lock into a position at right angles to the body and these make the sticklebacks difficult for predators to swallow. Studies have shown that pike learn not to feed on stickles if other suitable species are available." In addition their little mouths are well fortified with sharp teeth.

Their nesting habits are especially fascinating, for they do make nests in somewhat the same manner as birds.

Those who have observed sticklebacks during nest building and spawning describe their behaviour as determined, purposeful and laborious. There are differences between species, but they share some behaviour.

In the spring and early summer they seek out places well grown with aquatic vegetation. Males, the architects of the homes under construction, select pieces of fine grasses and other fibrous material such as tiny sticks. They carry these to the fronds of water weeds where they lace them together to form hollow, rounded or conical-shaped nests with an opening at both top and bottom. This material is held together with mucus which they apply by rubbing against the sides of the structures, and which quickly acts as a hardening agent. Some observers say that the nests are held together by threads like spider silk secreted from their kidneys.

When all is in readiness each male seeks out a female and leads her into the nest where she lays small clusters of tiny, yellowish eggs. The male immediately fertilizes these and the female departs. The male assumes full responsibility for guarding the nests.

Whenever water flow is insufficient to supply the necessary aeration to the eggs, the male forces a current of water over them by fanning its pectoral fins. The eggs hatch in six to twelve days; the young are kept inside the nests for about a month, or until they can fend for themselves. This parental care is carried out with great pugnacity, and woe betide the intruder who dares to cross the family threshold. Nest building, courting and spawning behaviour vary, depending on the species, but the procedures are essentially similar. They take place in shallow water from April to July, although they may occur at other times throughout the summer.

Sticklebacks vary greatly in coloration, but during the spawning season most males develop pronounced reddish hues, generally on the belly and flank.

Most species of sticklebacks have access to tidal waters and some are anadromous. Despite their diminutive size the anadromous forms have an extraordinary ability to migrate. They move freely in and out of fresh, brackish and salt water over considerable distances—a remarkable feat for creatures so small.

Sticklebacks live on a wide variety of foods such as plankton, small crustaceans, algae, insect larvae, and the eggs and fry of their own and other fish. They, in turn, are preyed upon by larger fish and birds. Sticklebacks have no commercial value, but are often used as bait and are important food for larger fish, especially cutthroat trout.

Scott and Crossman make an interesting observation about one member of the family: "The threespine stickleback is well known to behaviourists and psychologists, as well as fishery biologists, because of its wide use as a laboratory animal. Not only will this small fish build a nest and spawn in an aquarium, but sexually mature males and females can be induced to perform their mating rituals by being presented with approximately shaped dummies simulating the opposite sex."

Species that occur in Canadian waters include: brook stickleback (*Culaea inconstans*); ninespine stickleback (*Pungitius pungitius*); fourspine stickleback (*Apeltes quadracus*); threespine

Species that occur in Canadian waters include: brook stickle-back (*Culaea inconstans*); ninespine stickleback (*Pungitius pungitius*); fourspine stickleback (*Apeltes quadracus*); threespine stickleback (*Gasterosteus aculeatus*); and blackspotted stickleback (*Gasterosteus wheatlandi*).

The white stickleback of the Maritime provinces and the two forms of newly evolving Enos Lake sticklebacks of Vancouver Island have yet to be formally described. The giant stickleback, a species found only in the Queen Charlotte Islands, also awaits formal classification. It is part of the unique ecosystem of the islands, and its presence there gives added weight to the recognition of that archipelago as Canada's equivalent of the Galapagos Islands.

Canada's Aquatic Heritage

Dr. Robert R. Campbell

Most life forms on this planet are dependent on water in one form or another, but few are so dependent as the fishes. These animals have been successful in adapting to diverse habitats and may be found almost anywhere a water body exists, from subzero Antarctic marine waters to desert pools with temperatures of over 40°C.

Canada, as the world's second largest country, is blessed with an abundance of aquatic resources. It has the longest marine coastline, fronts on three oceans and includes 25 percent of the earth's fresh water. Nearly a thousand species of fish are found in Canadian waters; about 20 percent of these are strictly freshwater species. The exact number of forms is not known. Scientists are still exploring our fish fauna and discovering new species. In the last two decades more than thirty-five new species have been recorded from the Canadian Arctic and more than fifty species from the Pacific coast.

Even though blessed with abundant freshwater resources, the

country is not rich in species diversity. Probably this is a result of the relatively recent retreat of the Pleistocene ice and the north temperate to polar climate (depending on latitude) dictated by our geography. Our freshwater fish fauna is represented by some twenty-four families and about a hundred and eighty-one species, if the introduced brown trout, carp (*Cyprinus caprio*), goldfish (*Carassius auratus*), and tench (*Tinca tinca*) are included. In comparison, there are fifty families and some seven hundred and seventy-five species in the US. About five families (Salmonidae, Cyprinidae, Catostomidae, Percidae and Cottidae) actually contain 70 percent of the fauna. Although energy flows through the aquatic ecosystems do not provide the basis for a more diverse aquatic fauna, they are sufficient to support an abundance of most forms present. Also, what we lack in quantity is made up in quality. Canada has some of the finest salmon, trout, and charr populations in the world, not to mention large and smallmouth bass (*Micropterus salmoides, Micropterus dolomieui*), northern pike (*Esox lucius*), muskellunge (*Esox masquinogy*), and walleye (*Stizostedion vitreum glaucum*).

Prior to the advent of European settlement, aboriginal peoples depended on these resources for food, using the resource prudently and not upsetting the balance of nature. Beginning with colonization—and culminating with intensive agriculture and industry in the twentieth century—urbanization, deforestation, impoundments, drainage modifications, and agriculture have led to significant changes in the quantity and quality of available habitat. The addition of human and industrial wastes, contaminants, nutrients, and toxic chemicals to our waters has left many water bodies unfit either to support aquatic life or to be sources of water for human consumption.

Often the effects of such alterations, particularly those involving chemical compounds, are slow or not readily apparent in their effect. They may take decades or more to be noticed, or may go unnoticed until it is too late to take appropriate action. All too often such effects are more widespread and insidious than the dramatic oil spills which are localized and unduly publicized by the media.

The impoundment of waterways has created impassable barriers to fish populations and led to the extirpation of economically important stocks of commercial and sport fish populations. The creation of a dam on the Tusket River in Nova Scotia is partially responsible (acid rain, exploitation and habitat degradation are other factors) for the demise of the endangered Atlantic whitefish (*Coregonus huntsmani*). Diversions of important rivers in many parts of the country, particularly British Columbia, have necessitated the expenditure of millions of dollars in design and construction of fishways to permit the passage of spawning species such as salmonids, species which make a significant contribution to the economies of our coastal provinces. To maintain species diversity in the face of such habitat changes, fish hatcheries have been established for most West Coast salmonids. The construction of dams to power mills on Lake Ontario tributaries blocked spawning runs of Atlantic salmon (*Salmo salar*); native salmon were extirpated by 1900. Impoundments also create other hazards for fish and man as witnessed in Ontario on the English-Wabigoon system and in Quebec with the La Grande project. Dams lead to accumulation and settling of heavy metals, particularly mercury, compounds that not only have the potential to weaken the fecundity of aquatic species, but also pose serious health hazards for man.

Often, the effects of change resulting from the influence of man go unnoticed, particularly at the lower trophic levels or amongst species with no commercial value. Some species have become extinct (Banff longnose dace, *Rhinichthys cataractae smithi*; gravel chub, *Erimystax x-punctata*) or endangered (Salish sucker, *Catostomus* sp.), not through exploitation but as incidental victims of human activity resulting in habitat loss or degradation. Some (Banff longnose dace, gravel chub) are small, obscure species. Others—such as the Aurora trout, *Salvelinus fontinalis*

timagamiensis, which virtually disappeared from its Ontario habitat because of lake acidification, and the Atlantic whitefish which
is threatened by acidification of its Nova Scotia habitat—are of
interest to anglers because of their appeal as sports fish. Acid rain
is particularly pernicious in its threat. Quiet and unseen, it affects
all trophic levels within an aquatic ecosystem. In fish it reduces
fecundity, hatchability of eggs, and bone calcification. In molluscs, mussels and even plankters, it leads to death. This deprives
organisms at higher trophic levels of a source of food . . . and leaves
pristine lakes devoid of life.

In addition to the direct and indirect effects of civilization
on habitats, species are also affected by exploitation and the
effects of poorly regulated patterns of use. This is exemplified
in the loss of the blue walleye, *Stizostedion vitreum glaucum,*
from lakes Ontario and Erie. This species, which once supported a fishery landing millions of kilograms annually, had
disappeared by 1965 before any efforts could be brought to
bear on its behalf. Other species such as the deepwater cisco
(*Coregonus johannae*) have faced a similar fate, while others
like the Atlantic whitefish (*Coregonus huntsmani*), blackfin,
shortjaw and shortnose ciscoes (*Coregonus nigripinnis, Coregonus reighardi* and *Coregonus zenithicus*) have been pushed
close to extinction.

Sometimes the process of extinction is a natural biological
phenomenon as in the case of the threatened margined
madtom, *Noturus insignis.* Many species exist in Canada at the
northern fringe of their range. Others survived the Pleistocene
ice *in refugia,* but have evolved isolated from their kin; they are
now relict populations with restricted distributions and low
numbers. Such species, because of their natural rarity, low
numbers and restricted distributions, are vulnerable to natural
(and man-made) catastrophes. The committee on the Status of
Endangered Wildlife in Canada (COSEWIC) has examined the
status of many such species. Those found to be vulnerable are
listed on the accompanying table (page 281).

Despite man's ability to alter habitats and exploit natural resources, the overall Canadian story is not one of doom and gloom. Granted, there are the horror stories associated with the loss of freshwater species such as the blue walleye, and the present decline of important commercial marine species such as northern cod, *Gadus morhua*. But the diversity of Canadian freshwater and marine fauna has changed little over the period of recorded history.

Of the nearly one thousand species of fish known to inhabit Canadian waters only three freshwater species—deepwater cisco, Banff longnose dace and blue walleye—have become extinct in historic times, and an additional two—gravel chub and paddlefish (*Polyodon spathula*)—extirpated. Only three other species—Aurora trout, Atlantic whitefish and salish sucker—are endangered; twelve others are threatened—Lake Simcoe whitefish (*Coregonus clupeaformis* sp.), the blackfin, shortnose and shortjaw ciscoes, black and copper redhorse (*Moxostoma dusquesnei* and *Moxostoma hubbsi*), Eastern sand darter (*Ammocrypta pellucida*), channel darter (*Percina copelandi*), margined madtom, Enos Lake stickleback, shorthead sculpin (*Cottus confusus*), and deepwater sculpin (*Myoxocephalus thompsoni*). Although northern cod stocks are in decline, the overall status of the species does not place populations in risk of imminent extinction as long as the present threats to the species remain in check.

The good news is that concern for species and spaces remains a high priority for most Canadians, a concern which goes back to the last century and was well developed by the beginning of the twentieth century. We are all familiar with the heroic efforts to save the whooping crane (*Grus americana*), but probably few realize that the Fisheries Act dates to 1867 and provides the basis for regulations regarding the conservation of aquatic species and their habitats.

Since 1979, the plight of species at risk in Canada has been brought to the attention of the appropriate management jurisdictions and the public through the efforts of the Committee on the Status of Endangered Wildlife in Canada (COSEWIC). In 1988 government agencies charged with protecting species designated by COSEWIC established a strategy for the recovery of endangered species and an organization, Recovery of Nationally Endangered Wildlife (RENEW), to apply it. Since the outset, RENEW has been concerned only with terrestrial vertebrates; the mandate for responsibility for fish, marine mammals, plants and invertebrates was unclear or, as in the case of fish, already under the jurisdiction of federal and provincial agencies. The Department of Fisheries and Oceans (DFO) and the Province of Nova Scotia have undertaken joint operations to ensure the maintenance and recovery of the Atlantic whitefish. In Ontario, attempts are underway to re-establish populations of aurora trout in their native habitat. Ontario has also taken steps, through regulation of the commercial chub fisheries, to ensure stabilization and rehabilitation of cisco stocks in the Great Lakes. In Quebec, efforts have been directed to further research on the copper redhorse and other species to provide management information. Federally, DFO has established strategies and policies (Fish Habitat Policy, Arctic Marine Conservation Strategy) which provide infrastructure for federal-provincial programs directed at the preservation, maintenance and rehabilitation of aquatic habitats and species. These are currently applying comprehensive research and management regimes to ensure stabilization and rehabilitation of northern cod stocks.

On other fronts the federal and provincial governments have been concentrating on legislation and agreements to reduce sulphur and nitrous oxide emissions, leading contributors to acid rain. Transboundary Air Pollution pacts have been signed with our neighbours to the south and, internationally, attempts are underway to curb persistent problems related to the long-range transport of airborne pollutants. Canada has been a leading supporter of the Convention on International Trade in Endangered Species of Wild Fauna and Flora (CITES) and, more recently, has played a lead role in the initiation and implementation of the Biodiversity Convention.

While more Canadians are becoming concerned about species and spaces, many rest in their complacency that our vast wilderness provides all the protection that is required. Not surprisingly, however, some of the best aquatic habitats coincide with the best land available for development. Preservation of habitat for wildlife becomes an ever more costly business which will only be viable if more people believe it is worthwhile.

Although the situation in Canada may not be as bleak as in some other areas of the globe, much remains to be accomplished. A new sense of political will has led to some new approaches. What remains is to follow through on those initiatives already in place, continue to develop new ones, pursue revitalized policies, design new management regimes and do sound, applied research to aid and support these efforts. Much work lies ahead; much effort is needed. Such projects require not only the political will of federal and provincial or territorial politicians, but also the co-operation and support of the public and all organizations and institutions with an interest in the conservation of the resources. For the process of review, renewal and reform to fully benefit Canadians, it must have their active participation.

Lake, River and Sea-Run Fishes of Canada is an authoritative, definitive work and an important contribution to the literature and natural resource heritage of the country. If it serves to pique the interest of the uninitiated, or adds to the knowledge of the consummate angler, it has only partly filled its purpose. I hope that it will introduce many to the importance of Canada's fishes, emphasizing not only their socioeconomic commodity value but, more importantly, the intangible benefits of enjoying a quiet moment waiting for a "strike," and the pride we can take as Canadians in proprietorship of this wonderful resource. Proprietorship brings responsibility, however. Every Canadian must accept this responsibility, not only for the future of the fishes of Canada and their habitat, but for all forms of life and the land on which it exists. If we do not, in the long run, the lost opportunities for angling aurora trout in Ontario or Atlantic whitefish in Nova Scotia will be less crucial than our own survival in this biosphere.

DR. R.R. CAMPBELL,
Chairman,
Committee on the Status of Endangered Wildlife in Canada
(COSEWIC)
Fish and Marine Mammals Subcommittee,
Canadian Wildlife Service,
Environment Canada

Freshwater and anadromous fish species assigned COSEWIC status to April 1994.

Species	Scientific Name	Status	Date Assigned
Vancouver lamprey*	*Lampetra macrostoma*	Vulnerable	April 1986
Chestnut lamprey	*Ichthyomyzon castaneus*	Vulnerable	April 1991
Northern brook lamprey	*Ichthyomyzon fossor*	Vulnerable	April 1991
Shortnose sturgeon	*Acipenser brevirostrum*	Vulnerable	April 1980
Green sturgeon	*Acipenser medirostris*	Vulnerable	April 1987
White sturgeon	*Acipenser transmontanus*	Vulnerable	April 1990
Spotted gar	*Lepisosteus oculatus*	Vulnerable	April 1983[a]
Spring cisco*	*Coregonus sp.*	Vulnerable	April 1982
Squanga whitefish*	*Coregonus sp.*	Vulnerable	April 1988
Kiyi	*Coregonus kiyi*	Vulnerable	April 1987
Redside dace	*Clinostomus elongatus*	Vulnerable	April 1987
Silver chub	*Macrhybopsis storeriana*	Vulnerable	April 1985
Pugnose shiner	*Notropis anogenus*	Vulnerable	April 1985
Bigmouth shiner	*Notropis dorsalis*	Vulnerable	April 1985
Silver shiner	*Notropis photogenis*	Vulnerable	April 1983[b]
Rosyface shiner	*Notropis rubellus*	Vulnerable	April 1994
Pugnose minnow	*Opsopoedus emiliae*	Vulnerable	April 1985
Speckled dace	*Rhinichthys osculus*	Vulnerable	April 1980[c]
Umatilla dace	*Rhinichthys umatilla*	Vulnerable	April 1988
Central stoneroller	*Campostoma anomalum*	Vulnerable	April 1985
Banded killifish (Newfoundland)	*Fundulus diaphanus*	Vulnerable	April 1989
Blackstripe topminnow	*Fundulus notatus*	Vulnerable	April 1985
Lake chubsucker	*Erimyzon sucetta*	Vulnerable	April 1994

Species	Scientific Name	Status	Date Assigned
Bigmouth buffalo	Ictiobus cyprinellus	Vulnerable	April 1989
Black buffalo	Ictiobus niger	Vulnerable	April 1989
Spotted sucker	Minytrema melanops	Vulnerable	April 1983[a]
River redhorse	Moxostoma carinatum	Vulnerable	April 1983
Greenside darter	Etheostoma blennioides	Vulnerable	April 1990
Brindled madtom	Notorus miurus	Vulnerable	April 1985
Redbreast sunfish	Lepomis auritus	Vulnerable	April 1989
Warmouth	Lepomis gulosus	Vulnerable	April 1994
Orangespotted sunfish	Lepomis humilis	Vulnerable	April 1989
Fourhorn sculpin (Arctic Islands)	Myoxocephalus quadricornis	Vulnerable	April 1989
Giant stickleback*	Gasterosteus sp.	Vulnerable	April 1980
Unarmoured stickleback*	Gasterosteus sp.	Vulnerable	April 1983
Lake Simcoe whitefish*	Coregonus clupeaformis ssp.	Threatened	April 1987
Blackfin cisco	Coregonus nigripinnis	Threatened	April 1988
Shortnose cisco	Coregonus reighardi	Threatened	April 1987
Shortjaw cisco	Coregonus zenithicus	Threatened	April 1987
Black redhorse	Moxostoma dusquesnei	Threatened	April 1988
Copper redhorse*	Moxostoma hubbsi	Threatened	April 1987
Eastern sand darter	Ammocryupta pellucida	Threatened	April 1994
Channel darter	Percina copelandi	Threatened	April 1993
Margined madtom	Gasterosteus insignis	Threatened	April 1989
Enos Lake stickleback*	Gasterosteus sp.	Threatened	April 1988
Shorthead sculpin	Cottus confusus	Threatened	Nov. 1983
Deepwater sculpin (Great Lakes)	Myoxocephalus thompsoni	Threatened	April 1987

Species	Scientific Name	Status	Date Assigned
Atlantic whitefish*	*Coregonus huntsmani*	Endangered	April 1983
Aurora trout*	*Salvelinus fontinalis timagamiensis*	Endangered	April 1987
Salish sucker	*Catostomus sp.*	Endangered	April 1986
Paddlefish	*Polyodon spathula*	Exirpated	April 1987
Gravel chub	*Erimystax x-punctatus*	Exirpated	April 1987[d]
Deepwater cisco	*Coregonus johannae*	Extinct	April 1988
Banff longnose dace*	*Rhinichthys cataractae smithi*	Extinct	April 1987
Blue walleye	*Stizostedion vitreum glaucum*	Extinct	April 1985

* Endemic to Canada

[a] Updated April 1994—no status change.
[b] Updated April 1987—no status change.
[c] Updated April 1984—no status change.
[d] Updated April 1987—previous status of "Endangered" assigned April 1985.

Literature Cited

Armstrong, Herbert H. "Dolly Varden char (*Salvelinus malma*)." In *Trout.* The Wildlife Series. Stackpole Books, 1991.

Barnhart, Roger A. "Steelhead (*Oncorhynchus mykiss*)." In *Trout.* The Wildlife Series. Stackpole Books, 1991.

Bartram, William. *Travels Through North and South Carolina, Georgia, East and West Florida.* Originally published 1791.

Burns, Ted. *Coastal Cutthroat Trout in British Columbia.* Fish and Wildlife Branch, BC Ministry of Environment.

Campbell, R.R., ed. "Rare and Endangered Fishes and Marine Mammals of Canada." COSEWIC Fish and Marine Mammals Subcommittee. Status Reports: IV. *The Canadian Field Naturalist,* 1988.

Crossman, E.J., and J.M. Casselman. *An Annotated Bibliography of the Pike, Esox lucius (Osteichthyes: Salmoniformes).* Royal Ontario Museum, 1987.

Curtis, Brian. *The Life Story of the Fish—His Morals and Manners.* New York: Harcourt, Brace and Co., 1949.

Downes, Stephen, and Martin Knowelden. *The New Compleat Angler.* Stackpole Books, 1983.

Dunfield, Robert. *Atlantic Salmon in the History of North America.* Canadian Special Publication of Fisheries and Aquatic Sciences 80. Ottawa: Department of Fisheries and Oceans, 1985.

Dymond, J.R. *The Trout and Other Game Fishes of British Columbia.* Ottawa: Department of Fisheries, 1932.

Eales, J.G. "The Eel Fisheries of Eastern Canada." Fisheries Research Board of Canada, Bulletin 166.

Green, C. Willard. "The Smelts of Lake Champlain." In *A Biological Survey of the Champlain Watershed*. Supplement, 19th Annual Report, New York State Conservation Department, 1929.

Groot, Cornelis. Personal communications.

Haig-Brown, Roderick. *Fisherman's Spring*. Vancouver: Douglas & McIntyre, 1990.

Haig-Brown, Roderick. *Fisherman's Summer*. Vancouver: Douglas & McIntyre, 1990.

Hart, J.L. *Pacific Fishes of Canada*. Bulletin 180. Fisheries Research Board of Canada, 1973.

Healey, M.S. "Life History of Chinook Salmon (*Oncorhynchus tschawytscha*)." *Pacific Salmon Life Histories*. UBC Press/Department of Fisheries and Oceans, 1991.

Hoffmann, Richard C. "The Protohistory of Pike in Western Culture." In *An Annotated Bibliography of the Pike, Esox lucius (Osteichthyes: Salmoniformes)*. A Life Sciences Miscellaneous Publication. Toronto: Royal Ontario Museum, 1987.

Idyll. C.P. *Abyss—The Deep Sea and the Creatures That Live in It*. New York: Thomas Y. Crowell Co., 1964.

Johnson, Lionel. "The Arctic Charr, *Salvelinus alpinus*." In *Charrs: Salmonid Fishes of the Genus Salvelinus*, ed. Eugene K. Balon. The Hague: Dr. W. Junk bv Publishers, 1980.

Kuehne and Barbour. *The American Darters*. University Press of Kentucky, Lexington, 1983.

Machidori, S., and F. Kato. "Spawning Populations and Marine Life of the Masou Salmon (Oncorhynchus masou)." International North Pacific Fisheries Commission, Bulletin 43, 1984.

McAllister, Don. E. *A Revision of the Smelt Family, Osmeridae*. National Museum of Canada, 1963.

McAllister, Don. In *Freshwater Fishes of Northwestern Canada and Alaska* (McPhail and Lindsey). Bulletin 173, Fisheries Research Board of Canada, 1970.

McClane, A.J. and Gardner, Keith. *McClane's Game Fish of North America*. Times Books, 1984.

McPhail, J.D., and C.C. Lindsey. *Freshwater Fishes of Northwestern Canada and Alaska*. Bulletin 173, Fisheries Research Board of Canada, 1970.

Morton, William. "Charr or char: a history of the English name for members of the salmonid genus Salvelinus." In *Charrs: Salmonid Fishes of the Genus Salvelinus*, ed. Eugene K. Balon. The Hague: Dr. W. Junk bv Publishers, 1980.

Neave, Ferris. "The Origin and Speciation of Oncorhynchus." *Transactions of the Royal Society of Canada*. Vol. LII; Series 111, June, 1956.

Nelson, J.S., and Martin J. Paetz. *The Fishes of Alberta*. 2nd ed. University of Alberta Press/University of Calgary Press, 1992.

Nelson, Joseph S. *Fishes of the World*. 2nd ed. John Wiley & Sons, 1984.

Nelson, Joseph S. *Fishes of the World*. 3rd ed. John Wiley & Sons, 1994.

Newsome, G.E., and Jean Tompkins. "Yellow Perch Egg Masses Deter Predators." *Canadian Journal of Zoology.* 63(12): 2882–2894, 1985.

Outram, Donald N. *Canada's Pacific Herring.* Department of Fisheries and Oceans, 1965.

Power, Geoffrey. "The Brook Charr, *Salvelinus fontinalis.*" In *Charrs: Salmonid Fishes of the Genus Salvelinus,* ed. Eugene K. Balon. The Hague: Dr. W. Junk bv Publishers, 1980.

Ptolemy, Ron. Personal communication.

Raymond, Steve. *Kamloops: An Angler's Study of the Kamloops Trout.* New York: Winchester Press, 1971.

Salo. Ernest O. "Life History of Chum Salmon (*Oncorhynchus keta*)." *Pacific Salmon Life Histories.* UBC Press/Department of Fisheries and Oceans, 1991.

Sawyer, Frank. *Keeper of the Stream.* London: Adam and Charles Black, 1952.

Schultz, Leonard P., with Edith M. Stern. *The Ways of Fishes.* New York: D. Van Nostrand Co., Inc., 1948.

Scott, W.B., and E.J. Crossman. *Freshwater Fishes of Canada.* Bulletin 84, Fisheries Research Board of Canada, Ottawa, 1973. New edition published by Department of Fisheries and Oceans, Ottawa, in the *Canadian Bulletin of Fisheries and Aquatic Sciences* series, 1983.

Thoreau, Henry David. *A Week on the Concord and Merrimack Rivers.* 1849.

Thorpe, John E. *The Atlantic Salmon Journal.* Winter, 1988.

Van Dyke, Henry. *Fisherman's Luck.* New York: Scribner's, 1902.

Vladykov, Vadim D. *Cods—Fishes of Quebec.* Album No. 4: 1–12 pp. Department of Fisheries, Quebec. 1955.

Vladykov, Vadim D. *Eels—Fishes of Quebec.* Album No. 6: 1–12 pp. Department of Fisheries, Quebec. 1955.

Vladykov, Vadim D. *Speckled Trout—Fishes of Quebec.* Album No. 1. Department of Fisheries, Quebec. 1953.

Vladykov, Vadim D. *Sturgeons—Fishes of Quebec.* Album No. 5: 1–11 pp. Department of Fisheries, Quebec. 1955.

Walden II, Howard T. *Familiar Freshwater Fishes of America.* New York, Evanston, and London: Harper and Row, 1964.

Walton, Izaak. *The Compleat Angler.* Toronto: Musson, 1906.

References

Balon, Eugene K., ed. *Charrs: Salmonid Fishes of the Genus Salvelinus.* The Hague: Dr. W. Junk bv Publishers, 1980.

Barnhart, Roger A. "Species Profiles: Life Histories and Environmental Requirements of Coastal Fishes and Invertebrates (Pacific Southwest)." *Steelhead.* US Fish and Wildlife Service, 1986.

Beamish, F.W.H., P.J. Healey, and D. Griggs. *Freshwater Fishes in Canada. Report on Phase 1 of a National Examination.* Ottawa: Canadian Wildlife Federation, 1986.

Benke, R.J. *Native Trout of Western North America.* American Fisheries Society, 1992.

Berst, Alfred, Peter E. Ihssen, George R. Spangler, G. Burton Ayles, and G. William Martin. "The splake, a hybrid charr, *Salvelinus namaycush* x *S. fontinalis.*" In *Charrs: Salmonid Fishes of the Genus Salvelinus.* Ed. Eugene K. Balon. The Hague: Dr. W. Junk bv Publishers, 1980.

Burns,Ted. *Coastal Cutthroat Trout in British Columbia.* Fish and Wildlife Branch, BC Ministry of Environment.

Carl, G. Clifford, W.A. Clemens and C.C. Lindsey. *The Freshwater Fishes of British Columbia.* 3rd ed. Victoria: BC Provincial Museum, 1959.

Cavender, Ted M. "Taxonomy and Distribution of the Bull Trout, Salvelinus confluentus (Suckley), from the American Northwest." California Fish and Game 64(3):139–174.

Foerster, R.E. "The Sockeye Salmon, *Oncorhynchus nerka.*" Fisheries Research Board of Canada, Bulletin 162, 1968.

Groot C., and L. Margolis, eds. *Pacific Salmon Life Histories.* UBC Press/Department of Fisheries and Oceans, 1991.

Groot, C., "Modifications on a Theme: A Perspective on Migratory Behaviour of Pacific Salmon." Salmon and Trout Migratory Behaviour Symposium. June, 1981.

Harris, J.R. *An Angler's Entomology.* London: Collins, 1952.

Hart, J.L. *Pacific Fishes of Canada.* Bulletin 180. Fisheries Research Board of Canada, 1973.

Hartman, G.F. *Reproductive Biology of the Gerrard Stock Rainbow Trout.* Victoria: BC Fish and Wildlife Branch.

Hass, Gordon R., and J.D. Mcphail. "Systematics and Distribution of Dolly Varden (*Salvelinus malma*) and Bull Trout (*Salvelinus confluentus*) in North America." *Canadian Journal of Fisheries and Aquatic Sciences.* Vol. 48, 1991.

Healey, M.S. "Life History of Chinook Salmon (*Oncorhynchus tshawytscha*)." *Pacific Salmon Life Histories.* UBC Press/Department of Fisheries and Oceans, 1991.

Heard, William R. "Life History of Pink Salmon (*Oncorhynchus gorbuscha*)." *Pacific Salmon Life Histories.* UBC Press/Department of Fisheries and Oceans, 1991.

Hickman, Cleveland P. *Biology of the invertebrates.* Saint Louis: C.V. Mosby Company, 1967.

Immes, A.D. *A General Textbook of Entomology.* 9th ed. London: Methuen & Co. Ltd., 1970.

Johnson, Lionel. "Arctic char (*Salvelinus alpinus*)." In *Trout.* The Wildlife Series. Harrisburg, Pa.: Stackpole Books, 1991.

Johnson, Lionel. "Systems for Survival: Of Ecology, Morals and Arctic Charr." Trondheim: Keynote address to the International Arctic Charr Symposium, June, 1994.

Johnson, W.E., and C. Groot. "Observations on the Migration of Young Sockeye Salmon (*Oncorhynchus nerka*) through a Large, Complex Lake System." *Journal of the Fisheries Research Board of Canada* 20(4), 1961.

Kasterner, Joseph A. *Species of Eternity.* New York: Alfred A. Knopf, 1977.

Klausewitz, Wolfgang. "Problems of sensitivity to pain and ability to suffer in fish." *Fischokologie* 1(1):65–90, 1989.

Kwain, W. "Record Size of Freshwater Pink Salmon." *North American Journal of Fisheries Management,* 1987.

Kwain, W., and George A. Rose. "Spawning Migrations of Great Lakes Pink Salmon (*Oncorhynchus gorbuscha*). Size and Sex Distributions." *Journal of Great Lakes Resources.* 12(2):101–08. International Association of Great Lakes Resources, 1986.

Kwain, W., and S.J. Kerr. "Return of 1-year-old Pink Salmon in Michipicoten River, Eastern Lake Superior." *North American Journal of Fisheries Management* 4:335–337, 1984.

Kwain, Wen-hwa, and Andrew H. Lawrie. *Pink Salmon in the Great Lakes.* American Fisheries Society, 1981.

Lamb, Andy, and Phil Edgell. *Coastal Fishes of the Pacific Northwest.* Madeira Park, BC: Harbour Publishing, 1986.

Larkin, P.A. "Maybe You Can't Get There from Here: A Foreshortened History of Research in Relation to Management of Pacific Salmon." London, Ont.: Fry Lecture, delivered to the Annual Meeting of the Canadian Society of Zoologists, May 17, 1978.

MacCrimmon, Hugh R., and T.L. Marshall. "World Distribution of Brown Trout, *Salmo trutta.*" *Journal of the Fisheries Research Board of Canada.* 25(12):2527–2548, 1968.

Machidori, S., and F. Kato. "Spawning Populations and Marine Life of the Masou Salmon (*Oncorhynchus masou*)." *Bulletin* 43, International North Pacific Fisheries Commission, 1984.

MacPhail, J.D., and C.C. Lindsey. "Freshwater Fishes of Northwestern Canada and Alaska." Fisheries Research Board of Canada Bulletin 173, 1970.

McAllister, Don E. Syllogeus 64. *A List of the Fishes of Canada.* Ottawa: National Museum of Natural Sciences, 1990.

McKenzie, R.A. *Smelt: life history and fishery.* Fisheries Research Board of Canada, 1964.

Mowat, Farley. *Sea of Slaughter.* Toronto: McClelland and Stewart, 1984.

Moyle, Peter B. *Inland Fishes of California.* University of California Press, 1976.

Neave, Ferris. "Ocean Migration of Pacific Salmon." *Journal of the Fisheries Research Board of Canada* 21(5), 1964.

Nelson, Joseph S. "Distribution and Nomenclature of North American Kokanee (*Oncorhynchus nerka*)." *Journal of the Fisheries Research Board of Canada* 25(2), 1968.

Nelson, Joseph S. *Fishes of the World.* 2nd ed. John Wiley & Sons, 1984.

Nelson, Joseph S. *Fishes of the World.* 3rd ed. John Wiley & Sons, 1994.

Nelson, Joseph S., and Martin J. Paetz. *The Fishes of Alberta.* 2nd ed. University of Alberta Press/University of Calgary Press, 1992.

Netby, Anthony. *Salmon—The World's Most Harrassed Fish.* London: Andre Deutsch, 1980.

Netby, Anthony. *The Atlantic Salmon—A Vanishing Species?* London: Faber and Faber, 1968.

Newsome, G.E., and Jean Tompkins. "Yellow Perch Egg Masses Deter Predators." *Canadian Journal of Zoology* 63:2882–2894, 1985.

Parker, B.J., and C. Brousseau. "Status of Aurora Trout, *Salvelinus fontinalis timagemiensis.* A Distinct Stock Endemic to Canada." *The Canadian Field Naturalist.* COSEWIC Status Report, 1988.

Power, Geoffrey. "The Brook Charr, *Salvelinus fontinalis.*" In *Charrs: Salmonid Fishes of the Genus Salvelinus,* ed. E.K. Balon. The Hague: Dr. W. Junk bv Publishers, 1980.

Radinsky, Leonard B. *The Evolution of Vertebrate Design.* Chicago: University of Chicago Press, 1987.

Richards, W.O., and R.G.Davies. *A General Textbook of Entomology.* 9th ed. London: Methuen and Co., 1970.

Salo. Ernest O., "Life History of Chum Salmon (*Oncorhynchus keta*)." *Pacific Salmon Life Histories*. UBC Press/Department of Fisheries and Oceans, 1991.

Schultz, Leonard P., with Edith M. Stern. *The Ways of Fishes*. New York: D. Van Nostrand Company, Inc., 1948.

Scott, W.B., and E.J. Crossman. *Fishes Occuring in the Fresh Waters of Insular Newfoundland*. Toronto: Royal Ontario Museum, 1964.

Scott, W.B., and E.J. Crossman. *Freshwater Fishes of Canada*. Bulletin 84, Fisheries Research Board of Canada, Ottawa, 1973. New edition published by Department of Fisheries and Oceans, Ottawa, in the *Canadian Bulletin of Fisheries and Aquatic Sciences* series, 1983.

Scott, W.B., and M.G. Scott. "Atlantic Fishes of Canada." *Canadian Bulletin of Fisheries and Aquatic Sciences* 219:731, 1988.

Trotter, Patrick C. *Cutthroat: Native Trout of the West*. Colorado Associated University Press, 1987.

Wilder, D.C. "A Comparative Study of Anadromous and Freshwater Populations of Brook Trout (*Salvelinus fontinalis* (Mitchill))." *Journal of the Fisheries Research Board of Canada* 9(4), 1952.

Withler, I.L. "Variability in Life History Characteristics of Steelhead Trout (*Salmo gairdneri*) Along the Pacific Coast of North America." *Journal of the Fisheries Research Board of Canada* 23(3):365–393, 1966.

Wooding, Frederick H. *Canada's Atlantic Salmon*. Ottawa: Department of Fisheries, 1956.

Wooding, Frederick H. *The Angler's Book of Canadian Fishes*. Toronto: Collins, 1959. Rev. ed. Toronto: McGraw-Hill Ryerson, 1974.

Wulff, Lee. *The Atlantic Salmon*. New York, A.S. Barnes and Company, 1958.

Additional:

Common and Scientific Names of Fishes from the United States and Canada. 5th ed. American Fisheries Society Special Publication 20. Bethesda, Maryland, 1991.

The Canadian Field Naturalist, publ. quarterly by The Ottawa Field Naturalists' Club, Ottawa. Various issues.

Bulletins of the International North Pacific Fisheries Commission.

Special Acknowledgments

To the following publishers who have granted me permission to quote from publications bearing their imprint, I extend my grateful appreciation:

Adam and Charles Black, London, England, for permission to use extracts from Frank Sawyer's *Keeper of the Stream;* Dr. Brian Curtis and his publisher, Harcourt, Brace & Co., New York, for permission to use extracts from Dr. Curtis's book *The Life Story of the Fish;* Douglas & McIntyre Ltd., Vancouver, for permission to use extracts from "The Protohistory of Pike in Western Culture" by Professor Richard C. Hoffmann, quoted in *An Annotated Bibliography of the Pike, Esox lucius (Osteichthyes: Salmoniformes),*" by E.J. Crossman and J.M. Casselman.

I am grateful to the Department of Fisheries and Oceans, Ottawa, for permission to draw freely on *Freshwater Fishes of Canada* by Scott and Crossman, *Freshwater Fishes of Northwestern Canada and Alaska* by McPhail and Lindsey, *The Atlantic Salmon in the History of North America* by R.W. Dunfield and numerous special publications under the imprint of the Fisheries Research Board of Canada. I appreciate, as well, the permission of the University of British Columbia Press, Vancouver, to use excerpts from *Pacific Salmon Life Histories,* edited by C. Groot and L. Margolis, and the permission of the editor of *The Atlantic Salmon Journal* to use an extract from an article written by Dr. John Thorpe, Freshwater Fisheries Laboratory (Pitlochry), Scotland.

I want, as well, to warmly thank Ted Davis (my angling friend and master fly-tyer), Michael E. Wooding, Dr. D.S. Kober, Dr. Lionel Johnson, R.A. (Ron) Ptolemy, and Lorry and Erica Harrison, all of whom—throughout the book's stages of development—advised me sensitively and well. Their help will be long remembered.

Index